Political Conflict and Economic Interdependence
Across the Taiwan Strait and Beyond

Studies in Asian Security

A SERIES SPONSORED BY THE EAST-WEST CENTER

Muthiah Alagappa, Chief Editor
Distinguished Senior Fellow, East-West Center

The **Studies in Asian Security** book series promotes analysis, understanding, and explanation of the dynamics of domestic, transnational, and international security challenges in Asia. The peer-reviewed publications in the Series analyze contemporary security issues and problems to clarify debates in the scholarly community, provide new insights and perspectives, and identify new research and policy directions. Security is defined broadly to include the traditional political and military dimensions as well as nontraditional dimensions that affect the survival and well being of political communities. Asia, too, is defined broadly to include Northeast, Southeast, South, and Central Asia.

Designed to encourage original and rigorous scholarship, books in the *Studies in Asian Security* series seek to engage scholars, educators, and practitioners. Wide-ranging in scope and method, the Series is receptive to all paradigms, programs, and traditions, and to an extensive array of methodologies now employed in the social sciences.

★　　　★　　　★

The East-West Center is an education and research organization established by the U.S. Congress in 1960 to strengthen relations and understanding among the peoples and nations of Asia, the Pacific, and the United States. Funding for the Center comes from the U.S. government, with additional support provided by private agencies, individuals, foundations, corporations, and the governments of the region.

Political Conflict and Economic Interdependence Across the Taiwan Strait and Beyond

Scott L. Kastner

STANFORD UNIVERSITY PRESS
Stanford, California

Stanford University Press
Stanford, California

Printed in the United States of America

Library of Congress Cataloging-in-Publication Data

Kastner, Scott L.
    Political conflict and economic interdependence across the Taiwan Strait and
beyond / Scott L. Kastner.
    p. cm. — (Studies in Asian security)
    Includes bibliographical references and index.
    ISBN 978-0-8047-6203-8 (cloth : alk. paper)—
    ISBN 978-0-8047-6204-5 (pbk : alk. paper)—
        1. China—Commerce—Taiwan.   2. Taiwan—Commerce—China.   3. China—
Foreign economic relations—Taiwan.   4. Taiwan—Foreign economic relations—China.
5. China—Economic policy—2000–.   6. Taiwan—Economic policy—1975–.   I. Title.
II. Series.
    HF3838.T28K37   2009
    337.5105124'.9—dc22   2008042370

This book is printed on acid-free, archival-quality paper.

Typeset at Stanford University Press in 10/13.5 Bembo

Special discounts for bulk quantities of Stanford Security Series are available to
corporations, professional associations, and other organizations. For details and
discount information, contact the special sales department of Stanford University
Press. Tel: (650) 736-1783, Fax: (650) 736-1784

For Dina

Contents

Acknowledgments

This book has benefited from the helpful comments and advice of many colleagues and friends. I am especially grateful to David Lake, who has given me excellent advice, feedback, and much-needed encouragement at every stage of this project. Michael Hiscox has also provided great feedback and advice throughout the process. Chad Rector read several versions of the manuscript, and it has benefited greatly from his many insightful comments. Tom Christensen, Miles Kahler, Susan Shirk, Barry Naughton, Miranda Schreurs, Neal Beck, Stephanie Rickard, and Stephanie McWhorter also provided very helpful comments on, and critiques of, earlier versions of the manuscript.

I benefited enormously from a year at Princeton as a fellow in the Princeton-Harvard China and the World Program. In addition to giving me a year away from teaching to work on this book, the fellowship and particularly my discussions at Princeton with Tom Christensen, Lynn White, Xu Xin, Ian Chong, Min Ye, and Yanliang Miao helped to make the manuscript stronger. I am likewise very grateful to have had the chance to spend a year as the China Security Fellow at National Defense University's Institute for National Strategic Studies. INSS was a great environment, and I especially wish to thank Phil Saunders for his helpful advice and encouragement. I also thank the General Research Board at the University of Maryland for providing support for this project.

My colleagues in the Department of Government and Politics at the University of Maryland, College Park, have been very supportive, and I thank in particular Margaret Pearson, Karen Kaufmann, Ken Conca, Virginia Haufler, Paul Huth, and Ric Uslaner for their mentorship and book-publishing advice. I thank Robert

Chyou, Janice Wang, and Kwei-Bo Huang for their friendship, support, and advice on my several trips to Taiwan over the past eight years. And Yue Liu, Chris Kim, Grace Kim, and Sarah King provided very helpful research assistance on this project.

I thank Muthiah Alagappa for his interest in my manuscript and his encouragement as I made revisions, and I am grateful to the series editorial committee and the anonymous reviewers for their comments, which helped to make this a stronger book. At Stanford I thank Geoffrey Burn for his many suggestions and for being very generous with his time, and I thank Jessica Walsh and John Feneron for their help getting the manuscript through the publication process. I am also indebted to Jeffrey Wyneken for his great job copyediting the manuscript.

Finally, I wish to thank my family, without whose support and love this book would never have been possible. My mother, Karin Klein, has been a constant source of encouragement and has always been there for me—as have my grandmother, Irmgard Klein, my sister, Lisa Kastner, and my late grandfather, Bruno Klein. My father, Larry Kastner, has encouraged me to keep a positive attitude (with admittedly mixed results). And my wife, Dina, has been a source of inspiration since I met her; she has helped me to keep things in proper perspective.

S.K.

Political Conflict and Economic Interdependence
Across the Taiwan Strait and Beyond

1

Introduction

International political conflict can have a chilling effect on commerce. Governments sometimes impose economic sanctions on political adversaries to influence their behavior. State leaders sometimes limit economic ties with enemies, or potential enemies, because they worry that trade and investment ties will make those rivals stronger militarily. And the possibility that political conflict today could escalate to military violence tomorrow makes trade in the presence of conflict a potentially risky undertaking. Many well-known empirical cases demonstrate clearly the negative effects political conflict can have on commerce. During the Cold War, Western countries, led by the United States, placed strict limits on trade with the Eastern Bloc. Trade between India and Pakistan declined drastically in the years after partition. United States technological exports to China are more regulated and controversial than similar exports to U.S. allies.[1] Political conflict across the Middle East has been a barrier to commercial integration in that region for decades. And numerous recent quantitative studies have found that international political conflict, measured in a variety of ways, harms trade.[2] In short, it appears that trade, at least some of the time, tends to follow the flag.

But the effect of conflict on commerce is hardly universal. Rather, economic relations can blossom, and sometimes flourish, even in the face of intense political and military rivalry. On the eve of the First World War, for example, Great Britain and Germany had an extensive commercial relationship (Papayoanou 1996). During the Cold War, West Germany sought enhanced, rather than reduced, levels of trade with rivals in Eastern Europe (Davis 1999); South Korea pursues similar policies toward North Korea today. Economic integration between Singapore and Malaysia is substantial despite the sometimes icy relationship shared by the two states. And economic ties between China and Taiwan flourish despite intense political rivalry. Indeed, economic integration across the Taiwan Strait actually accelerated even as political relations grew considerably worse after the mid-1990s.

Why is it that political conflict sometimes undermines commercial relations between countries but that, at other times, economic ties can come to flourish despite even intense political hostility? The question is important. Economic flows between countries can have a large impact on the well-being of those countries' inhabitants. In the China-Taiwan case, for example, inflows of foreign investment and access to foreign markets have become central to China's rapid economic development (Lardy 2002), and Taiwan has been a major supplier of overseas capital for the Mainland. Had conflict interfered more with cross-Strait economic integration, the development paths of both economies over the past twenty years could well have been significantly different. Furthermore, many argue that economic integration reduces the likelihood of military conflict (e.g. Russett and Oneal 2001). To the extent that economic integration does make military violence less likely, it is important to understand how economic ties can come to thrive in the shadow of political conflict to begin with.

1. Conflict and Economic Integration in Three Contemporary Military Rivalries

Consider, briefly, the relationship between political conflict and economic integration in three contemporary cases characterized by political tensions and military rivalry: India and Pakistan; North and South Korea; and Mainland China and Taiwan. At the heart of all three rivalries is a dispute relating to territorial sovereignty: the status of Kashmir in India-Pakistan relations; the terms of reunification in the relationship between the two Koreas; and the sovereign status of Taiwan in the relationship across the Taiwan Strait. In all three cases, conflict is serious and persistent, and has at times become militarized. Political conflict has influenced the nature of economic interactions in each relationship. But the effects of conflict have varied greatly across the cases.

The relationship between India and Pakistan epitomizes the detrimental effect international political conflict can have on cross-border economic flows. At the time of partition, when British India was divided into the two new states, trade between India and Pakistan was substantial. Roughly 45 percent of Pakistan's total imports came from India, for example. Yet bilateral trade declined drastically in the turbulent years that followed partition and has typically represented less than

1 percent of both countries' total trade since the 1950s. Over the years leaders from both sides have been quite willing to politicize economic flows between the two countries. Officials in Pakistan, for example, have repeatedly linked a normalized trading relationship with India to a resolution of the Kashmir dispute. At times of heightened crisis, moreover, both governments have had a tendency to undermine bilateral linkages as a means to punish the other side or to demonstrate resolve. For example, both sides severed bilateral trade ties when war erupted in 1965. Likewise, when tensions rose in 2001, both sides severed transportation links between the two countries. In short, political frictions between India and Pakistan have had a profound and lasting impact on their bilateral economic relations.

On the surface, the relationship between the two Koreas appears quite similar to the India-Pakistan case. Here too economic linkages remain sparse against a backdrop of intense political rivalry. Until the late 1980s South Korea banned all trade with the North, and even in recent years bilateral flows represent a fraction of a percent of South Korea's total trade. Though inexpensive labor, combined with shared culture and language, should make North Korea an ideal destination for South Korean investments, these too remain limited. The North remains one of the most autarkic countries in the world. Pyongyang's unwillingness to commit strongly and credibly to deep economic reforms, along with its tendency to allow political and security concerns to drive its economic interactions with the South, mean that investment in North Korea is fraught with uncertainty and risk.

But a closer inspection reveals some cracks in the ice. In particular, South Korea's economic policies toward the North have changed dramatically in recent years. After authorizing bilateral trade in the late 1980s, and loosening investment restrictions to some extent in the mid-1990s, Seoul in 1998 adopted a new policy—called the Sunshine Policy—that actively encouraged economic linkages with the North. Under the policy, South Korea refrains from using economic instruments to punish North Korean behavior; this effort to keep politics and economics on separate tracks remained in effect even during the recent standoff involving the North's nuclear weapons program. Seoul's engagement policy has achieved some successes: trade, though still limited, has nearly doubled. Thousands of South Korean tourists visit Mount Kumgang in North Korea each year. And over twenty South Korean firms have set up operations in an industrial park in North Korea, which was constructed using South Korean funds. Economic ties remain weak, but there are some signs that things may be changing. Things have certainly changed dramatically on the south side of the border.

Like the other two cases, the relationship across the Taiwan Strait is characterized by intense political conflict and military rivalry. Chinese missile tests off the coast of Taiwan in 1996 and Beijing's steady buildup of offensive military capabilities directed at Taiwan since the early 1990s provide continuing evidence that cross-Strait political conflict is serious. As in the other two cases, bilateral political conflict has had an impact on the bilateral economic relationship. Largely because relations with the Mainland have been tense, Taiwanese leaders have tried to limit the extent of cross-Strait economic integration; they worry in part that the Taiwanese economy might become too dependent on the Mainland's, and hence vulnerable to explicit or implicit sanctioning threats. Taiwanese officials also express concern that high-tech investments in China by Taiwanese firms may tilt the military balance in Beijing's favor.

Despite these concerns, cross-Strait commercial relations have grown rapidly; Taiwanese economic policy toward the Mainland has in fact varied considerably since the late 1980s. Broadly speaking, the scope of Taiwanese restrictions on cross-Strait trade and investment flows has decreased over time. And since the late 1980s, Taiwanese investors have flocked to a booming Chinese economy that is increasingly integrated into global markets and that has welcomed these investors with open arms. Mainland China is, by far, the largest recipient of Taiwan's foreign direct investment, and in recent years China surpassed the United States to become Taiwan's largest trade partner. Taiwanese companies continued to pour investments into the Mainland market even as bilateral tensions rose substantially in the run-up to and aftermath of the 2004 Taiwanese presidential election. Taiwanese businesses, evidently, are confident that their Mainland investments will remain secure and profitable even during times when bilateral political relations sour considerably.

These three cases illustrate the basic question that motivates this book: Why does international political conflict sometimes suffocate international economic flows, as in the case of India–Pakistan relations, but not at other times? In the case of China and Taiwan, economic ties have come to flourish despite a hostile political landscape. When tensions grow in India–Pakistan relations, both sides sometimes signal their resolve by taking steps—like severing transport links—that harm bilateral economic ties. But during times of turbulence in the cross-Strait case, Chinese leaders appear to bend over backwards to emphasize their commitment to protect the rights and interests of Taiwanese investors. To an increasing extent, it seems, the political and economic relationships across the Taiwan Strait operate in separate spheres. This book explores how such a state of affairs can arise.

2. Existing Approaches

The relationship between international political conflict and economic interdependence has long attracted substantial scholarly interest, and remains the subject of vigorous debate. Much of the recent literature focuses more specifically on the relationship between trade and military conflict, in particular the extent to which increased trade between countries reduces the likelihood of military conflict. At the forefront of recent interest in the subject has been a series of works by Oneal and Russett, who make the liberal case that trade (in addition to democracy and international organizations) has a pacific effect (Oneal and Russett 1997; 1999a; 2001; Russett and Oneal 2001). Nonetheless, the liberal hypothesis remains controversial on both theoretical and empirical grounds (e.g. Barbieri 1996; 2002; Gartzke 2003).[3] In Chapter 6, I consider the impact of economic interdependence on military conflict and examine whether the growing economic relationship across the Taiwan Strait reduces the danger of war there. But the primary purpose of this study is to treat economic interdependence as the dependent variable—to consider, that is, how and when conflict influences international economic ties.

Studies considering this reverse relationship again tend to focus primarily on trade and military conflict in particular. Recent studies have shown, for example, that militarized interstate disputes (MIDs) have a negative impact on trade (Keshk et al. 2004; Oneal et al. 2003), though Morrow and others (1998) find that MIDs have an insignificant impact on trade flows in a study limited to the great powers. Morrow (1999) suggests that this result might arise because forward-looking economic actors anticipate potential disputes and thus limit exposure prior to the fact; Li and Sacko (2002) find empirical support for this proposition, showing that unexpected military disputes have a negative effect on trade while expected ones do not. More-recent studies have used simultaneous models to assess the direction of causality between militarized disputes and trade. Keshk and others (2004) apply such a model to a large sample and find that, while military disputes have a negative impact on commerce, trade has no significant effect on the likelihood of a militarized dispute.[4] Other studies suggest that wars, and especially major-power wars, also have a negative impact on trade (Anderton and Carter 2001; Glick and Taylor 2005), though this effect does not appear to be universal: Levy and Barbieri (2004; Barbieri and Levy 1999) demonstrate that wartime trade sometimes thrives, suggesting that war's impact on trade is likely contingent on a host of other factors.

But it is also clear that conflict does not have to be militarized to affect trade. Pollins (1989a; 1989b), for example, has used events data to show that pairs of countries with relatively cooperative political interactions tend to trade more with each other than pairs of countries with more hostile interactions. Other studies show that states with conflicting interests or goals—operationalized in a variety of ways—trade less with each other, on balance, than states whose goals are not in conflict. Simmons (2005), for example, finds that territorial disputes have a negative impact on trade, and Long (2003a) finds that strategic rivalry also has a negative effect. Some studies suggest that allies trade more with each other than with other states, though the findings here are mixed.[5] Other studies investigate the impact of conflict using more general proxies for state interests. For example, Dixon and Moon (1993) find that the United States trades more with countries that vote as it does in the United Nations General Assembly than with states that do not. Morrow and others (1998) show that countries with similar alliance portfolios—taken as a broad indicator of national security interests—trade more with each other than do countries with dissimilar portfolios.

The existing literature on the effects of conflict on economic interdependence has several shortcomings, which this study seeks to address. First, there has been little effort to explain *variation* in the relationship between conflict and commerce. Most existing studies have simply asked whether conflict affects trade, and if so, by how much.[6] But growing economic integration across the Taiwan Strait, despite very intense political conflict, suggests that it is equally important to consider *when* conflict affects trade. The primary purpose of this study is to develop and test hypotheses in this regard.

Second, as also suggested by Barbieri and Schneider (1999), existing studies have not gone far enough in linking the relationship between conflict and trade to the expansive literature on the *domestic determinants of trade policy*. This is a curious omission given the similarity of the dependent variable in the two literatures. The role of protectionism, for example, should at a minimum be controlled for in quantitative analyses, and may in fact intervene in the relationship between conflict and trade in important ways. This project explicitly links the study of conflict and trade to the vast literature on the domestic determinants of foreign economic policy (e.g. Frieden 1991; Rogowski 1989; Simmons 1994; Hiscox 2001).

Finally, the literature on conflict and trade is dominated by large-sample quantitative analyses, with less attention paid to the detailed study of particular cases. This may indeed be why so little attention has been paid to the puzzle laid out above. Quantitative analysis is an important component of hypothesis testing, and is utilized in Chapter 7 of this study. But detailed case studies can help identify causal processes that are difficult to capture in very large-sample analyses, which is particularly pertinent in a study like this where the relevant question is not whether conflict affects trade but, rather, when it does.

3. Defining Conflict

As the previous section should make clear, conflict can be thought of in different ways. For the purposes of this project, I choose to define conflict broadly, as the extent to which the political goals or interests of two countries diverge. Conflict defined in this way can be thought of as a continuum. At one end, conflict is low between states that share a range of interests to which they are deeply committed. Here we might think of cases like the United States and the United Kingdom, or the United States and Canada. This is not to suggest that there is no conflict in such relationships but rather that conflicting interests are generally minor compared to shared interests. At the opposite end of the continuum, conflict is high between states that share few interests, and where each state pursues goals that cannot be attained without undermining the objectives of the other state. The three case studies considered in this book—China-Taiwan, India-Pakistan, and North Korea–South Korea—all involve conflict that lies at this end of the continuum, as I will explain more fully in later chapters. In Chapter 2, I discuss this measure of conflict in more detail, considering some of its benefits and drawbacks.

4. The Argument in Brief

The primary hypothesis advanced in this study is that the effect of conflict on economic interdependence is contingent on the nature of domestic ruling coalitions within the states enmeshed in conflict. I begin my argument by drawing from the existing literature to specify two broad causal mechanisms through which conflict might affect international economic ties. First, economic ties between countries can have security-related consequences (Gowa 1994). Trade, for example, can supply an enemy with important military technologies, or it can make a country vulnerable to sanctioning threats. As such, state leaders sometimes place restrictions on foreign economic ties in the presence of conflict. Second, conflict makes international economic exchange more risky for the firms engaged in such exchange: states with conflicting interests sometimes engage in costly competitions (like war, in extreme cases) that can be disrupting to economic flows. The added risk leads to reduced levels of economic integration in the presence of conflict (Morrow 1999).

I hypothesize that conflict's effects on international economic flows are more muted when the leaders of the countries in question are politically accountable to internationalist economic interests—those that support and gain from integration into the world economy. There are two reasons for this.

First, leaders accountable to internationalist economic interests confront a trade-off when considering restrictions on commerce, which leaders less accountable to such interests do not face. Suppose a leader who is politically accountable to internationalist economic interests recognizes that commercial ties with a strategic competitor undermine her ability to achieve her goals that are in conflict with that second state. Imagine, for example, that her country's exports include products with military applications that can improve the military capabilities of the second state. Imposing restrictions on commerce with the second state may help the leader attain her international goals, but doing so may also undermine her domestic political support—since restrictions on foreign commerce inflict losses on her political supporters. A leader who is not accountable to internationalist economic interests, when facing the same international situation, would be less concerned by the domestic political implications of imposing commercial restrictions. Since she does not draw support from the potential losers resulting from foreign commercial restrictions, she need not in this instance worry about a trade-off between pursuing her international goals and maintaining political support domestically. The trade-off faced by leaders accountable to internationalist economic interests suggests that they are less likely than other leaders to impose restrictions on foreign economic ties in the shadow of conflict.

Second, for similar reasons, when leaders accountable to internationalist economic interests wish to signal resolve to strategic competitors, they try to do so in ways that are not detrimental to foreign commerce. In demonstrating commitment to an international goal, leaders have a variety of means at their disposal. Some, such as sanctions, embargos, border-closings, and the like, are damaging to foreign economic ties. Others, like military buildups and exercises, recalling diplomats, and so forth, are less directly detrimental to international commerce. Though they do not always possess the flexibility to do so, leaders accountable to internationalist economic interests generally prefer to signal resolve in ways not detrimental to cross-border commerce. An action detrimental to foreign commerce is reserved as a last resort, when the stakes are very high, as a signal that is both very costly and very informative. Other leaders, who are less constrained politically, may choose to signal resolve in a way that is damaging to cross-border commerce in a much broader range of disputes—even when the stakes are low—because such signals are less costly. Independent economic agents factor this into the risk associated with commerce in the shadow of conflict. That is, the risk of commercial disruptions is lower when conflict is between internationalist regimes than when conflict is between non-internationalist regimes.

5. Plan for This Study

The next chapter lays out my core theoretical argument. After expanding on the definition of conflict sketched out earlier, the chapter considers in more detail why conflict might be expected to affect cross-border economic flows. I then develop this study's primary hypothesis, that the effects of conflict on commerce are conditioned by the nature of governing coalitions in the countries involved, in particular the extent to which internationalist economic interests exercise political power within such coalitions.

Chapters 3–6 then present an extensive case study of the political and economic relationship across the Taiwan Strait. Chapter 3 describes in more detail the nature of political conflict across the Taiwan Strait and discusses recent economic trends in the relationship. I argue that this case, in some respects, resembles a "least likely" test case for my hypotheses, and as such some generalization is possible. Chapter 4 examines evolving Taiwanese economic policies toward Mainland China since the late 1980s. These policies have generally become more liberal over time, with some important exceptions. This is somewhat puzzling, since there is good reason to believe that cross-Strait economic integration may have negative security implications for Taiwan. Though numerous factors have shaped Taiwanese policies, I show evidence that policy shifts can be explained in part by changes in the political strength of internationalist economic interests in Taiwan.

Chapter 5 considers Mainland China's policy toward Taiwan. Given intense cross-Strait political conflict, how has the People's Republic of China (PRC) been able to make credible its promises to protect the interests of Taiwanese investors? Crucially, while Beijing often tries to signal its resolve on the issue of Taiwanese sovereignty, it generally has aimed to do so in a way that does not affect the cross-Strait economic relationship. The PRC is governed by an increasingly internationalist coalition; signaling in a way that damages cross-Strait economic ties would be extremely costly. Beijing's signaling behavior on the issue of Taiwan's sovereignty, then, is broadly consistent with the theoretical argument developed in Chapter 2. Nonetheless, I also emphasize in Chapter 5 that the PRC's cross-Strait economic policies are not simply a consequence of domestic political constraints faced by Chinese leaders. Rather, a realist logic also governs Beijing's behavior: PRC officials seek to reassure Taiwanese investors—even during times of intense cross-Strait conflict—in part because they hope that growing economic ties will reinforce Beijing's influence over Taiwan. Examining the PRC's policies toward one class of Taiwanese investors—those sympathetic to Taiwan's Democratic Progressive Party—offers an opportunity to sort out the relative importance of the realist logic and the political constraints logic in driving the PRC's signaling behavior toward Taiwan. It appears that both causal logics are salient, and the chapter concludes with a reassessment of my core theoretical argument in light of the cross-Strait case.

Chapter 6 then examines the implications of burgeoning cross-Strait economic ties for the political relationship between Mainland China and Taiwan (does economic interdependence make a cross-Strait military confrontation less likely?) and for the "economic interdependence promotes peace" hypothesis more generally. My approach here is to begin by identifying the precise causal mechanisms, drawn from the extant literature, through which growing economic ties could lead to peace. I then explore whether these different causal processes are operating across the Taiwan Strait, while considering simultaneously the broader implications the cross-Strait experience might have for theories of commercial liberalism.

Chapter 7 considers how well the theoretical argument developed in Chapter 2 generalizes beyond the Taiwan Strait. The chapter begins with a quantitative analysis of trade flows among seventy-six countries over the years 1960–1992. The findings are encouraging, though I emphasize that considerable qualification is necessary due to difficulty in measuring key concepts in a large-sample framework. The chapter then considers the two other cases introduced earlier: India-Pakistan relations and the relationship on the Korean Peninsula. The India-Pakistan relationship represents an interesting contrast to the cross-Strait case; here, internationalist economic interests have been more marginalized politically in the two countries, and conflict, in turn, has had a more substantial impact on bilateral economic exchange. The relationship between North and South Korea is more of a mixed dyad, where internationalist economic interests appear completely marginalized in the North, and more influential in the South. Economic integration remains limited in this case, but South Korea has promoted increased exchange in recent years. Taken together, the two cases offer further support for my primary hypothesis.

Finally, Chapter 8 provides a brief summary of my main findings in this study and offers some suggestions for future research.

International Conflict, Domestic Politics, and Economic Interdependence

Theory and Hypotheses

Under what conditions can economic ties flourish despite conflict between countries? Existing literature suggests two reasons why international political conflict might be expected to have a negative impact on commerce—this study's dependent variable—in the first place: conflict makes governments more attentive to the security externalities that economic integration potentially entails, and conflict increases the risks faced by economic agents considering international commercial and financial ventures. These processes that dampen economic ties between rival states, however, are not constant; they may be stronger or weaker in different circumstances. This chapter introduces the central argument of the book: conflict between countries ruled by leaders who are relatively accountable to internationalist (pro-trade) economic actors is less likely to interfere with bilateral economic relations than it is in other cases.

The chapter begins by expanding on the definition of conflict presented in Chapter 1, emphasizing that it is useful to distinguish between conflict and violence or other costly contests. Section 2 considers why conflict might be expected to harm international economic flows to begin with. Then, Section 3 develops the core hypothesis, that conflict's effects on commerce are contingent on leadership accountability to internationalist economic interests. Section 4 concludes.

1. Conceptualizing International Political Conflict

In the Introduction (Chapter 1) I defined conflict broadly, as the extent to which the political goals or interests of two countries diverge. In thinking of conflict in this way, I am following Gartzke (2003) in distinguishing it from the costly contests (like war, in extreme cases) that states sometimes pursue to resolve their points of conflict. This may seem like a strange or academic distinction, but the difference between conflict generally and violence in particular is critical to understanding why states that are adversaries might have deep economic ties.

More specifically, not all serious conflicts escalate to shooting wars; many states that are adversaries go through long "cold wars" without ever getting to violence. However, it is difficult—or perhaps impossible—to know in advance whether or not any one particular conflict will turn violent (Gartzke 1999). The possibility of war is therefore in the minds of leaders and businesses considering trading in the shadow of conflict (this is detailed more fully later).

Certainly violence itself is likely to have a direct impact on commercial exchange, but what about conflict without violence? There is good reason to believe that even the possibility of violence—arising from serious conflicts of interest—might also affect trade,[1] and this impact may vary substantially across cases. Consider the relationship across the Taiwan Strait. The core puzzle in this case, as outlined in the previous chapter, is that economic ties between Mainland China and Taiwan flourish despite intense political tension over the issue of Taiwan's sovereign status. The issue is important in both Beijing and Taipei, so important that leaders in Beijing have repeatedly vowed to fight a costly war to prevent the legal independence of Taiwan. The situation, in short, is potentially explosive; that commerce between the two sides thrives nonetheless—despite the catastrophic consequences war would entail—demands explanation. Conceptualizing conflict as the extent to which states' core interests diverge allows for an examination of this puzzle in a way that a focus on costly contests, such as militarized disputes or war, does not, because the relationship in the Taiwan Strait has been free of military violence for decades.

Moreover, a focus on militarized disputes, or war, also has the disadvantage of limiting the scope of inquiry to only the most serious conflicts. By thinking of conflict as a continuum, however, it is possible to investigate more fully how the severity of conflict affects commerce. As I explain later, even when states bargain over issues that have little or no chance of escalating to military violence the potential for some commercial disruption exists. While the disruption might be small relative to the disruption likely to occur in disputes that could escalate to war, it is nonetheless interesting and worth considering. On a conceptual level, in short, it makes sense to treat conflict as a continuum and to define it as the extent to which the goals of two countries diverge. In this approach, all international relations are likely to involve at least some conflict, but the severity of conflict should vary greatly across relationships.

The primary drawback to an interest-based, rather than an observed outcome-based, definition of conflict centers on issues of operationalization. While such an approach is useful analytically, it is not straightforward to measure conflicting state interests systematically. I thus devote considerable space in the following chapter to examining the nature and evolution of conflict in the relationship across the Taiwan Strait. Later, in the quantitative tests introduced in Chapter 7, I test my hypotheses using different variables that act as proxies for conflicting interests. The use of multiple measures allows for an investigation into how sensitive findings are to one particular measure of conflict.

2. Why Might International Political Conflict Affect International Economic Relations?

This section considers *why* international political conflict might be expected to have an impact on international economic relations; the remainder of the chapter then considers more specifically *when* these effects are likely to emerge. Political conflict can harm economic ties between countries for at least two overarching reasons. First, economic integration sometimes generates political, that is to say, security, externalities (Gowa 1994). In other words, trade or investment flows can make it harder for a country to achieve political objectives that conflict with those of another country; in these instances, leaders can be expected to impose restrictions on those flows. Second, when states with conflicting political goals compete over those objectives, the actions that they take (such as war or economic sanctions) can be detrimental to their economic ties. Commerce in conflictual dyads will thus tend to be lower because of the higher risk premium associated with market-based exchange (Morrow 1999).

The Political Externalities of Economic Integration

Though generally welfare-enhancing to states economically, commercial and financial integration at times generates externalities that affect the ability of states to achieve their political objectives vis-à-vis other countries (Gowa 1994). Externalities are simply costs or benefits from a transaction that fall on third parties and that are not taken into account by those engaging in the transaction (Parkin 1990). For example, a firm, pursuing higher returns, may generate more pollution than is socially desirable, since most of the costs of pollution are not incorporated into the price of the firm's products. Likewise, a firm may discount the negative political or security consequences of its behavior, since the costs of reduced security are borne by the citizens of the home country generally rather than by the firm in particular, and as such are not factored into the price of the firm's products. Cross-border economic flows can generate several distinct types of security externalities; moreover, countries for which these externalities are negative can sometimes benefit by imposing restrictions on the economic ties giving rise to the diseconomies, just as they may benefit by imposing restrictions on activities that generate pollution. Next I discuss several different types of political externalities that can arise from economic integration.

Trade in strategic goods can improve an adversary's military capabilities. Perhaps the most straightforward type of political externality concerns trade in goods with direct military applications—which I will refer to here simply as strategic goods. Clearly, exports of strategic goods can improve an adversary's military capabilities, and foreign investments in strategic industries can have similar effects. Policymakers, in turn, might block exports of strategic goods, or investments in strategic industries, that they believe are facilitating an adversary's military development. The conditions under which it would be worthwhile for them to do so, however, appear to be rather strict.

In many dyadic relationships, bilateral economic exchange will not generate this particular type of political externality. The externality will arise only if producers in country A wish to export to country B some strategic good that is produced at higher prices (or not at all) in B, or if capital owners in A wish to invest in a strategic industry in B. For example, A might be an oil producer and B an oil importer; or A might invest in high-technology industries in B that enable B to upgrade its weapons systems. Moreover, even if the externality is present, A's ability—by blocking the relevant bilateral economic exchanges—to have a meaningful impact on B's military capabilities hinges on the *substitution elasticity* of the goods or investments in question.[2] That is, if B can find relatively cheap substitutes for these goods or investments from A, then A's efforts to block bilateral exchange will have little effect. For example, if B can obtain a strategic good, currently exported by country A, from some third country C at only marginally worse terms, then A obtains only marginal security benefits by restricting exports of the good—unless it is able to cooperate with C in limiting exports of the good to B.[3]

Nonetheless, states sometimes do impose restrictions on sensitive exports or foreign investments because policymakers worry about enemies gaining easier access to strategic materials. The U.S. effort to limit the export of sensitive technologies to the Eastern Bloc during the Cold War is perhaps the most well-known example. Yet this example also illustrates the strict conditions under which this sort of dynamic holds. Technological advantages held by the United States meant that unregulated trade with the Eastern Bloc would entail security externalities, as such trade would make it easier for the Soviet Union to upgrade its military technologies. Accordingly, the United States passed laws, including the 1949 Export Control Act and the 1951 Battle Act, which were designed to limit strategic exports to the Soviet Bloc (McDaniel 1993, 5–6). Yet imposing controls on exports made little sense unless other advanced economies also limited exports to the Eastern Bloc. The United States thus tried to coordinate with other developed economies in limiting exports to the Soviet Bloc, leading to the establishment of the Coordinating Committee for Multilateral Export Controls (COCOM) in 1949 (McDaniel 1993, 2). In the early 1950s, COCOM members cooperated in a wide-ranging economic boycott of the Eastern Bloc; under pressure from other members, however, the United States after 1954 acquiesced to a more limited role, focusing on strategic exports (Mastanduno 1988). COCOM's effectiveness varied over the course of the Cold War (Mastanduno 1992), in part because of disagreements among members concerning the scope of exports that should be subject to restrictions. Throughout COCOM's existence, exports originating from nonmember advanced economies (generally neutral countries like Sweden or Switzerland) were a continual problem, which grew more substantial as the number of countries with the capacity to export high-technology products increased (McDaniel 1993; Bertsch and Elliott-Gower 1991). Thus, even in a case involving the world's largest economy, where unregulated trade in high-technology products would generate certain security-related externalities, the United States found it difficult to eliminate those externalities: restrictions on bilateral trade with the Soviet Bloc would have only marginal effects, since substitutes from other advanced economies were widely, and increasingly, available, and coordination between the United States and other potential exporters proved difficult.

Economic exchange can increase the wealth of potential adversaries. It is not only through trade (or investments) in strategic goods that economic integration can improve the relative military capabilities of an adversary. More broadly, the income gains that economic exchange produces are themselves fungible, and hence can be converted to military strength (Gowa 1994; Gowa and Mansfield 1993). Leaders in country A may simply worry that economic exchange with country B will yield greater economic benefits (such as faster growth) in B than in A. For example, if A is a developed economy and B is not, trade might enable B to catch up economically to A faster than it otherwise would. If relations with B are hostile, then A's leaders will be especially concerned about these sorts of "relative gains," since the increased economic benefit could potentially be translated into increased military capabilities in the long run (Grieco 1988).[4] As with the externalities arising from trade in strategic goods, however, in most circumstances A is unlikely to be capable of independently reversing externalities associated with relative gains. That is, if other countries are willing to trade with B on terms similar to A's, then A would need to obtain their cooperation (in restricting trade with B) in order to effect any meaningful change in B's development trajectory.[5]

Economic exchange can generate dependencies. A third type of political externality that can arise from economic exchange centers on the dependencies that economic integration sometimes generates. Economic integration opens the possibility for economic coercion: a state that comes to depend heavily on economic ties with a second state is potentially vulnerable to economic sanctions imposed by that second state. To avoid being the target of economic coercion, and having to make political concessions to avert economic sanctions, states can sometimes benefit by preventing economic ties with adversaries from developing in the first place.

On the surface, implementing restrictions to slow bilateral economic exchange in order to prevent sanctions against that exchange seems self-defeating and pointless: why deny yourself the gains of trade because your opponent *may* in the future threaten to deny those same gains? But further consideration reveals the fundamental importance, not of expected gains from economic interaction with a second country but rather, of (1) the marginal gains of that exchange versus the next best option, and (2) the specificity of the assets engaged in that exchange. If country A's return on some transaction with country B is only slightly better than the next best use of the assets employed in that transaction, then the costs of stopping the transaction with B before it occurs (and thereby driving the assets to pursue their second best use) are low. Completing the transaction, however, may entail investing assets that are specific to the bilateral relationship, meaning they hold value only in the context of the relationship and cannot be easily transferred to other countries (see Lake 1999, 55–57; Rector, 2009). If B can make a credible sanctioning threat against those assets, the value of the concessions A must deliver could easily exceed the costs it would have incurred from stopping the relationally specific assets from being deployed in the first place.

The logic is most obvious for foreign direct investments with relatively long-term time horizons. These sorts of investments are clearly vulnerable to opportunism by the host country because of the sunk costs that they entail: once a company from country A builds a factory in some foreign country B, it cannot move it elsewhere.[6] If government officials in A believe that B might use the factory as a hostage in bargaining with A—threatening to expropriate it if A fails to give ground on some issue—then country A would be better off prohibiting investments in B, especially if the marginal costs of investing elsewhere are small. This sort of logic also applies to commercial relations, since trade involves specialization. For example, if country A's economy specializes heavily in industries dependent on exports to B, then a severing of bilateral trade could entail substantial adjustment costs for A.[7] Again, if a state anticipates this sort of scenario, and expects that its trading partner is likely to act opportunistically after trade relations have been established, then it may choose to prevent commercial integration from proceeding in the first place. This dynamic is more likely to arise in the presence of an asymmetric distribution of relationship-specific assets within a particular dyad, as such asymmetry yields the less dependent state disproportionate bargaining power (Hirschman 1945; Keohane and Nye 1989; McLaren 1997). A small country dependent on the market of a large country, for example, is vulnerable to economic sanctions in a way that the large country is not (e.g. Hirschman 1945; Drezner 1999). In this type of situation, the negative political externalities associated with trade may drive the smaller country to diversify its foreign commercial relations away from the larger country—especially if leaders in the smaller country believe that the larger country will use its leverage (as might be the case, for example, if the two countries have seriously conflicting interests).[8]

Economic exchange can influence the power of different domestic political groups. Finally, trade can change the balance of power among competing domestic political coalitions. Trade makes the holders of a country's relatively abundant factors of production richer, and holders of its relatively scarce factors poorer; over time, groups that become wealthier are likely to become more powerful in domestic politics as well (Rogowski 1989). Furthermore, trade can spur the formation of groups that have a vested interest in liberal trade policies. Just as industries benefiting from a country's existing protectionist trade barriers tend to organize and lobby against reductions in those barriers, so too actors benefiting from a country's existing trade openness are likely to organize and oppose policies that might put trade openness at risk. These political externalities can exert a substantial impact on a government's trade policy under any circumstances. For example, a leader who depends on the support of protectionist economic interests may oppose liberal trade policies simply because trade would have the effect of undercutting his supporters and making his opponents stronger. The process could also work in reverse: a leader supported by actors benefiting from trade might push for deeper trade openness, thereby solidifying her own political standing.[9]

When international political conflict is present, trade's impact on the political strength of different domestic groups can become an especially salient concern for leaders, potentially resulting in trade restrictions that leaders would not consider in the absence of conflict. The reasoning is fairly straightforward. Suppose leaders in country A have goals that conflict seriously with the goals of country B, but not with the goals of country C. To the extent that commercial interests are motivated primarily by profits, and not by the goals at the root of the political conflict, economic links with country B are problematic for A's leaders in a way that economic ties with C are not. Economic interests in A that benefit from trade between A and

B would have reason to pressure leaders in A to adopt less confrontational policies toward B, since tense bilateral political relations could be destabilizing to bilateral commercial flows. In other words, the deeper the economic relationship between A and B, the more domestic political pressure leaders in A would be under (from actors in A benefiting from the bilateral economic relationship) to modify their goals that are in conflict with B's goals. Trade between A and C would not lead to similar pressures because the goals of those two states do not diverge. A leader committed to the goals at the heart of the rivalry between A and B might thus try to limit commercial integration between A and B, hoping in the process to prevent new vested interests opposed to those goals from emerging in A.

Here again asymmetry is likely to be important. If country A depends much more heavily on bilateral trade than does country B, then the actors with a vested interest in that trade will probably exert much more political influence in A than they do in B. In this type of scenario, leaders in A should be especially concerned about the political consequences of bilateral trade: here, trade increases pressures within A for a resolution to the bilateral political dispute without generating any corresponding pressures in B. In other words, leaders in A will face increased pressure to back down, while leaders in B will be free to remain resolved. Indeed, this is an effect that B might even try to cultivate by promoting trade with A (Hirschman 1945; Skalnes 1998; Abdelal and Kirshner 1999/2000; Kahler and Kastner 2006).

Summary. Though states generally benefit economically from international trade and investment flows, foreign economic ties can also generate a variety of political externalities that can influence the ability of states to achieve goals that are in conflict with other countries. In countries for which such political externalities are negative, leaders are faced with a tradeoff between the economic costs of restricting commerce on the one hand and the political consequences of permitting it on the other. The more substantial those negative consequences become, the more likely leaders are to opt for restrictions. As the discussion to this point should make clear, however, the extent to which trade generates political externalities varies considerably across dyads. In some dyads, commerce might have very few security-related externalities: for example, when two adversaries share a trading relationship that is limited, symmetrical, and that does not involve the trading of strategic goods, it is unlikely that their commercial relationship will have an impact on their political relationship in a meaningful way. In other cases, trade might have both positive and negative political externalities for a particular country. I return to these issues in Section 3. Next, however, I consider a second causal mechanism through which conflict affects international economic relations.

International Conflict and Risk

In addition to making governments more attentive to the political externalities of international economic exchange, international political conflict can also distort economic flows by increasing the risks faced by the firms undertaking international trade and investments. Simply put, interstate competition over conflicting goals can harm commerce. In extreme cases, of course, states with competing objectives sometimes fight destructive wars. But even in conflicts that do not escalate into military confrontations, states sometimes adopt other policies, like economic sanctions or border closings, that can be devastating to bilateral economic ties. Firms thus face greater risks when trading or investing in the presence of conflict, and these increased risks can distort international economic flows (e.g. Morrow 1999). In the remainder of this section, I consider in more detail why conflict may result in costly competitions that can harm commerce.

When a state's preferences over some issue conflict with those of another state, it is often uncertain how committed the other state is to its position on the issue. Consider as an example the main case study in this book, the relationship across the Taiwan Strait. Here (as is discussed in more detail in Chapter 3) the core issue of contention between the current Taiwanese leadership and the current leadership in Beijing is Taiwan's sovereign status. PRC officials aim, at a minimum, to keep Taiwan from formalizing its de facto independent status, and from taking steps that effectively preclude unification as a viable future scenario. On the other side, recent Taiwanese presidents have at times taken steps to further consolidate Taiwan's sovereign status. Former President Chen Shui-bian, for example, sought—ultimately unsuccessfully—to construct a new constitution for Taiwan. Though Mainland leaders have warned against steps they see as moving the island in the direction of formal independence, it is hard for Taiwanese officials to predict how the PRC would respond to such steps. PRC leaders might hint at a military response, but such a course of action would obviously be very costly; in any given instance it is hard for Taiwanese leaders to know whether such threats are real or bluff.

This example highlights a central point of the crisis-bargaining literature: when two states have conflicting interests, each side is often uncertain over the true level of the other side's resolve; that is, it is uncertain of the costs the other side is willing to pay in order to achieve a favorable outcome. This uncertainty gives states that are in reality unresolved an incentive to nonetheless act resolute—to bluff (Fearon 1995). Even states that are highly resolved, however, would prefer not to have to carry out the threats they are resolved to carry out, since doing so is costly. Far better would be for their adversaries to recognize this resolve and back down first. Thus, states that are truly resolved have every incentive to distinguish themselves from states that are bluffing, and one way to do this is to communicate—or "signal"—a willingness to accept costs in order to achieve a favorable outcome.[10] By sending costly signals, states convey information more credibly: since states that lack resolve are by definition unwilling to pay costs to achieve a favorable bargaining outcome, the demonstration of a willingness to pay some costs increases the likelihood that a state will be perceived as resolute.

Unfortunately for actors engaged in international commerce, the signals states choose to send can harm international economic flows: states sometimes impose economic sanctions, close borders, or enact embargoes in order to signal commitment to issues that are important to them.[11] Indeed, commercial integration between countries effectively expands the "menu" of signaling options available to states by making it possible to demonstrate resolve by harming trade (Gartzke 2003; Gartzke et al. 2001; Morrow 1999; 2003; Stein 2003). Of course, signals of resolve can still fail: some uncertainty will always remain (Schultz 2001), and thus wars—which are likely to be especially disruptive to commerce—can erupt when two highly resolved states fail to convince each other of their respective levels of commitment. That such dynamics might occur in the presence of conflict should lead private economic actors to place a risk premium on commerce in the shadow of conflict. At the margins, they should limit their exposure, especially when relationship-specific investments are under consideration.[12]

Conflict can have a negative impact on trade even when there is little potential for escalation to war or comprehensive trade sanctions, as states sometimes signal in ways that can harm trade even when they are bargaining over relatively low-level disputes. For example, after the 2001 spy plane incident between the United States and China, Beijing signaled its displeasure with U.S. reconnaissance policy—and Washington's handling of the incident—by suggesting it might purchase more Airbus planes and fewer Boeing planes in the future.[13] At a still lower level of conflict, countries sometimes adopt more restrictive entry and visa requirements to demonstrate dissatisfaction with entry requirements in other countries (and, conversely, sometimes relax visa requirements when relations with other countries improve).[14] The added costs associated with such restrictions could discourage commerce at the margins. Of course, the trade disruption that is likely to arise in minor disputes would be small compared to the disruption that could occur in serious disputes with the potential to escalate into war.

In summary, we have seen two causal pathways through which international political conflict can have a detrimental effect on international economic flows. In the first case, leaders restrict commerce because they believe economic integration potentially entails security externalities. In the second case, firms anticipate the possibility that leaders will choose to signal resolve in a way that damages commerce—such as by imposing sanctions or, in an extreme case, going to war.

Since the general effect of conflict on commerce should be negative (once other factors are controlled for), my initial baseline hypothesis is as follows:

H_1: *Holding all else equal, higher levels of political conflict between countries are associated with lower levels of economic exchange between those countries.*

The corresponding null hypothesis is:

H_0: *Political conflict between countries has no effect on those countries' economic relations.*

3. When Does International Political Conflict Affect Economic Exchange?

We know from prior studies that the effects of conflict on commerce appear to vary substantially across cases. In this section I argue that there is good reason to believe that conflict's effects are contingent, in part, on the nature of the governing coalitions within the countries enmeshed in conflict. In particular, the economic consequences of conflict are likely to be more limited to the extent that leaders are accountable to internationalist economic interests.

Leaders, of course, do not make foreign economic policy in a vacuum: the benefit that leaders derive from foreign economic policies depends on the policy preferences of their core constituents. It is clear, moreover, that international economic integration affects different groups within a particular society differently, and as such foreign trade and investment policies can be deeply contentious. The Stolper-Samuelson theorem predicts, for example, that the owners of relatively abundant factors of production will see their returns increase with trade liberalization, while owners of relatively scarce factors will see their returns decline with liberalization (Stolper and Samuelson 1941; Rogowski 1989; Frieden and Rogowski 1996). In this regard, a leader who depends heavily on labor for support may come to have drastically different trade policy preferences from a rival politician who draws more heavily from landowners or business for support. Conversely, to the extent that factors of production cannot easily be shifted across industries, trade policy preferences are more likely to vary by industry rather than by class: both capital holders and workers in internationally competitive industries will tend to support trade liberalization, while the reverse will tend to be true in industries that are not competitive internationally (Frieden 1991; Hiscox 2001; 2002; Solingen 1998, 22).[15] In short, international economic policies typically generate substantial domestic political conflict, and the actors who benefit from liberalization in foreign economic policies are likely to vary substantially across countries and also across time within countries—depending on variables such as the relative abundance of different factors of production, the mobility of those factors across industries, and the opportunity costs of closure (Frieden and Rogowski 1996). For my purposes here, I will refer to those actors who stand to benefit from liberal foreign economic policies as "internationalist economic interests" (e.g. Papayoanou 1996).

When devising foreign economic policies, leaders must surely consider the extent to which their policy decisions deviate from the interests of the coalitions that back them. By adopting policies at odds with core supporters, leaders run the risk of losing those supporters to defection (to alternative coalitions) or of being replaced by rivals more attentive to coalition interests. Thus, we might expect that leaders who draw support from internationalist economic interests prefer not to adopt policies that place the country's foreign economic ties in jeopardy, as doing so could alienate key supporters. In contrast, leaders who tend to draw support from more protectionist interests need not worry about angering supporters when implementing restrictions on foreign economic exchange; if anything, they may broaden support among core constituencies by doing so. In short, leaders should expect to pay higher political costs for pursuing policies detrimental to foreign economic exchange to the extent that they are backed by internationalist economic interests.

That leaders who draw support from internationalist economic interests would be expected to pursue more open foreign economic policies is straightforward. Solingen (2001) provides evidence showing that internationalizing coalitions do indeed tend to adopt more open trade policies. However, there is also reason to expect that an interactive effect between conflict and leadership accountability to internationalist economic interests exists. That is, the independent effects of international conflict on states' international economic ties should hinge, in part, on the extent to which leaders in those countries are accountable to internationalist economic interests. This intervening variable—leadership accountability to internationalist economic interests—should have an impact on both causal mechanisms described in the previous section, for the following reasons.

Consider first the case of security externalities. Imagine two countries, A and B, which have conflicting interests. The leader of state A recognizes that economic integration with B entails political externalities that are positive for B and negative for A. Suppose, for example, that absent political interference, A would export high-technology products to B and that those products would allow B to improve its military capabilities vis-à-vis A. Under certain conditions,[16] A's bargaining power relative to B improves if it restricts those high-tech exports, since such restrictions would have a negative impact on B's military capabilities. If the leader of state A depends on the political support of actors who benefit from trade, however, then at the margins she will pay higher domestic political costs for imposing trade restrictions than were she not accountable to such interests. In other words, such a leader faces a tradeoff between maximizing A's bargaining power vis-à-vis B and solidifying her own domestic political standing, a tradeoff that leaders not accountable to actors benefiting from trade do not face. She might still choose to impose the restrictions, but at the margins she is less likely to, given her own domestic political incentives; that likelihood decreases to the extent that she owes her political position to the support of internationalist economic interests.

With the second causal mechanism, the risks of trade in the presence of conflict, risk might also be lowered when internationalist economic interests hold strong political clout in the states involved. When states send signals to convey resolve, they in fact have a portfolio of methods from which to choose. Some of these methods directly and negatively affect bilateral economic relations (such as an economic sanction), while others do not (such as military exercises).[17] Because leaders who depend on the support of internationalist economic interests pay higher political costs (relative to other leaders) for taking actions detrimental to foreign commerce, these leaders will rank the costliness of various signals differently from how leaders not supported by internationalist interests would rank them. Specifically, leaders accountable to internationalist economic interests should view signals that are detrimental to commerce, like economic sanctions, as being more costly than would other leaders.

Consider again two states, A and B, enmeshed in a conflictual relationship in which, over time, a number of disputes arise. Assume further that A's leader is highly committed to some of these issues, and only moderately committed to others. In other words, A would be willing to bear high costs to obtain a favorable settlement with regard to the first set of issues, and only moderate costs to obtain a favorable settlement with regard to the second set of issues. If, on the one hand, economic sanctions (or some other signal that hurts economic ties) were relatively cheap—as would be the case if A's leader is not accountable to internationalist economic interests—then A would be willing to signal commitment using economic sanctions for the entire range of issues. That is, economic sanctions would always be on A's menu of possible signals through which to indicate commitment. If, on the other hand, A's leader depended on the political support of internationalist interests, then signaling through the use of economic sanctions would be relatively costly. Here, sanctions would be off the menu for the second range of issues—those to which A was only moderately committed—because the costs of sending a signal in this way would exceed the expected gains of achieving a favorable bargain for A. In other words, economic sanctions (or other types of signals that damage commerce directly) will be on the menu of signaling options

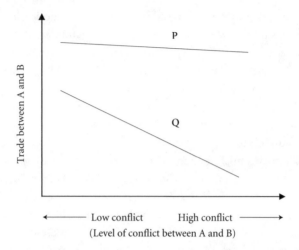

FIG. 1. Graphical illustration of H2's expectations. Line P represents trade between countries whose leaders are relatively accountable to internationalist economic interests; line Q represents trade between countries whose leaders are not highly accountable to internationalist economic interests.

in a smaller percentage of instances when A's leader depends on the support of internationalist interests. At the margins, then, private commercial actors should feel less threatened in the presence of conflict when leaders are accountable to internationalist economic interests than they otherwise would feel. They know that in these instances, leaders will only signal resolve in a way that hurts international commerce when the stakes are relatively high. Conversely, for leaders who do not depend on the support of free trade interests, these types of economically damaging signals are on the table in a much broader range of possible disputes that might arise in the context of a conflictual relationship.

My second hypothesis is thus as follows:

H_2: *All else equal, the negative effects of international conflict on international economic integration are less severe to the extent that leaders in the countries enmeshed in conflict are accountable to internationalist economic interests.*

To restate, the relationship posited by H_2 is an interactive one. Clearly, levels of trade should be higher when countries are governed by leaders accountable to internationalist economic interests, ceteris paribus. But H_2 also posits that international conflict should have a smaller independent effect on trade when such leaders are in power. Figure 1 provides a simple graphical illustration of H_2's expectations. Here, line P represents trade between two countries (A and B) governed by leaders relatively accountable to internationalist economic interests.

H_2 suggests that trade between the two countries should not be highly sensitive to the level of conflict between A and B; hence, the slope of line P is not strongly negative. Line Q represents trade between two countries whose leaders are not highly accountable to internationalist economic interests. Since leadership accountability to internationalist economic interests should have an independent effect on trade between A and B, line Q is lower than line P across all levels of conflict. But H_2 also predicts that conflict should have a greater independent effect on trade between A and B when leaders are not accountable to internationalist economic interests. The slope of line Q is thus more sharply negative than the slope of line P.

Measuring Leadership Accountability to Internationalist Economic Interests

As is the case with conflict, operationalizing leadership accountability to internationalist economic interests is hardly a straightforward task. Identifying which actors support, and which oppose, liberal foreign economic policies is itself a difficult undertaking yet represents only an initial step in understanding leadership accountability to such interests. As Solingen (1998, 24) writes, "The institutional context in which coalitions operate plays an important role in defining a coalition's political wherewithal ... and the very fate of liberalization." On a broad level, democracy may increase—on average—leadership accountability to internationalist economic interests, to the extent that median interests tend to be internationalist in orientation (Papayoanou 1996; 1999).[18] But leadership accountability to internationalist economic interests is likely to vary greatly even among democracies. Small district size in parliamentary systems, for example, can give regionally concentrated protectionist interests disproportionate political power (Rogowski 1987).[19] Highly popular leaders, or leaders who won landslide victories in elections, meanwhile, might simply feel less beholden to any specific component of their winning coalitions. And because the economic costs of closure are much higher in countries with small internal markets than in countries with large markets, internationalist economic interests are likely to be more marginalized in the latter than in the former.

Meanwhile, just as democracy does not guarantee that internationalist economic interests will wield substantial political clout, authoritarian political systems do not necessarily leave such interests marginalized. Rather, the influence of internationalist economic interests in nondemocratic systems should hinge on the composition of a particular country's "selectorate," the actors to whom top leaders are accountable (Shirk 1993; Roeder 1993). Shirk (1996) argues that in China, for instance, key components of the selectorate—such as provincial officials—had an increasing stake in access to global markets over the course of the 1980s. In other systems, such as some military juntas, leaders may have little or no accountability to internationalist economic interests.

In the empirical chapters that follow, I measure leadership accountability to internationalist economic interests in two ways. First, in the case studies, I proceed by examining the political institutions and processes in the countries involved. I identify internationalist economic interests based on observed policy positions (for example, which actors lobby openly for liberalization) and deduced preferences based on theory (Frieden 1999; Frieden and Rogowski 1996), and then assess how much influence such interests are able to exert in the political arena. Second, I draw inference based on countries' overall trade policy orientations, particularly in the quantitative analysis. My primary task in this book is to better understand when conflict between countries A and B will have an impact on economic relations between A and B. Obviously, it would be a tautology to measure the strength of internationalist economic interests based on economic exchange between A and B. But it is possible to draw some inference regarding the political clout of internationalist economic interests in A by examining A's overall foreign economic policies, not simply those directed at B in particular. That is, internationalist economic interests are likely to be stronger in countries that pursue, on balance, open foreign economic policies than they are in countries that pursue, on balance, relatively closed foreign economic policies. Of course, such an approach carries with it risks as well: for example, leaders who are relatively autonomous from competing economic interest groups might still pursue open trade policies. I return to these issues when describing the quantitative research design in Chapter 7.

Objections and Extensions

One potential objection to this line of analysis concerns endogeneity. More specifically, the work of Solingen (1998; 2003) suggests that conflict in a particular region is endogenous to the types of domestic coalitions governing countries in that region. Regions where countries are governed by strongly internationalizing coalitions are likely to be zones of stable peace. Internationalizing coalitions, for example, tend to avoid the sorts of destabilizing behaviors—such as mythmaking and bloated defense budgets—that are more common among statist/nationalist coalitions. Likewise, McDonald (2004) demonstrates quantitatively that countries with more open trade policies have a lower incidence of military conflict. These studies raise an important question: is it possible for conflict to persist even as leaders become more accountable to internationalist economic interests?

There can be little doubt that the relationships examined in this book are most likely characterized by substantial "feedback loops." Indeed, the possibility that increased economic flows reduce the likelihood of military violence (Russett and Oneal 2001) is in part what motivates this project. If trade does indeed facilitate peace, it is important to understand how economic ties can develop in the first place in dyads with a potential to engage in military conflict; H_2 has the potential to offer some leverage in this regard. But it is almost certainly the case that as internationalist economic interests become more powerful in domestic political systems, they often aim not simply to limit the impact of conflict on foreign economic policy but also to restructure those foreign policy goals that lie at the heart of conflict. Chapter 6 addresses this issue head-on by examining whether growing economic linkages across the Taiwan Strait influence, or are likely to influence in the future, the probability of cross-Strait military conflict. The chapter considers at length the possibility that economic ties can come to have a transformative impact on the foreign policy goals that drive cross-Strait political conflict. I also address this issue in the empirical chapters that follow by effectively holding the level of conflict constant—at least to some degree. In the cross-Strait case the conflicting goals at the center of the bilateral rivalry remained in place (and perhaps intensified during the presidencies of Lee Teng-hui and Chen Shui-bian) even as leadership accountability to internationalist economic interests on both sides fluctuated (and generally increased) in recent decades. Levels of conflict could, of course, decline in the future if internationalist interests become even more entrenched in the two polities (and such a process might even be starting to unfold under new Taiwanese president Ma Ying-jeou).

A separate issue concerns leaders who are not especially accountable to internationalist economic interests but who nonetheless pursue strongly internationalist foreign economic policies. For example, a leadership that is relatively insulated from societal pressures—perhaps operating in an autocratic setting—may yet be strongly committed to economic development, and might conclude that an internationalizing strategy is the best path to economic growth.[20] Are the independent effects of conflict on commerce likely to be mitigated when such leaders are in power, even though they are not necessarily accountable to internationalist economic interests?[21] The answer, I suspect, is yes, though I also believe that the effect is likely to be less dramatic. Such leaders, like those directly accountable to internationalist economic interests, will also face difficult tradeoffs that might lead them to try to separate international political and economic arenas, even though doing so could be counterproductive to their foreign political goals (such as a reluctance to limit trade in the presence of security externalities). But precisely because they enjoy more political autonomy domestically, they may be able more easily to set aside temporarily their development objectives when core international political objectives are challenged, in a way or to an extent that would be more difficult for a leader who is directly accountable to the interests that would be harmed by such a course of action.

Finally, it is important to emphasize that factors other than the domestic political influence of internationalist economic interests are also likely to condition the effect of international political conflict on cross-border economic flows. The discussion in the previous section suggests, for example, that conflict is likely to affect some types of economic exchange more than others. In particular, conflict should have a bigger impact on economic exchange that requires the deployment of relationship-specific assets. Since such assets (think of a large-scale factory) would be difficult or impossible to redeploy if conflict were to escalate, firms should be reluctant to undertake them at all in the presence of conflict.

Likewise, Section 2 suggested that there could be substantial variation across cases in the political externalities arising from commerce. These externalities sometimes tend to reinforce each other, and sometimes tend to cancel each other out. Consider, for example, a country A that benefits disproportionately from trade with country B, but at the same time depends more on bilateral economic relations than does B. The disproportionate gains that A reaps from the exchange enable A to invest more in its military, relative to B, than would otherwise be possible; in this regard, trade yields positive security externalities for A and negative externalities for B. At the same time, however, A's asymmetric dependence on the bilateral relationship makes A more vulnerable to economic coercion than B, a negative political externality for A and a positive one for B. In this scenario, even if conflict between the two countries becomes severe, neither has obvious reason to place limits on bilateral economic exchange since it is unclear whether security externalities on balance benefit A or B. Alternatively, if it were B, instead of A, that depended more on the bilateral economic relationship, the security externalities of economic exchange would uniformly benefit A and harm B. In this case, B would have more reason to impose restrictions on bilateral economic ties if political conflict between the two countries gave B reason to worry about trade's security externalities. In sum, the precise nature of trade's security externalities could influence the extent to which national leaders seek to impose restrictions on trade in the presence of conflict.

The empirical chapters that follow are sensitive to the reality that variables other than the one emphasized in H_2 could influence the extent to which conflict affects trade in a particular case. When other factors appear salient, I am up-front about it. But the focus, of course, is on testing H_2 and evaluating the extent to which the theoretical argument fleshed out above helps to make sense of trends in PRC-Taiwan relations.

4. Summary

Chapter 1 developed a straightforward research question: How are we to explain the substantial variation that appears to exist in the effects of international political conflict on international economic ties? To address that question, this chapter began by developing a broad framework that seeks to explain how conflict affects bilateral economic relations. That discussion culminated in a baseline hypothesis (H_1): the effect of conflict on commerce, all else being equal, will tend to be negative. Two causal mechanisms, drawn from the existing literature, give rise to this hypothesized effect. First, state leaders worry about the possible security externalities of economic interdependence in the shadow of conflict, which may in turn lead them to adopt policy restrictions on bilateral exchange. Second, private actors demand higher risk premiums for bilateral economic transactions when conflict is present. The remainder of the chapter considered the sources of variation in conflict's effects on economic exchange.

In developing an explanation for this variation, I focused on the domestic political determinants of conflict's impact on economic exchange. Though a substantial (and growing) literature considers the domestic political variables that affect countries' foreign economic policies, existing studies have largely ignored *interactions* between these domestic political variables and international conflict. But there are good reasons to believe that such interaction should be present; my argument along these lines culminated in the following hypothesis (H_2): the effects of conflict on economic exchange will be less severe when leaders are accountable to internationalist economic interests. The chapters that follow evaluate this hypothesis, first in the context of PRC-Taiwan relations and then more generally in Chapter 7.

Mainland China–Taiwan Relations as a Case Study

1. Introduction

The relationship across the Taiwan Strait in many ways epitomizes the puzzle outlined in Chapter 2. Political relations between Beijing and Taipei are, and have been, deeply strained. As one scholar has written, the issue at the heart of the rivalry—Taiwan's sovereign status—remains "the only issue in the world today that could realistically lead to war between two major powers."[1] Yet despite persistent and severe conflict in bilateral political relations, economic relations across the Taiwan Strait flourish. Trade flows have grown rapidly over the past twenty years, and Mainland China has recently displaced the United States as Taiwan's primary trading partner. The Mainland is also the primary destination for Taiwan's outward foreign direct investment by a large margin. This "perplexing duality" of economic integration and political standoff represents a "paradox for the student of international relations" that demands explanation.[2]

This chapter and the next three consider this intriguing case in the context of the theoretical arguments and hypotheses laid out in Chapter 2. The case study is not a formal scientific test: in a single case study like this, it is typically difficult to control fully for different, alternative explanations; some of the variables discussed abstractly in the previous chapter are difficult to operationalize or observe in practice; and as with any case study, questions of generalizability cannot be dismissed in a cavalier fashion. Despite these caveats, however, this case study is not simply a descriptive exercise. Rather, it aims to assess the extent to which the arguments made in Chapter 2 can help to explain trends and events in the relationship across the Taiwan Strait. In that regard, the case is potentially very useful. Given the severity of political conflict between Beijing and Taipei, relations across the Taiwan Strait approximate a "least likely" case, meaning that the processes mediating conflict's effects on commerce in this case may be present in other dyads characterized by conflict. In the next section I describe in more detail the nature of political conflict in Mainland China–Taiwan relations. The discussion is necessarily cursory, as entire volumes have been written on the issue of political conflict itself across the Taiwan Strait (e.g. Tucker 2005; Sheng 2001; Zhao 1999c). Here I simply provide a brief historical overview of cross-Strait political relations and discuss the core issues that generate cross-Strait political conflict. Section 3 then presents trends in the cross-Strait economic relationship. The chapter concludes with a discussion of the methodological issues surrounding this case study.

2. A Brief Summary of Political Conflict Across the Taiwan Strait

The issue of Taiwan's sovereign status has been at the heart of the cross-Strait rivalry ever since the Nationalist Party (the Kuomintang, or KMT) retreated to Taiwan in 1949 after being defeated by the Chinese Communist Party (CCP) in the Chinese Civil War. Even after retreating to Taiwan, Chiang Kai-shek's Nationalist regime (which continued to use the name The Republic of China, or ROC) still claimed to be the legitimate government of all China. Authorities in the newly established People's Republic of China (PRC), meanwhile, aimed to "liberate" Taiwan, and bring the island under Beijing's authority.[3] Though Beijing's hopes for a quick resolution were foiled when the Truman administration placed the United States Seventh Fleet in the Taiwan Strait following the outbreak of the Korean War, the eventual establishment of PRC sovereignty over Taiwan remained an important foreign policy objective. Cross-Strait relations, in turn, were characterized by repeated crises during the 1950s and 1960s.[4] During the 1960s, Chiang Kai-shek repeatedly asked for United States support in a military offensive against the PRC (Gu 1995, 35). And while Beijing began as early as the 1950s to emphasize "peaceful liberation" in its policy toward Taiwan,[5] Mainland officials in 1962 and 1975 devised contingency plans—never acted on, of course—to seize the island militarily (Gu 1995, 26–27).

The KMT leadership's claim as the legitimate government of all China remained largely unchanged through the 1970s, even following the ROC's loss of the Chinese seat in the United Nations in 1971 and the severing of diplomatic relations with the United States in 1979. However, Mainland China's policies toward Taiwan began to change in the late 1970s, and this shift—to an emphasis on "peaceful reunification" rather than confrontation—would lead to some improvement in cross-Strait relations during the 1980s. Beijing's changed stance on Taiwan became apparent in the "Message to Taiwan Compatriots" announced in 1979, in which the Mainland called for negotiations to resolve the Taiwan issue and promised "to respect the current situation in Taiwan and the views of Taiwanese in all walks of life." The statement also called for the establishment of economic linkages across the Taiwan Strait. In 1981, Marshall Ye Jianying expanded on these themes as he announced a "Nine Points" plan for peaceful reunification; the plan promised a high level of political autonomy for Taiwan—including keeping its own army—if it were to reunify with the Mainland.[6] This proposal, that Taiwan would maintain a high level of autonomy within a unified China, became known as "one country, two systems." China's 1982 state constitution formally authorized the formation of such a "special administrative region."[7]

Though the one country, two systems formula was dismissed by an ROC government that continued to reject official contact with the PRC,[8] Taiwanese policy toward the Mainland nonetheless exhibited some moderation of its own during the 1980s. For example, beginning in 1982 the Taiwanese government began to refer to Beijing as *Zhonggong dangju* (Chinese communist authorities) rather than *Gongfei* (Communist bandits); the ROC government also stopped using slogans such as "counterattack the Mainland" (Copper 1996, 165; Roy 2003, 148). More consequentially, the Taiwanese government began to allow its citizens to travel to Mainland China in 1987 (Copper 1996, 165), and later in the decade lifted bans on indirect trade and investment flows to China (a decision that will be discussed in more detail in the next chapter).

On the surface, at least, cross-Strait relations continued to stabilize to some extent during the early 1990s. In the Guidelines for National Unification, adopted in 1991, the ROC government affirmed that "both the mainland and Taiwan areas are parts of Chinese territory," and that "helping to bring about national unification should be the common responsibility of all Chinese people," though it emphasized too that unification must come about in the context of a "democratic, free and equitably prosperous China."[9] Shortly thereafter, Taiwanese president Lee Teng-hui (1988–2000) lifted the "Temporary Provisions Effective During the Period of Communist Rebellion," which had suspended the ROC constitution since the latter's being enacted in 1948. Lee also ended the "Period of National Mobilization for the Suppression of the Communist Rebellion," thereby declaring the civil war over and effectively legitimizing Communist rule on the Mainland (Roy 2003, 185).[10] In 1991, the ROC government established the Straits Exchange Foundation (SEF). Though formally a private organization, the SEF was created to serve as a semi-official intermediary in dealing with the Mainland (Goldstein 1999, 204; Roy 2003, 219). The PRC, in turn, formed a companion organization with similar function, the Association for Relations Across the Taiwan Straits

(ARATS). In 1992 ARATS proposed direct chairman-level talks between the two organizations; Taiwanese officials responded positively, leading to a 1993 meeting between C. F. Koo of SEF and Wang Daohan of ARATS in Singapore.[11]

Yet even as events like the Koo-Wang meeting suggested an improved cross-Strait political climate, the stage was being set for intensified conflict later in the decade. In part, renewed conflict emerged from political changes in Taiwan. Prior to the 1980s, the KMT had presided over a Leninist regime in which the ruling party penetrated all branches of the state, and in which opposition parties were banned (Chu 1994, 115). Moreover, though representing only about 15 percent of Taiwan's population, Mainlanders (people who emigrated to Taiwan after the mid-1940s, and their descendents) dominated the KMT leadership structure. In this type of environment, political leaders remained committed to the view that Taiwan in principle is a part of China while prohibiting contrarian public discourse on the subject. But a slow process of democratization began to accelerate in the 1980s; key breakthroughs included the government's 1986 decision to tolerate opposition parties and the 1987 lifting of martial law, which had been in place since the 1940s (Roy 2003, 172–75). Elections grew in importance, and after 1996 (when the first popular election was held for the presidency) all major executive and legislative positions—with the exception of the premier—were subject to election.[12] As the island democratized, more native Taiwanese (who compose roughly 85 percent of the island's population[13]) began to occupy official positions; Lee Teng-hui became the first Taiwan-born president of the ROC following the death of Chiang Ching-kuo in 1988. Democratization likewise enabled supporters of Taiwanese independence to organize and to voice their views openly. In 1991, Taiwan's largest opposition party, the Democratic Progressive Party (DPP), added a plank to its platform calling for the establishment of a "sovereign, independent, self-governing Republic of Taiwan."[14]

As he consolidated authority against this backdrop, Lee Teng-hui came to advocate a broader role in world affairs for Taiwan while distancing himself from the principle that Taiwan is a part of China. In an effort to reverse Taiwan's growing isolation as other countries broke ties with the ROC to establish relations with Beijing, Lee's government pursued a policy of "pragmatic diplomacy." The general aim was to maintain constructive relations with other countries, even if those countries established formal diplomatic relations with the PRC (Copper 1996, 150). In 1990, for example, after Saudi Arabia established relations with the PRC, Taipei did not respond (as it normally had done with other countries in the past) by breaking ties with Saudi Arabia. Rather, Saudi Arabia ultimately severed official ties with Taipei at Beijing's insistence (Zhao 1999b, 114). These efforts to improve Taiwan's international profile soon became more pronounced: in 1993,

Taipei began actively to seek re-entry into the United Nations, and in early 1994 Lee Teng-hui took a high-profile trip to Southeast Asia, meeting with officials along the way, in what was officially called a private vacation.[15] As Yun-han Chu (2000, 205) writes, "These moves amounted to a concerted effort to establish a separate international identity" for Taiwan.

Taipei's efforts in these regards were alarming to PRC leaders, who worried increasingly that Lee's ultimate goal was Taiwanese independence. These concerns were reinforced by Lee's harsh anti-PRC rhetoric following the 1994 murder of several Taiwanese nationals at China's Thousand Islands Lake, and by an interview in 1994 with a Japanese journalist in which Lee called the KMT an "alien regime" and compared himself to Moses (Zhao 1999b, 111; Swaine 2001, 315). Nonetheless, though warning against Taiwanese separatism, Beijing's policies remained generally conciliatory: in a speech in January 1995, Chinese president Jiang Zemin issued an "Eight Points" proposal that called for dialogue and that reiterated his previous statement that "under the premise that there is only one China, we can discuss any issues," including "all issues of concern to Taiwanese officials."[16] Lee responded to Jiang's speech with his own "Six Points" proposal in which he demanded that the PRC relinquish the use of force against Taiwan before negotiations could begin; in Beijing, the response was viewed as a "slap in the face" (Swaine 2001, 319). Shortly thereafter, in May 1995, Lee took a highly publicized trip to his alma mater, Cornell University. The trip left leaders in Beijing more convinced than ever that Lee was pursuing a separatist agenda, and furthermore that the conciliatory approach the PRC had been adopting was not working; after the trip, Beijing's policies toward the island toughened significantly. The Mainland cancelled a second round of Koo-Wang talks scheduled for later in the year, and engaged in a series of military exercises near Taiwan. The exercises culminated in missile tests near the island in early 1996, in the run-up to Taiwan's first presidential election.[17]

Though cross-Strait relations stabilized considerably after Taiwan's election in 1996, tensions spiked again in 1999 after Lee characterized relations with the Mainland as "special state-to-state relations." The formulation was hardly a major departure from past policy—Taiwanese officials had insisted since the early 1990s that the ROC and PRC represented two sovereign states (Chen 1999, 135). Still, Lee's announcement elicited a sharp reaction from the Mainland, culminating in early 2000 in a white paper that was harshly critical of Lee and which warned that indefinite delay on reunification would be a legitimate reason for the PRC to resort to military force (Swaine 2001, 330).[18] Mainland leaders staunchly opposed Lee's efforts to redefine the cross-Strait relationship along the lines of the Cold War German model or the Korean model, where both sides possess equal sovereignty. For Beijing, the Taiwan Strait situation is fundamentally different; unlike Germany or Korea, where division was the product of international forces, Taiwan's separation from China was a relic of the Chinese Civil War and as such remained an internal affair.[19]

The election of Chen Shui-bian of the officially pro-independence Democratic Progressive Party (DPP) as Taiwanese president in 2000 had the potential to further destabilize cross-Strait relations. But Chen initially adopted a cautious strategy in dealing with the Mainland: in his inauguration he announced that his administration would follow a policy of "5 No's," which included no official independence for Taiwan, no public referendum on the issue of independence, and no change in the ROC's name (e.g. Keum and Campbell 2001, 76). Still, Chen steadfastly refused to acknowledge support for the one-China principle in any form, and cross-Strait tensions began to rise again after an August 2002 speech in which Chen emphasized that "Taiwan is a sovereign, independent country" and that each side of the Taiwan Strait constitutes a separate country (*yi bian, yi guo*) (Bush 2005, 69; Su 2003, 242). By the fall of 2003, as Taiwan's 2004 presidential election loomed, cross-Strait relations again appeared heading toward crisis. In 2003, Taiwan's Legislative Yuan passed a referendum law that allowed for direct referenda under restrictive conditions; Chen seized on a loophole in the law, that a president can hold a defensive referendum when Taiwan's national security is at risk, to announce a referendum on the same day as the 2004 presidential election. Ultimately, under strong pressure from the United States, Chen chose not to make the referendum overly provocative, instead asking two relatively innocuous questions. The KMT and other opposition parties led a boycott of the referendum, and in the end both questions failed to get enough participation for the results to be valid; nonetheless the precedent of direct votes in Taiwan on issues relating to national security was deeply disturbing from Beijing's perspective. After his narrow electoral victory, moreover, Chen vowed to push for a new constitution in his second term; he further indicated that he believed Taiwan had already achieved "an internal consensus that insists on Taiwan being an independent, sovereign country."[20]

As the year-end legislative elections approached in Taiwan, Chen tried to rally support for the DPP and its ally, the Taiwan Solidarity Union (TSU), by placing heavy emphasis on Taiwan's sovereignty in the fall campaign.[21] He campaigned for a new constitution to replace the ROC constitution dating back to the Chinese Civil War, and for a "rectification" of Taiwan's internationally used name, the ROC (e.g. Christensen 2005, 3). As Christensen writes, Chen's re-election, combined with his renewed emphasis on the sovereignty issue in the fall 2004 campaign, led to a deep sense of pessimism in Beijing, with many officials and scholars coming to believe that war was becoming inevitable (Christensen 2005).[22] Though this pessimism subsided to a considerable degree after the DPP and its allies failed to win control of the Legislative Yuan, it became hard to imagine a significant breakthrough in bilateral relations occurring during the remainder of Chen's presidency. And, indeed, Chen continued to place emphasis on the sovereignty issue. In early 2006, for example, his government declared that the National Unification Guidelines would "cease to apply" (*zhongzhi shiyong*) and the National Unification Council would "cease to operate" (*zhongzhi yunzuo*).[23] More recently, Chen backed a controversial referendum endorsing Taiwan's entry into the United Nations under the name "Taiwan" to be voted on at the same time as the 2008 presidential election; the planned referendum sparked sharp criticism from the United States.[24]

The DPP ultimately suffered landslide defeats in the 2008 legislative and presidential elections, and a large majority of Taiwanese voters refused to participate in the controversial referendum—ensuring its defeat.[25] Cross-Strait relations appear likely to stabilize—at least to some extent—under new president Ma Ying-jeou of the KMT. Ma campaigned on a pragmatic platform: he pledged to seek neither legal independence nor unification while president, and he called for renewed cross-Strait dialogue under the rubric of the "'92 consensus."[26] At the time of this writing in June 2008, cross-Strait relations have improved significantly under the new Ma administration; whether the two sides will seize the opportunity to effect a broader transformation in the cross-Strait relationship remains unclear, however.[27]

To summarize, the issue that lies at the heart of cross-Strait political conflict concerns Taiwan's sovereign status. Since the early 1990s, Taiwanese leaders—first Lee Teng-hui and then Chen Shui-bian—sought to enhance Taiwan's international profile and sovereign status. Like Lee before him, Chen viewed Taiwan as an independent, sovereign state of equal stature to the PRC. For leaders in Beijing, who view Taiwan as being legally a part of a single China and for whom de facto reunification remains a cherished long-term goal, this claim is unacceptable.

3. Growing Economic Ties Across the Taiwan Strait

Despite persistent conflict in relations across the Taiwan Strait, economic ties between Taiwan and Mainland China have burgeoned since the late 1980s. Before the mid-1980s, the economic incentives for Taiwanese businesses to interact with the Mainland were quite limited. Taiwan had followed a development strategy focusing on the export of labor-intensive manufactures; the primary target market for these exports was the United States. At the same time, China's economic reforms had only begun in the late 1970s. Though the Mainland decided to allow Taiwanese goods to enter the country duty-free in 1980, Taiwan's response was limited since, according to Barry Naughton (1997, 84), "a minimum essential degree of marketization had probably not been achieved" in China. And incentives for cross-Strait integration remained limited even though unit labor costs in Taiwan grew quickly in the 1970s and early 1980s. This was true in part because the New Taiwan dollar remained steady against the US dollar through the 1970s, and even depreciated considerably against the dollar in the early 1980s (Naughton 1997).

Under pressure from the United States, the Taiwanese government allowed the New Taiwan dollar to appreciate after the mid-1980s, resulting in a rise of 48 percent against the US dollar between 1986 and 1988 (Chu 1994, 121–22). The appreciation of Taiwan's currency clearly had the potential to undermine the competitiveness of the island's labor-intensive exports; businesses thus had strong new incentives to move such production into low-wage, overseas areas. Continued economic reform in China, combined with the Mainland's shared culture, labor abundance, and geographic proximity, made it an attractive site (Chen 1994). Investments in the late 1980s and early 1990s were largely undertaken by small, labor-intensive enterprises. Investments were small-scale, often involved used or rented equipment, and were expected to lead to profits within a relatively short span of time (Taylor 1999; La Croix and Xu 1995; Hsing 1998). At the time, Taiwanese businesses pursued primarily a "two ends remain outside" (liangtou zaiwai) strategy: Taiwanese investors in China imported materials and equipment (mostly from Taiwan) and exported finished products (Hsing 1998, 129; Yan 1992, 52). As China's economic reform and opening accelerated after 1992, however, larger Taiwanese firms began to enter the Mainland market in greater numbers: the number of major Taiwanese firms with officially reported investments in China grew from forty-six in 1993 to eighty-three in 1996 (Chu 1997, 242).[28] Moreover, China's large internal market began to motivate investments to a greater extent, and the expected time span for investments to turn a profit increased.[29] The average size of individual investment projects also grew sharply in the mid-1990s.[30] Meanwhile, over the course of the 1990s the nature of Taiwanese investments in China shifted toward more capital-intensive and high technology sectors. From 1991 to 1998, approximately 21 percent of Taiwan's approved investments in China were in the electronics and electric appliances sectors; by decade's end this percentage approached 50 percent.[31]

Trade flows, dominated by Taiwanese exports to the Mainland, have grown rapidly since the late 1980s: cross-Strait trade was less than US$1 billion in 1986, but by 2006 exceeded US$88 billion (see Figure 2).[32] Indeed, Mainland China in

FIG. 2. Cross-Strait trade (billions US$). Based on data reported in *Liang'an Jingji Tongji Yuebao*, No. 176.

FIG. 3. Approved Taiwan investment in Mainland China (millions US$). Based on data reported in *Liang'an Jingji Tongji Yuebao*, No. 176. Does not include values of previously unreported investments that were added onto totals reported for 1993, 1997, 1998, 2002, and 2003 (as reported in *Liang'an Jingji Tongji Yuebao*, No. 155).

2003 replaced the United States as Taiwan's largest trading partner.[33] Investment flows have also grown rapidly—much more rapidly than official statistics suggest. This is because a large percentage of Taiwanese investments in China are illegal under Taiwanese law, and hence go unreported. So, while official Taiwanese and Mainland statistics place accumulated Taiwanese investment on the Mainland through 2006 at US\$55 billion and US\$44 billion, respectively, many estimate that Taiwanese investments in China actually exceed US\$100 billion.[34] Figure 3 plots cross-Strait investment flows since the early 1990s according to official Taiwanese statistics.

4. Using Mainland China–Taiwan Relations as a Test Case

In the context of prior work on conflict and economic interdependence, rapidly growing cross-Strait economic ties in the presence of severe cross-Strait political conflict are puzzling for two reasons. First, why is economic integration not more adversely affected by the security externalities that such integration gives rise to? In this case, as I show in the following chapters, officials in *both* Taiwan and Mainland China have recognized that the security externalities of economic integration benefit China to the detriment of Taiwan's security; in that regard, it is on the surface surprising that the Taiwanese government does not do more to stem the flow of cross-Strait trade and investment. Chapter 4 deals with this issue by analyzing the determinants of Taiwanese economic policy toward Mainland China in light of the theoretical arguments I advanced in Chapter 2. The second puzzle concerns Taiwanese businesses engaged in cross-Strait economic exchange: why do these firms flock to the Mainland market despite the conflict? Do they not fear—particularly since the mid-1990s, when cross-Strait tensions over the sovereignty issue rose—that Beijing might employ economic sanctions as a signal that the Mainland is resolved in blocking an independent Taiwan? Chapter 5 addresses this issue, again in light of the theoretical arguments made in Chapter 2, by examining PRC signaling behavior toward Taiwan. These chapters rely on information from a variety of sources, including newspapers, scholarly articles and books, government documents, and interviews that I conducted with government officials, scholars, and policy analysts in Taipei (fall 2000–spring 2001; spring 2004; summer 2005), Beijing (spring 2002), and Shanghai (summer 2004).

It would be disingenuous to suggest that I picked the Mainland China–Taiwan relationship as a case study for scientific reasons. Rather, I picked the case because it is one that interests me; the reason the case originally drew my interest is, in large measure, its importance in contemporary international affairs. In that regard, any light this case study sheds on the dynamics of relations across the Taiwan Strait will hold intrinsic value. That said, the case is also useful from the perspective of evaluating the arguments made in Chapter 2. As noted earlier, Mainland China–Taiwan relations resemble a "least likely" case study because of the intensity of political conflict across the Taiwan Strait (George and Bennett 2005). If domestic political factors reduce conflict's effects on economic integration even here, then these effects could generalize to other cases (especially those in which conflict is less severe). Moreover, as will be shown in the next chapter, not only have economic flows across the Taiwan Strait varied over time, but Taiwan's economic policies toward Mainland China have also varied. As such, the case is effectively transformed into multiple observations—meaning that it is possible to consider the extent to which different independent variables, such as the accountability of leaders to internationalist economic interests or the importance of security externalities, co-vary with Taiwanese policy.

Yet the case study also carries with it a number of methodological problems that need to be addressed up front. First, as King and others (1994, 209–12) caution, rigorous hypothesis-testing in the context of single case studies—even in least-likely, "crucial" scenarios—is fraught with difficulties. Alternative explanations, for example, cannot be systematically examined. In this case study, variation in Taiwan's policies over time does allow me to engage some alternative explanations, but I nonetheless remain cautious in claiming that findings here generalize elsewhere. As with any case, in cross-Strait relations there are simply too many features that are quirky or relatively unique. For example, that the two sides of the Taiwan Strait share a language and a culture, or that the political conflict is in part residual of a civil war and concerns the issue of national unification, or that Taiwan's foreign policy goals are a highly contentious issue domestically in Taipei could all conceivably exert an important influence on the relationship between conflict and commerce across the Taiwan Strait. The case study, therefore, is not a rigorous test of the hypotheses outlined in Chapter 2; rather, it is—to paraphrase Lake (1999, 71)—an "exercise in theory-driven" analysis of a contemporary case, where available evidence from the case is considered against the backdrop of the theoretical arguments made in Chapter 2. It is my hope that these theoretical arguments can provide new insights into the dynamics of cross-Strait relations over the past two decades.

The case study faces additional methodological challenges. One of the primary independent variables introduced in Chapter 2—the extent to which leaders are accountable to internationalist economic interests—is a relatively abstract concept that was useful in theory-development but that is difficult to operationalize in an empirical analysis. In this case, I assess leadership accountability to internationalist economic interests based on my understanding of the Taiwanese and Chinese domestic political systems; I am also up-front throughout that my assessments are characterized by a considerable degree of uncertainty arising from possible measurement error. However, I do not arrive at my assessments based on a circular logic, inferring back from observed policy changes; that is, I take care throughout the case study to avoid tautology.

A separate issue concerns the evidence that I use in this case study. Ideally, in addition to demonstrating correlation between the independent and dependent variables, I would also show evidence indicating a causal link—that is, I would be able to demonstrate that the observed relationship between the variables of interest is not spurious. I attempt to draw these causal links where possible—for example, by searching for official statements that provide evidence concerning the motivations of policy. At times, however, the evidence I provide is circumstantial, simply because I was unable to find a "smoking gun." In these cases, I am again frank about the limitations of my analysis. In the end, it is my belief that the case study serves its purpose quite well: it shows that the theoretical arguments presented in Chapter 2 can shed additional light on the dynamics of the relationship across the Taiwan Strait, and it offers some preliminary confirmation of those theoretical arguments.

4

Changing Taiwanese Economic Policy
Toward Mainland China

1. Introduction

This chapter examines Taiwan's economic policy toward Mainland China. Ultimately in this study I am interested in levels of economic integration that arise in conflictual relationships. But the theoretical argument developed in Chapter 2 shows that one mechanism through which conflict can affect international economic flows centers on national foreign economic policies. States sometimes place restrictions on economic relations with adversaries because international economic flows sometimes have security-related externalities. As such, this chapter considers the restrictions that Taiwan has placed on cross-Strait economic exchange, and the factors that have led to changes in these restrictions over time.[1]

Indeed, Taiwan has maintained a range of restrictions on cross-Strait economic ties, and evidence suggests that these restrictions have been motivated to a considerable extent by security concerns: Taiwanese policymakers worry that economic integration with China has security externalities that are negative for Taiwan. But the scope of Taiwanese restrictions on cross-Strait economic ties has varied considerably since the mid-1980s, and changes in the level of conflict are not sufficient to explain this variation. For example, though cross-Strait tensions remained high in 2000–2001, newly elected Taiwanese president Chen Shui-bian repeatedly advocated removing restrictions on economic exchange with the Mainland; in 2001 his government announced a major liberalization of cross-Strait economic policy. More generally, even though recent administrations in Taiwan have been concerned that deepening economic integration with China could hamper their international political goals, they have been unwilling—and perhaps unable—to adopt the strict controls necessary to scale back cross-Strait economic ties; to the contrary, economic integration has continued to grow rapidly.

My core argument in this chapter is that the political clout of internationalist economic interests within Taiwan's ruling coalition has acted as an important intervening variable influencing the relationship between cross-Strait political conflict and Taiwan's cross-Strait economic policy. In this case, I focus on those economic interests that benefit directly from cross-Strait commercial integration. As the political influence of these interests increased, Taiwanese officials were less willing to impose restrictions on commerce with China, despite a high level of cross-Strait political conflict.

The next section discusses how Taiwanese policymakers have viewed commercial relations with the Mainland under the shadow of political rivalry. In particular, I consider why Taiwan has implemented policies designed to reduce the scope of cross-Strait economic relations. Sections 3–5 examine the evolution of Taiwanese economic policy toward the Mainland since the mid-1980s, using evidence from newspapers, interviews, and secondary publications[2]; Section 6 concludes.

2. National Security Concerns and Taiwanese Restrictions on Cross-Strait Commerce

Though there has been considerable variation in Taiwan's commercial policy toward the Mainland over the past two decades, and though the scope of restrictions has generally declined over time, substantial restrictions remained in place throughout the Lee Teng-hui and Chen Shui-bian administrations. For example, most direct travel, shipping, and communications links with the Mainland (the "three links") were prohibited, which meant that travel and trade had first to pass through other locations, such as Hong Kong. Only recently, under the Ma Ying-jeou administration, has there been significant progress on opening up the three direct links. Taiwanese investment on the Mainland remains subject to restrictions (though these too are being relaxed under Ma), and the island's barriers to Chinese investments and exports remain considerable. Taiwan has maintained these various restrictions in part because officials (particularly in the Lee and Chen administrations) have worried that cross-Strait economic integration could make it harder for the island to pursue its international political objectives. That is, cross-Strait economic ties potentially have security externalities that are negative for Taiwan.

Taiwanese policymakers have expressed concern about several types of security externalities that could arise from cross-Strait economic integration.[3] First, economic ties with China make Taiwan vulnerable to sanctioning threats that Beijing might issue in the future. This vulnerability arises in large part because of the asymmetric nature of cross-Strait economic integration: cross-Strait trade represents a much larger percentage of Taiwan's overall trade flows (nearly 22 percent in 2007) than is the case for Mainland China (only 4.7 percent in 2007). Cross-Strait investment flows are even more imbalanced: Taiwan's approved investments in China have in recent years represented more than 60 percent of Taiwan's total approved foreign investments. But contracted Taiwanese investments in China have represented less than 10 percent of the PRC's total contracted investment inflows.[4] While the Mainland has until now largely eschewed sanctions (for reasons that will be explored in the next chapter), the possibility that Beijing could impose sanctions in a crisis may increase the Mainland's bargaining leverage over the island.[5]

Second, some officials (particularly in previous administrations) have been concerned that, over time, economic integration could come to have a transformative impact on the island's politics, making it more likely that future governing coalitions in Taiwan will identify more with China and be less interested in protecting and promoting Taiwan's sovereign status. On the one hand, growing cross-Strait exchanges have the potential to blur Taiwanese identity, leading more Taiwanese to identify with China over time.[6] On the other hand, the Taiwanese business community, as it becomes more integrated with the Chinese market, could become an important constituency opposing a more assertive Taiwanese sovereignty (preferring instead stability in cross-Strait relations). Especially worrying is the possibility that Beijing might pressure Taiwanese businesses to play such a role, a concern emphasized by former foreign minister Tien Hung-mao: "In the [2000] election, China came to realize that businessmen can play a very strong role in Taiwanese politics. So China has begun politicizing the economic relationship between the two countries."[7] Former president Lee Teng-hui himself warned in 1996 that the Mainland was using Taiwanese investors as a tool to influence Taiwan's government.[8] My own interviews also pointed toward this mechanism as a source of concern. One government official whom I interviewed in 2000, for example, argued that Taiwanese investments on the Mainland give Beijing a channel through which to influence Taiwanese politics. He noted in particular that Mainland officials might pressure Taiwanese companies to lobby the Taiwanese government for policies favorable to Beijing; other interviewees echoed this same concern as a factor behind restrictions on cross-Strait commerce.[9]

Third, some Taiwanese officials have worried that certain types of Taiwanese investments in China, especially high-tech and infrastructure investments, have the effect of making China more economically and militarily powerful, and hence more of a threat to Taiwan. One official I interviewed in 2001 noted that policymakers were especially concerned about technology transfers to China: Taiwanese firms alter the strategic balance by taking technology, which they developed using money raised in Taiwan, over to the Mainland. He emphasized that a motivating factor behind the "Go Slow, Be Patient" policy—a policy devised by Taiwan in 1996, which I will discuss further on—was officials' worry that cross-Strait commerce was making China stronger at a time when relations were hostile.[10] In addition to reinforcing existing bans on Mainland investments in high-tech or defense-related industries by enacting stiffer penalties for violators, the Go Slow, Be Patient policy prohibited Taiwanese firms from investing in Mainland China's infrastructure development.[11] Public statements made as the new regulations were announced in 1996 and 1997 likewise indicate clearly that security externalities were a motivating factor behind the new restrictions. Pin-kung Chiang, then chairman of Taiwan's Council for Economic Planning and Development, asserted that "China is trying to attract more investment from Taiwan to increase their economic power and to reduce our economic power. . . . They haven't said that, but it's very obvious they have political motivations."[12]

New Taiwan president Ma Ying-jeou is clearly less concerned than his predecessors about the security externalities of cross-Strait economic integration. Indeed, Ma believes that deepening cross-Strait economic ties also give Taiwan an opportunity to influence the PRC's political development.[13] Moreover, the restrictions on cross-Strait economic ties that were imposed by Ma's predecessors were not always motivated entirely by security concerns. For example, barriers to imports—such as agricultural goods—certainly benefit specific import-competing Taiwanese producers; that is, protectionism is a motivation for restrictions on imports from China. As more and more Taiwanese companies have shifted production facilities to the Mainland, officials have also worried about a "hollowing out" of Taiwan's economy that might undermine long-term growth prospects (my interviews). Lee Teng-hui likewise articulated this concern when he began to warn companies to slow their investment activities in China in 1996. He argued at a conference that companies should "grow roots in Taiwan," and expressed alarm at the trend of increasing Taiwanese investments on the Mainland while domestic investment decreased. Nonetheless, economic worries do not appear to be the primary reason behind the adoption of restrictions on cross-Strait investment flows. During the mid-1990s—just as the Go Slow, Be Patient policy was being formulated—Taiwanese officials encouraged *expanded* Taiwanese investments in Southeast Asia through the "Go-South" strategy.[14] Policymakers in Taipei, it seems, were less interested in preventing the outflow of capital from Taiwan than they were in keeping that capital from flowing into China.

In summary, national security concerns have been a key reason behind many of Taiwan's restrictions on cross-Strait economic relations. However, the discussion to this point has not considered why Taiwanese restrictions on cross-Strait commerce have varied over time. Why, for example, did Taiwanese policymakers decide to implement the Go Slow, Be Patient policy in 1996–97, after several years of gradual liberalization? Why did Chen Shui-bian's government relax that same policy in 2001, even though China's general policy stance toward Taiwan did not change? The next sections describe changes in Taiwanese policy over time, and argue that domestic political conditions account for some of the variation.

3. The Late 1980s and Early 1990s: Liberalizing Trends

Taiwan banned all contact with Mainland China before the mid-1980s; during the later 1980s, it began to liberalize many of its restrictions on cross-Strait commerce. In this section I describe and explain these changes: I begin by summarizing changes in Taiwanese economic policy toward Mainland China in the late 1980s into the early 1990s. I then consider political change in Taiwan as a factor contributing to these changes. In particular, democratization in Taiwan raised the political costs to leaders for maintaining economically costly restrictions on cross-Strait commerce, and also increased the political influence of big businesses. I emphasize, however, that increasing political clout for big businesses was not the decisive factor leading to reduced restrictions on cross-Strait commerce in the late 1980s and early 1990s. This is because most Taiwanese investors on the Mainland at the time were small businesses with limited political clout. A more important factor, which I consider next, was that the security costs associated with integration were not high at the time precisely because the types of businesses that wished to invest in China in the late 1980s typically were small, labor-intensive operations. As such, the value of relation-specific assets that these businesses tended to invest on the Mainland was limited, and security externalities were probably limited as well.

Changing Cross-Strait Commercial Patterns and Taiwanese Policies

Prior to the mid-1980s, economic interaction between Taiwan and Mainland China was very limited. Several factors, including limited marketization of the Mainland's economy and an undervalued New Taiwan dollar (NT$), reduced the economic incentives of Taiwanese firms to trade with or invest in Mainland China. Importantly, Taiwan's tight political restrictions on cross-Strait commerce also had a dampening effect on the level of economic interaction across the Taiwan Strait. Through the early 1980s, the island's official stance toward the Mainland consisted of no contact, no negotiation, and no compromise—the "three no's" policy (La Croix and Xu 1995, 126). Beginning in the mid-1980s, however, Taiwan began to soften its restrictions on cross-Strait interaction. In 1985, the ROC government modified the three no's policy to "no contact, no encouragement, and no inter-vention"; the change effectively legitimized indirect trade with the Mainland (Yan 1992, 86; La Croix and Xu 1995). Far more wide-reaching changes in Taiwan's policy occurred in 1987 when President Chiang Ching-Kuo lifted martial law on Taiwan and allowed the island's residents to visit relatives on the Mainland (Chiu 1995, 148). The new policies signaled a more relaxed atmosphere regarding eco-nomic interaction with China.

In 1987, the Taiwanese government began to allow a very limited number of agricultural and raw materials to be imported indirectly from Mainland China (Yan 1992, 86), and in 1989 it announced the "Mechanisms for Managing Goods from the Mainland Area" (*Dalu Diqu Wupin Guanli Banfa*). The new regulations made explicit the requirements for importing products from the Mainland— including the provisions that any imports from the Mainland must be indirect (that is, pass through some third country or territory), must not harm Taiwan's national security or economic development, and must be on the list of allowable imports generated by the Ministry of Economics (Yan 1992, 87). In 1990, the Taiwanese government announced the "Mechanisms for Managing the Indirect Export of Products to the Mainland Area" (*Dui Dalu Diqu Jianjie Shuchu Huopin Guanli Banfa*) and the "Mechanisms for Managing Indirect Investment or Techni-cal Cooperation in the Mainland Area" (*Dui Dalu Diqu Congshi Jianjie Touzi huo Jishu Hezuo Guanli Banfa*) (Yan 1992, 86). The new regulations provided legal sanc-tion to indirect exports to, and investments in, Mainland China and detailed crite-ria that such exports and investments must meet in order to conform to Taiwanese law. Again, the regulations required that all exports to and investments in China be indirect, not undermine Taiwan's national security or economic development, and be in product categories approved by the Ministry of Economics (Yan 1992, 88–90).

In the years that followed, Taiwanese authorities continued to prohibit direct transactions with the Mainland, but they gradually relaxed restrictions on the types of products allowed to be traded and the types of industries acceptable for investment. For example, by 1992 the list of allowable import product categories had expanded from 29 (when the list was first announced in 1987) to 693 (out of a total of 7,083 product categories) (Yan 1992, 89); though Taiwan continued to prohibit the importing of over 90 percent of all product categories from the Mainland, substantial liberalization had clearly occurred. Similarly, the govern-ment initially authorized 3,353 product categories for indirect investments in China when it legalized such investments in 1990, but it expanded this list by 326 product categories in 1991 and by another 58 in 1992 (Yan 1992, 90). Substantial restrictions remained: larger projects received considerable scrutiny (Schive 1995,

33–34), while investments in a number of sectors continued to be banned.[15] Still, the 3,737 product categories approved for investments in China represented nearly 53 percent of all product categories (Yan 1992, 90), and almost all industries that were by the early 1990s noncompetitive in Taiwan were allowed to invest in China (Chiu 1995, 149). In the wake of these policy changes, approved Taiwanese investment on the Mainland—according to Mainland statistics—grew from under US$100 million in 1987 to over US$5 billion in 1992 (Chiu 1995, 150), while Leng Tse-Kang (1996, 110) estimates that cross-Strait trade over the same time frame grew from US$3.6 billion to US$14.5 billion. In short, changes in Taiwan's cross-Strait commercial policies during the late 1980s and early 1990s were clearly substantial, and they demand explanation.

Explaining Commercial Liberalization: The Impact of
Political Changes in Taiwan

Chapter 3 described the economic changes that spurred cross-Strait commercial integration starting in the late 1980s; reform on the Mainland and a revaluation of the New Taiwan dollar were especially important factors driving small- and medium-sized, labor-intensive firms to invest in China. Chinese policy shifts were likewise important; Beijing suggested as early as 1978 that the two sides should engage in indirect trade and in 1988 announced special incentives to Taiwanese investors in the "Regulations on Encouraging Investment by Taiwanese" (Chiu 1995). But political change in Taiwan also appears to have played a role in chang-ing the island's commercial policy toward the Mainland.

Prior to the 1980s, the ruling KMT banned opposition parties; though local officials were popularly elected, almost no central government positions were subject to elections (Chu 1994, 115). Before Chiang Kai-shek's forces retreated to Taiwan, the National Assembly had in 1948 passed the "Temporary Provisions Effective During the Period of Communist Rebellion," which suspended the ROC constitution and transferred sweeping powers to the president (Roy 2003, 83). The KMT later declared martial law on Taiwan; the party would rule Taiwan under martial law and a suspended constitution for the next four decades.

During the 1980s, however, Taiwan began a gradual transition to democra-cy—as discussed briefly in the previous chapter. The process of democratization can be traced most clearly to 1986, when the KMT began to tolerate opposition parties. Several opposition leaders had announced the formation of the Demo-cratic Progressive Party (DPP) in that year; though the government declared the new party illegal, it did not actively crack down by, for example, arresting the founding members (Roy 2003, 172–73). The KMT lifted martial law on the island in 1987, and in 1991 President Lee Teng-hui lifted the "Temporary Provisions."

Meanwhile, the number of central government positions subject to elections grew steadily. The number of seats subject to election in Taiwan's Legislative Yuan (the principal law-making body) increased in the late 1980s, and beginning in 1992 all seats were democratically elected (the National Assembly, then responsible for amending the ROC constitution, was fully elected starting in 1991). Taiwan's first presidential election, won in a landslide by KMT candidate Lee Teng-hui, was held in 1996.[16]

Democratization meant that Taiwanese officials would be more accountable for economic performance than in the past, and it meant that people and groups could openly criticize the government when unpopular policies were implemented. Once the government made the decision to shed its protectionist policy of a severely undervalued New Taiwan dollar, the economic opportunity costs of preventing labor-intensive industries from investing on the Mainland grew considerably—since many such industries could no longer compete in world markets if confined to Taiwan. Higher levels of accountability in a democratic setting undoubtedly made policymakers more sensitive to those economic costs, and hence unwilling to expend the resources necessary to clamp down on cross-Strait commerce.

Furthermore, democratization increased the political power of societal, and especially business, interests; groups could now organize freely and lobby on behalf of their interests. Chyuan-Jeng Shiau argues that during the predemocratic era, the Taiwanese state allied itself with two major partners to bolster its legitimacy and support: local factions and businesses. Local factions—originally consisting primarily of landlords and gentry—helped to stabilize local populations; in return, the state gave them access to considerable patronage benefits. Shiau describes the state-business relationship as more of a "passive partnership." To secure business support, the state implemented a policy of heavy protectionism; businesses, though, "were not permitted to play an active role in the political arena" (Shiau 1996, 215–18). Yun-han Chu makes similar observations, noting that the KMT gained cooperation and loyalty from important business actors by granting them rights to oligopoly arrangements. Still, Chu writes that business elites remained on the "fringe of the KMT power structure." Businesses themselves had limited representation within the government, and senior officials from economic bureaucracies such as the Ministry of Economic Affairs (MOEA) "did not enjoy the same political standing of their counterparts in the military, security, and foreign policy agencies" (Chu 1994, 116–17). Rigger (1999, 75–76) characterizes Taiwan's interest-group system in the authoritarian era as party-state corporatism. Organizations, including business associations, were state structured and controlled. Rigger notes that 95 percent of the general managers of Taiwan's industrial organizations were KMT members. The result, she writes, was that the "associations became far more effective at communicating the state's policies to their members than articulating or promoting the members' interests vis-à-vis the state" (1999, 76). Before the 1980s, therefore, while the KMT was able to maintain business support through protectionist policies and patronage, businesses had limited access to central policymakers in Taiwan and limited leverage over the policy-making process.

After the mid-1980s, however, business access to politics began to grow in conjunction with democratization. Tse-Kang Leng outlines several mechanisms through which businesses were able to influence political decisions by the early 1990s. Perhaps most importantly, elections for the Legislative Yuan and other important posts—such as county magistrates—opened the door for influence buying (Leng 1996, 86; Chu 1994, 125). Moreover, Taiwan's single nontransferable vote (SNTV) electoral system encouraged legislative candidates to cultivate a personal vote.[17] Under the system, voters chose only one candidate. As most districts had several seats, party label was not sufficient because parties typically nominated several candidates within the same district (Cox and Niou 1994). Candidates thus needed outside resources through which to cultivate a personal vote, and local businesses were typically an obvious source. One estimate put the cost of running a campaign for Taiwan's legislature in the mid-1990s at between 2 and 4 million US dollars on average (Robinson 1999). Magnifying business influence in the early 1990s was the widespread practice of vote buying—at US$20 to US$80 per vote—which clearly increased campaign expenses significantly (Nathan 1993, 429; Leng 1996, 86).

Business actors also began to participate in politics directly, often running as candidates for elected office.[18] Meanwhile, starting in the late 1980s, KMT and state-owned businesses began to cooperate much more closely with an array of private business groups. Prior to the late 1980s, KMT enterprises typically entered into joint ventures with state-owned firms. But after 1988, the KMT entered into a large number of joint ventures with private firms as well. Leng (1996, 87) notes that the new arrangements were mutually beneficial: the KMT gained more financial resources with which to compete in elections (necessitated by democratization), while the private business groups that joined with the KMT obtained political access and protection.

In short, by the early 1990s, business access to the political arena had grown considerably, meaning that the political costs of ignoring business interests had grown as well. However, the importance of business's political influence in shaping changes in cross-Strait economic policy before 1992 should not be overstated. This is chiefly because small businesses remained more marginalized politically at the time. They were less organized than big business, and they generally did not possess sufficient resources to support candidates individually (Chu 1994, 133–34).[19] But it was small- and medium-sized firms that benefited most from cross-Strait commerce until the early 1990s, and it was they that had the most to gain from Taiwan's decision in the late 1980s and early 1990s to relax restrictions on cross-Strait trade and investment. In other words, the actors with the strongest internationalist economic interests—at least with regard to cross-Strait economic ties—continued to have limited political influence in the late 1980s and early 1990s. I will argue further on, in Section 4, that business influence in Taiwanese politics became a more decisive factor influencing cross-Strait commercial policy after 1992, when Taiwan's larger firms—those with increasing political clout— began to seek entrance into the Mainland market.[20]

Relation-Specific Assets and Business Strategies for Coping in the Uncertain Cross-Strait Political Environment

While economic and political changes largely sparked shifts in Taiwan's economic policies toward the Mainland during the late 1980s and early 1990s, the security externalities of Taiwanese investments in China at the time were probably limited. Recall from Chapter 2 that the extent to which political behavior can be linked successfully to economic ties depends in large degree on the value of assets specific to the bilateral relationship. Recall also that until the early 1990s, most Taiwanese firms that invested in the PRC were of the small-scale variety, which would be incapable of sinking a large amount of fixed assets in the Mainland market.

Moreover, in a study of the behavior of Taiwanese firms in Xiamen (in Fujian Province, directly opposite Taiwan), La Croix and Xu demonstrate that those firms took explicit steps to lower the likelihood and costs of opportunism by Mainland authorities. The authors note, for example, that Taiwanese investors tended to employ used machinery when possible in order to reduce the value of fixed assets in Mainland factories. In 1991, 93 percent of the Taiwanese firms surveyed employed used machinery in their production facilities on the Mainland. Often this machinery had become illegal in Taiwan because of tougher environmental protection laws, or had become obsolete in Taiwan's relatively high-skilled labor market. La Croix and Xu argue that the use of such equipment reduced the expropriation fears of Taiwan's investors, since the opportunity costs—and hence the costs of confiscation—of this equipment were low (La Croix and Xu 1995, 133–34). In a case study examining Taiwanese investments in Jiangsu Province in the late 1980s to early 1990s, Richard Pomfret similarly notes that Taiwanese companies typically imported used machinery from Taiwan. This machinery was sometimes over a decade old and unprofitable at Taiwanese wage rates (Pomfret 1995, 170–71). Facilitating this type of behavior was the "two ends remain outside" (*liang tou zai wai*) strategy pursued by Taiwanese firms, which enabled them to limit the amount of relation-specific assets they poured into the Mainland.[21] Utilizing this strategy meant that they didn't have to invest a large amount of capital or technology in China, nor did they have to invest in personal networks that would be necessary in order to produce for the Chinese domestic market (Yan 1992, 52; Hsing 1998, 129). Finally, La Croix and Xu emphasize in their study that Taiwanese firms generally invested in Xiamen through affiliates in third locations—such as Hong Kong or the United States. Because China had signed investment protection agreements with governments from these locations (thereby pledging not to expropriate investments from companies based in these locales), Taiwanese firms were able to obtain some guarantee against expropriation despite the lack of a similar agreement between Taiwan and the Mainland (La Croix and Xu 1995, 132–33).

In summary, it is not clear that Taiwanese investments in Mainland China through the early 1990s entailed substantial negative security externalities for Taiwan. Such externalities were insignificant due in large part to the limited value of relation-specific assets employed in Mainland production facilities by Taiwanese firms, and the generally small-scale nature of Taiwanese businesses that were investing in China. At the same time, by investing through affiliates in third countries, Taiwanese firms blurred their ties to the island: any Chinese threats directed at those investments would potentially involve other countries as well, perhaps increasing the costs to Beijing of actually carrying out a threat. Furthermore, since firms investing on the Mainland were typically small, labor-intensive operations, it is unlikely that the types of products and technologies flowing to China would have implications for the cross-Strait balance of power. In short, while political and economic changes raised the costs associated with Taiwanese restrictions on cross-Strait commerce and helped drive liberalization, the commercial links were not of the sort that would have had serious security implications for Taiwan.

4. Deepening Economic Integration and Taipei's Response: The Go-South and the Go Slow, Be Patient Policies

Beginning in the early 1990s, and especially after 1992, the pattern of Taiwanese investment in Mainland China began to change. Specifically, Taiwan's larger firms started to enter the Mainland market, and the scale of investment projects increased considerably. Taiwanese officials expressed concern about the security implications surrounding the new patterns of investment, and they adopted strategies to cope. Beginning in late 1993, the Taiwanese government embarked on the Go-South policy, whereby it encouraged Taiwanese investors to consider investing in Southeast Asia rather than in China; the policy was part of a general strategy of diverting large investments away from the Mainland while trying to avoid direct bans that would raise opposition from large businesses (recall from the previous section that the political influence of big business—in contrast to small business—had grown substantially by this time). Then, in late 1996, Taiwan adopted the Go Slow, Be Patient policy, which placed explicit limits on large-scale investments on the Mainland. In this section I first consider the changing structure of Taiwanese investments in China and then discuss the Go-South strategy and the Go Slow, Be Patient policy. I emphasize that Lee Teng-hui decided to implement the more stringent conditions of the Go Slow, Be Patient policy only after he had consolidated his authority through an overwhelming victory in the 1996 presidential race, meaning that he enjoyed greater leverage vis-à-vis the business community and could afford to confront it directly.

The Changing Structure of Cross-Strait Commerce and Its Security Implications

In 1990, the head of Taiwan's Formosa Group, Y. C. Wang, announced plans to build a US$5 billion petrochemical complex in Mainland China near Xiamen.[22] The announcement signaled the beginnings of a new trend in cross-Strait economic relations: that Taiwan's larger—and politically more powerful—business groups were starting to eye China's market. Before 1992, the Formosa Group plan was a relatively isolated case; starting in 1993, however, the number of large business groups investing in China, and the scale of the investments themselves, began to increase. In 1993, for example, only 46 of Taiwan's 350 major companies had reported investments on the Mainland. By mid-1996, this number had risen to 83 (Chu 1997, 242). Mainland officials reported in 1996 that the average size of Taiwanese investments had risen over the previous year from an average of US$1 million to an average of US$5 million; by 1996, moreover, it was not uncommon to find individual Taiwanese investments exceeding US$60 million or US$70 million, while some even exceeded US$100 million.[23] In the mid-1990s, the Taiwanese industries with the largest amount of investment on the Mainland were electronics, food and beverages, and metals, though the largest-scale individual projects tended to be in the petrochemicals industry.[24] To an increasing extent, Taiwanese firms were investing large sums of money in upstream production facilities and even infrastructure projects on the Mainland.[25]

Sparking the decision by Taiwan's larger corporations to enter the Mainland market was the resurgence of reform in China following the post-Tiananmen retrenchment. After the Tiananmen Square crackdown of 1989, conservatives gained the upper hand in the making of Chinese economic policy; the growth rate dropped to 3.9 percent in 1990 behind a program of macroeconomic auster-ity (see Naughton 1996, 8). However, following Deng Xiaoping's symbolic trip to South China in early 1992 and the Fourteenth Party Congress's decision to ratify a proclamation that China would become a "socialist market economy," it was clear that reformist elements had regained control of economic policy-mak-ing (Naughton 1996, 288). The acceleration of reform and the return of high growth rates, in turn, began to lure in Taiwan's larger firms. This was particularly the case given that China had opened much of its coastal region to foreign invest-ment—meaning that Taiwanese investors could access relatively skilled workers in addition to inexpensive labor and land (Chu 1997, 241).[26] Moreover, the deeper commitment to reform on the Mainland led some of Taiwan's larger firms to invest there with an eye toward the domestic Chinese market itself (rather than primarily producing for export) (Leng 1996, 90).

As noted earlier, in Section 2, many Taiwanese officials viewed the new cross-Strait commercial environment with alarm. The large-scale investments associated with the post-1992 wave of cross-Strait integration, and firms' desire to produce for China's domestic market, suggested that the per-company value of relation-specific assets pouring into China was on the rise. It was in this environment that President Lee Teng-hui expressed concern that Beijing might use Taiwanese inves-tors as a tool to influence Taiwan's government.[27] At the same time, however, recall that while democratization had not greatly increased the political clout of small businesses before the mid-1990s, the clout of big business had grown consider-ably.

Indeed, though Taiwanese officials were often concerned about the new trends in cross-Strait integration, Taiwan's larger corporations were exerting pressure on politicians to further liberalize the cross-Strait economic environment. In contrast to smaller businesses, by the 1990s big businesses had several outlets through which to influence cross-Strait economic policy-making in Taiwan. Most importantly, they tended to maintain close political connections to top leaders: the Evergreen Group, for example, maintained a close relationship with President Lee Teng-hui.[28] Organizations that represented the interests of big business—such as the Chinese National Federation of Industries—were also included in the decision making concerning lists of permitted investments in the Mainland and imports from the Mainland (Yan 1992, 92–93). Specifically, the Board of Foreign Trade and the Bureau of Industry within the Ministry of Economic Affairs would accept requests from businesses and business organizations to expand the list of items permitted for import from the Mainland or investment in the Mainland. These bureaus would review the requests, and before making a decision would hold a meeting to consider the advantages and disadvantages of the request at hand. In addition to relevant government officials, affected businesses and business organizations would be invited to attend these meetings and offer opinions (Yan 1992, 92–94; Leng 1996, 90–93). Furthermore, business groups (such as the Chinese National Federation of Industries) met frequently with government officials at informal meetings to offer economic policy advice; business representatives would sometimes use these meetings as an opportunity to criticize government policy toward China and to demand the opening of direct links with the Mainland.[29]

Government officials were probably not keen to ignore the advice and demands of big businesses given their increasing political influence. This was especially the case since the leadership of the KMT itself had been split after the death of President Chiang Ching-kuo in 1988. The party divided into two major factions, the Mainstream Faction (which supported President Lee Teng-hui) and the more conservative Non-Mainstream Faction (some members of which broke away to form the New Party in 1993). Numerous other factions also characterized the party in the legislature and at all other government levels (see, e.g., Kau 1996, 292–94). In this environment, one might expect that large corporations would be capable of exercising considerable political leverage thanks to the financial backing they could provide to political competitors. Indeed, during the early to mid 1990s, Taiwanese policymakers—despite their qualms about the security implications of the new cross-Strait economic trends—began to consider further relaxing the restrictions in place on cross-Strait commerce. In early 1995, for example, Taiwanese officials announced that they would begin to loosen bans on direct links with China; though the proposed changes were relatively small, they nonetheless signaled to the business community that its concerns were being addressed (Chu 1997, 243–44).[30]

In short, through the first half of 1996, Taiwanese policymakers avoided new restrictions on cross-Strait commercial ties despite the security ramifications of an increasing number of large investments on the Mainland; to the contrary, they contemplated further liberalization in the face of considerable pressure from big business. But policymakers also adopted alternative strategies to cope with deepening integration, which would not require that they take on the business community and suffer the political costs of doing so. Most notably, they offered businesses positive incentives either to stay in Taiwan or to invest abroad in locations other than China.

Positive Incentives and the Go-South Strategy

For Taiwan's policymakers, offering positive incentives (subsidies, low-cost loans, and so forth) for companies to stay in Taiwan or to invest in places other than Mainland China offered a strategy with lower political costs than imposing direct restrictions on cross-Strait commerce. The costs to Taiwan's overall economy would be similar to simply imposing restrictions on ties to the Mainland; the total loss in both cases equals the amount by which the foregone gains of investing in China exceeded actual gains from investing elsewhere. In both strategies, the gains (increased security) are diffuse. But by offering positive incentives, the costs become diffuse as well (since they represent government efforts ultimately paid for through the tax system) and would therefore be less likely to trigger opposition from Taiwan's business community. So while the government kept many existing restrictions on cross-Strait investment in place in the early 1990s, it sought to stem increasing investment flows in part through positive incentives rather than by imposing new restrictions.

To provide these incentives the Taiwanese government took several steps aimed at making Taiwan a more attractive investment site for Taiwan's larger companies. For example, officials sometimes provided tax incentives to companies choosing to invest in Taiwan,[31] while implementing policies that lowered the price of industrial land and that loosened environmental regulations (Chu 1997, 242–43). Conversely, government officials also bargained directly with firms to convince them to stay in Taiwan. After news broke of Y. C. Wang's decision in 1990 to build a petrochemical complex on the Mainland, for example, Taiwanese officials pressured him to delay the plan. Ultimately, the government was able to convince Wang to postpone the project indefinitely; in exchange, the government approved and helped subsidize a similar complex in Taiwan. Under the deal, the government agreed to provide low-cost financing for the project and also offered low-cost water supplies and a five-year tax break (Leng 1996, 96).[32] In other words, the government to a large extent sought to buy off Wang's Formosa Group rather than simply ban the company's investment plans.[33]

Meanwhile, for companies that clearly wanted to invest abroad to take advantage of lower labor costs, the Taiwanese government developed a strategy—which would become known as the Go-South policy—to encourage firms (and to give them incentives) to invest in Southeast Asia as an alternative to the Mainland. The ROC began to publicize the strategy in 1993, when officials announced that they would actively support more extensive economic ties with Southeast Asia. Economics Minister P. K. Chiang stated on December 27 of that year that the economics ministry would "make promotion of the south expedition program a major task in 1994," further noting that the ROC government would help Taiwanese firms establish multinational enterprises in Southeast Asia.[34] In February 1994, moreover, Lee Teng-hui made a highly publicized visit to Southeast Asia—with stops in Indonesia, Thailand, and the Philippines—in an effort to promote closer ties between Taiwan and the region.[35] The Taiwanese government also took a number of concrete steps to encourage investors to invest in Southeast Asia instead of China.

In the Philippines, Taiwan cooperated closely with the Philippine government in developing a major industrial park at Subic Bay. The Ministry of Economic Affairs used its International Economic Cooperation Development Fund (IECDF) to provide a US$23.6 million loan to help finance first-phase construction of the site, which began in March 1994. Also, two KMT-run enterprises, the China Development Corporation and the Central Development Corporation, were part of the joint venture that developed the park.[36] The China Development Corporation, moreover, agreed in 1995 to provide loans to Taiwanese companies seeking to relocate to Subic Bay.[37] In the spring of 1997, the Taiwanese government highlighted its continued support of Subic Bay by clearing a US$20 million long-term, low-interest loan to finance second-phase construction of the park. Taiwan's support of the project to some extent achieved its desired effect: by 1997 more than one hundred Taiwanese firms had registered to move some operations to the park, with a total commitment of over US$200 million worth of investments.[38]

The Taiwanese government took an active role in promoting economic interaction with other Southeast Asian nations as well. In Vietnam, for instance, the ROC government provided Hanoi with a US$10 million loan to help attract Taiwanese investors to the Hanoi Industrial Park—a site similar to Subic Bay, only smaller. The loan was in turn used by Hanoi to provide low-cost loans to Taiwanese firms planning to invest there.[39] The IECDF also provided a US$30 million loan to help the Vietnamese government finance infrastructure support for the project.[40] As of 1996, twenty-six Taiwanese firms (mostly small and medium sized) were planning to establish operations in the park.[41] Taipei also actively pursued investment protection and promotion agreements with other Southeast Asian countries, including Indonesia and Thailand.[42]

Ultimately, the onset of the Asian financial crisis in 1997 caused the Go-South strategy to fizzle. But we might draw two conclusions from Taipei's adoption of the strategy from 1993 to 1996. First, as Taiwan's larger firms began to move into the Mainland market, Taiwanese policymakers preferred not to incur the political costs of confronting those businesses directly. Instead, they pursued more indirect methods of slowing the flow of cross-Strait investments, which would not risk angering the business community. At the same time, they kept most pre-existing restrictions in place while paying lip service to limited liberalization schemes. Second, efforts to divert investment to Southeast Asia suggest that—contrary to the statements of some officials at the time—the primary concern associated with burgeoning cross-Strait investments lay not in the possible "hollowing out" of the

Taiwanese economy but rather in the security implications of those investments flowing to China in particular (see Section 2, earlier). If capital outflow per se were the primary concern, Taiwanese officials would not have been encouraging investors to dip into the Southeast Asian market. Beginning in the second half of 1996, however, the Taiwanese government *was* willing to adopt more direct restrictions on cross-Strait commerce, a subject to which I now turn.

The Go Slow, Be Patient Policy

Starting in 1996, Taiwanese economic policy toward the Mainland shifted as the government began first to signal its clear displeasure with the proliferation of large-scale investments on the Mainland, and then to tighten policy restrictions on those investments. In the first half of the year, two Mainland investment projects in particular attracted the attention of policymakers. Y. C. Wang's Formosa Group was again at the center of one of the proposals: Wang signed an agreement in May 1996 to invest US$3 billion in the construction of a power plant in Fujian Province.[43] The second high-profile case was President Group's plan to invest US$100 million in a Wuhan power project.[44] On August 15, 1996, President Lee Teng-hui signaled his disapproval of trends in cross-Strait commerce when he called on businesses to "go slow and be patient" (*Jieji Yongren*) in dealing with Mainland China. At the same time, policymakers pressured the Formosa Group and President Group to put their high-profile investments on hold; both firms complied.[45] Although Lee initially denied that Taiwan would impose new restrictions on cross-Strait investments,[46] by later in the year he had instructed government policymakers to work on a set of new regulations that would come to be known as the Go Slow, Be Patient policy. In particular, Lee asked officials to draft guidelines regarding appropriate ceilings on any particular firm's Mainland investments, as well as appropriate levels of overall Taiwanese investment on the Mainland as a percentage of total overseas investment (Tso 1996).

The new restrictions went into effect in 1997 and were targeted primarily at Taiwan's larger firms. Investments on the Mainland exceeding US$50 million were banned, as were all investments in major infrastructure projects (such as power stations, highways, or airports).[47] Taiwanese officials also placed upper bounds on the amount of overall capital a listed company could invest on the Mainland, and banned the raising of capital in Taiwan for investment in China.[48] Moreover, Taiwanese officials publicly emphasized that illegal investments would be punished. In February 1997, for example, the Ministry of Economic Affairs warned that businesses not reporting Mainland investments risked fines or even the imprisonment of their officials.[49] Fines for violating the Go Slow, Be Patient policy could be as high as US$650,000, with a five-year maximum jail term.[50]

Though the new restrictions signified a stark policy change in Taipei, their effect should not be exaggerated: even officials conceded that it was extremely difficult to enforce them by tracing the flow of funds through third locations and overseas companies. But the new restrictions did spark anger in the business community, and that community would for the next several years lobby against the Go Slow, Be Patient policy.[51] It is unlikely that they would have expended efforts opposing the policy if it would not constrain their behavior at all: at a minimum the new restrictions would have increased the hassles facing businesses wishing to invest in the PRC. Recognizing that the business community strongly opposed Go Slow, Be Patient, we might ask why it is that Taiwanese officials chose to change course and adopt such a policy.

Several factors appear to be important. First, as just discussed, the increasing scale of Taiwanese investments on the Mainland was undoubtedly a key underlying cause: projects like Wang's power plant scheme were particularly galling to Taiwanese policymakers worried about deepening dependence on the Mainland market. Taiwan's investments in China increasingly entailed security externalities that were negative for Taiwan.[52] Second, magnifying the salience of these security externalities, cross-Strait political conflict had become more intense following Lee Teng-hui's 1995 trip to Cornell University and the Mainland's tough response. A third event, the March 1996 Taiwanese presidential election, helps to explain why Lee waited until the summer of 1996 to change policy. In the election, Lee obtained 54 percent of the vote in a four-way race; the DPP candidate Peng Ming-min finished a distant second with 21 percent. Lin Yang-kang, a prominent member of the KMT Non-Mainstream Faction who was supported by the New Party, managed to receive only 15 percent of the vote (Cheng 1997).[53] Lee's landslide victory, combined with his stated intent not to run again in 2000, probably reduced the leverage that business actors would have felt they held vis-à-vis Lee. As Ho and Leng (2004, 737) write, "Lee was at the peak of his power" when he announced the Go Slow, Be Patient policy in the summer of 1996; he was effectively able to "[bypass] all relevant agencies in making the policy announcements."

For businesses dissatisfied with restrictions on cross-Strait investment and the lack of progress on opening direct transport and shipping links, few political "exit" options were available—at least over the short term. On the one hand, the New Party and what remained of the Non-Mainstream Faction supported cross-Strait commercial policies more in line with the preferences of investors in China,[54] but the poor showing by Lin in the election hardly suggested it would be worthwhile to switch loyalties in that direction. On the other hand, Peng Ming-min was a staunch advocate of Taiwanese independence (Wu 1999)—obviously not a position conducive to improving the cross-Strait economic environment. Though many in the DPP would push for a more pragmatic approach to cross-Strait issues in the aftermath of Peng's poor showing (Kuo 1998),[55] it is unlikely that businesses in 1996 would have viewed the party as a viable promoter of their interests related to Mainland China. This political environment likely contributed to Lee's willingness to adopt cross-Strait policies clearly at odds with business preferences. Officials were quite blunt in telling businesses that this was a time when their individual interests were in conflict with national security interests, and though they had the freedom to complain, they should understand that they "are part of the country, and should still put national interests first."[56] Lee could not have ignored such well-financed and well-connected "individual interests" had his political standing not been so strong.

In summary, two major variables help to explain the course of Taiwanese economic policy toward the Mainland in the early to mid 1990s. The first is the value of fixed assets that Taiwanese firms had planted in China. The growing value of those fixed assets starting in the early 1990s led Taiwanese policymakers to become more worried about the security ramifications of deeper integration with China (the spike in tensions from 1995 to 1996 could only have heightened those concerns). As a result, policymakers devised strategies to slow the pace of cross-Strait economic integration. Second, the changing political clout of internationalist economic interests affected the political costs to leaders of imposing restrictions on cross-Strait economic exchange; such costs factored into their calculus when devising strategies to cope with the security ramifications of deepening integration. Big businesses with a desire to invest in China held more political influence by the early 1990s than they had in the past, a result in large measure of Taiwan's democratic reforms; such influence made policymakers wary of imposing new direct restrictions on cross-Strait commerce. As an alternative, they focused on indirect incentives to steer businesses to other locations, particularly Southeast Asia. Lee's landslide victory in the 1996 presidential election, however, may have reduced—at least in the short term—the leverage that big business interests could exert vis-à-vis the president.

5. Taiwanese Policy Under Chen Shui-bian: Deepening Economic Integration and Ambiguous Policy Changes

In the second half of the 1990s, despite the presence of more stringent restrictions on cross-Strait commerce, Taiwanese integration with the Mainland economy continued to deepen. Among the most notable trends was the shift in Taiwanese high technology production to Mainland factories. Meanwhile, major political changes were afoot in Taiwan. In 2000, following a split in the KMT, the DPP candidate Chen Shui-bian won the Taiwanese presidency with 39 percent of the vote. The vote ended fifty-five years of KMT rule on the island. On the surface, one might have expected the new president to pursue cross-Strait economic policies similar to those of his predecessor. Indeed, Chen's party continued to embrace Taiwanese independence in its platform; Chen himself, though now emphasizing pragmatism in dealing with cross-Strait issues, had in the past leaned toward a pro-independence point of view. Chen, in short, might have been expected to view economic integration with the Mainland with the same suspicion that Lee did: as potentially undermining the sovereignty of the island through its potential to be linked to politics either directly (through sanctioning threats) or indirectly (through a pro-China business lobby).

To the contrary, Chen soon publicly advocated lifting some of the restrictions on cross-Strait commerce. He indicated a desire to open direct links with the Mainland, and his administration also began to review the Go Slow, Be Patient policy, suggesting a willingness to lift those restrictions as well. After considerable speculation, Chen announced in the fall of 2001 that the Go Slow policy would be scrapped, to be replaced by a policy of "aggressive opening and effective management." In 2002, Taiwan further relaxed its restrictions on investment in China. For the remainder of Chen's term, however, there was only limited policy liberalization, and his government demonstrated a greater willingness to enforce existing restrictions on investment in China. Though some progress was made under Chen on the three links issue—including the establishment of direct links between Taiwan-controlled Jinmen and Matsu and the Mainland—it was limited.

Taiwan's economic policy toward China under Chen begs two questions. First, why, given his own and his party's position on the issue of Taiwan's sovereignty, did Chen initially pursue liberalization? Second, why did liberalization efforts grind to a halt after 2002? I argue in this section that Chen, initially facing a precarious political position combined with worsening economic conditions, pursued a political strategy of capturing the center of Taiwan's political spectrum. This strategy, in turn, gave the business community in Taiwan substantial leverage, for reasons I will detail. However, after 2002, Chen largely abandoned this political strategy and focused instead on consolidating core "pan-green" supporters as he headed into the 2004 election campaign. In turn, the support of the business community became less crucial for Chen, and its influence over policy declined somewhat. I begin with a brief overview of trends in cross-Strait economic relations and Taiwan's changing policies under the Chen administration.

Changing Cross-Strait Economic Trends and Changes in Taiwan's Policy

The factors that led many of Taiwan's larger firms to invest in China in the early 1990s began to push the island's high-tech sectors to invest on the Mainland to an increasing extent in the late 1990s and early 2000s. By 2000, over half of Taiwan's investments in China were in the electric and electronics industry (Lee 2003, 119).[57] Among the Mainland's primary lures: a common language, a skilled and relatively cheap labor force, inexpensive land, and a huge potential market in which firms hoped to get a foothold. Furthermore, after 1997, the attractiveness of Southeast Asia as a site for investment declined sharply in the aftermath of the Asian financial crisis. Even before the crisis, firms had sometimes grumbled about the government wanting to drive their investment to places without a common language and without the Mainland market's huge potential.[58] China's ability to emerge from the crisis relatively unscathed only underscored the advantages of investing in China instead of elsewhere. Moreover, as some larger computer producers began moving production facilities to the Mainland, many smaller companies quickly followed; such a "ripple effect" derives from the close network of supporting companies that is characteristic of computer production. When, for instance, Taiwan-based Delta Electronics opened a factory in Dongguan, it estimated that about thirty smaller companies followed suit.[59] By 1998, Taiwanese companies produced 29 percent of their computer-related products on the Mainland, more than double the percentage just three years earlier.[60] Taiwan's information technology industry produced roughly half of its output in China by 2002, up from 23 percent in 1997 (Chao 2004, 696).[61]

Growing high-tech investment on the Mainland occurred despite the continued presence of stringent controls on such investment. Under the Go Slow, Be Patient policy, the Taiwanese government continued to ban investment in cutting-edge technologies on the Mainland, and likewise banned the importing of many high-tech products produced in China, even those made by Taiwan-based companies (in order to discourage them from shifting production to the Mainland[62]). Moreover, listed companies were allowed to invest only 20 percent of their net worth in the Mainland market.[63] Such restrictions were clearly a barrier to investors, but Taiwanese companies employed a range of strategies to dodge them. For example, companies would often under-report profits on the Mainland and then reinvest the unreported portion without approval. Or to avoid violating restrictions on high-tech production, companies would assemble all but the finishing touches of a certain product on the Mainland and complete the process back in Taiwan.[64] Alternatively, as Ho and Leng (2004) explain, some Taiwanese high-tech companies have been able to avoid government restrictions by becoming "hybrid

firms." Ho and Leng use the Semiconductor Manufacturing International Corporation (SMIC), a company headquartered in Shanghai but founded by a Taiwanese
businessman, as an example. The company has been able to circumvent Taiwan's
limits on semiconductor investments in China because it is registered in the Cay-
man Islands (Chase et al. 2004, 121) and because its founder, Richard Chang, holds
a U.S. passport.[65]

Against this backdrop of increasing cross-Strait economic integration and limited effectiveness of Taiwanese restrictions on those ties, new president Chen Shui-
bian advocated more open economic links with the Mainland. In September 2000,
for example, Chen called on the Mainland to enter into negotiations with Taiwan
in order to open direct shipping and communications links across the Taiwan
Strait.[66] He also noted that he desired to give high-tech companies more leeway
regarding their investments on the Mainland, and made a point of emphasizing
that the normalization of cross-Strait relations must begin with the normalization
of economic relations.[67] The government announced repeatedly its intention to
relax the Go Slow, Be Patient policy, [68] and in January 2001 Premier Chang Chun-
hsiung ordered the cabinet to prepare for the ramifications of changing policy.[69]
However, actual policy change was not immediately forthcoming: officials whom
I interviewed in the three opposition parties in the winter of 2001 suggested that
Chen's call for policy change was insincere.[70] Some emphasized in particular that
influential components of Chen's own DPP, such as the New Tide Faction, were
opposed to relaxing the commercial restrictions.

A breakthrough on investment policy occurred in August 2001, when Chen
endorsed the Economic Development Advisory Conference's recommendation
that Go Slow, Be Patient be scrapped in favor of a policy of "aggressive opening" and "effective management."[71] In particular, the conference recommended
removing the US$50 million limit on individual investment projects in China.[72]
In November, the government announced details of the new policy. In addition
to lifting the $50 million ceiling on individual investments, all investments smaller
than US$20 million would be automatically approved; larger projects would
be approved on a case-by-case basis under a streamlined application procedure.
Moreover, the ceiling on cumulative investments by listed companies was raised
from 20 percent of net worth to 40 percent. The new policy also eliminated dis-
incentives for businesses to repatriate Mainland capital by, for example, allowing
companies to deduct remitted stocks or surplus from the accumulated amount of
Mainland investments. The policy called for the gradual implementation of other
measures, including lifting the prohibition against direct investments in China,[73]
and allowing the financial services sector to set up branch offices or subsidiaries on
the Mainland. As part of the "effective management" component of the new pol-

icy, the government began to require that companies investing more than US$20 million on the Mainland file regular reports on their overseas investments.[74]

In 2002 the Taiwanese government decided to lift its ban on semiconductor investments in China. Under the new policy, Taiwanese companies would be allowed to invest in Mainland facilities that produced 8-inch diameter silicon wafers; companies were still barred from investing in more advanced 12-inch wafer production facilities.[75] Several other conditions applied to the new policy. Initial priority was given to companies wishing to invest used wafer manufacturing equipment. Only companies that had already built 12-inch wafer production facilities in Taiwan that had reached stable levels of production would be eligible to apply under the new policy. The Taiwanese government would approve no more than three 8- inch wafer factories in China by 2005 (the number represented the total for all Taiwanese companies, not for a single company). And the government made clear that it would increase penalties for violators of Taiwan's restrictions on high-tech investments in China.[76] As of 2005, the only company to take advantage of the new policy was Taiwan Semiconductor Manufacturing Company (TSMC); the company built a US$898 million plant in Shanghai, which began manufacturing chips in late 2004.[77]

As Yang and Hung (2003) write, the decision to lift the ban on semiconductor investments in China was a highly contentious political issue in Taiwan. Chen Shui-bian himself favored lifting the ban, and was backed by the economics bureaucracy and, of course, the semiconductor industry itself (Yang and Hung 2003, 695). Yet a coalition soon emerged to mount a high-profile campaign to block liberalization. The most visible opponent of lifting the ban was former president Lee Teng-hui, who relied primarily on national security arguments to make his case.[78] The new Taiwan Solidarity Union (TSU), which viewed Lee as its mentor and "spiritual" leader,[79] also opposed the policy shift, as did the head of the Mainland Affairs Council, Tsai Ing-wen (Yang and Hung 2003, 695). Others opposed lifting the ban for more protectionist reasons. The Council of Labor Affairs warned that allowing even 8-inch wafer investments in China would cost Taiwan eighteen thousand jobs.[80] The Taiwan Professional Engineers Association likewise opposed liberalization, fearing that lifting the ban would cause engineering jobs to shift to China. Noted the vice president of the association, Hsu Wen, "We will not have better jobs, or better pay. If we want that, we will have to go to China. I want to stay here" (Yang and Hung 2003, 691). In early March, in the streets of Taipei, approximately one thousand Taiwanese protested government plans to lift the ban.[81] Though Lee and others failed to block the policy shift, the liberalization plan ultimately adopted by the government reflected a compromise with opponents of liberalization: TSU officials claimed, for example, that requiring

12-inch processing facilities to be established first in Taiwan represented a cave-in by the cabinet to their demands.[82]

The Chen administration took other steps to liberalize cross-Strait investment flows during 2002. As noted earlier, the government lifted the ban on direct investments that summer; in August, the Ministry of Economic Affairs also announced that it was lifting the ban on an additional sixty-eight investment categories in China, including civil air transport, legal services, and real estate brokering.[83] After 2002, however, the trend toward liberalization in the Chen administration's investment policies toward China came to an end; Chen's government did not pursue substantial liberalization for the remainder of its tenure.

Indeed, even as policy opening proceeded in 2002, it was clear that the Chen administration took the "effective management" component of the 2001 policy reform seriously. Over the summer, the Mainland Affairs Council announced plans to increase penalties for violators of Taiwan's prohibitions against Mainland investments.[84] Furthermore, Taiwanese officials opened an investigation into whether any Taiwanese companies preempted the lifting on the ban of semiconductor investments in China; the government focused in particular on reports that the United Microelectronics Corporation (UMC) had illegally invested in a silicon wafer production facility in Suzhou through the He Jian Technology Company.[85] In early 2005, investigators searched UMC's offices and arrested Shyu Jiann-hwa, chief executive of He Jian.[86] The probe of UMC, combined with the decision to fine SMIC founder Richard Chang NT$5 million for investing illegally in China, suggested at least a somewhat serious effort to crack down on illegal investments in cutting-edge technologies in China.

Moreover, the Chen administration in 2002 began crafting a law—the National Technology Protection Law—to limit more explicitly sensitive technology transfer to China. A more controversial provision in the proposed law sought to impose more stringent personnel controls, requiring scientists and engineers working in high-tech industries to apply for permission from the government before taking jobs in China (Chase et al. 2004, 32–35). The Executive Yuan approved a draft of the bill in late 2002 and submitted it to the Legislative Yuan for approval (Chase et al. 2004, 39). However, the Legislative Yuan has not passed the bill as of 2006,[87] and approval in the foreseeable future seems unlikely given the pan-green alliance's minority status in that body.

The Chen administration had indicated in early 2005 that it was planning to relax restrictions on Mainland investments in small-sized liquid crystal display panel manufacturing, as well as semiconductor packaging and testing operations. However, after China passed its antisecession law in March, the Taiwanese government decided to delay indefinitely on the policy shift.[88] And in his 2006 New

Year's speech, Chen suggested that his administration would move more aggressively to manage cross-Strait economic relations. Henceforth, the policy of "proactive liberalization and effective management" would become instead "proactive management and effective liberalization": emphasis, in other words, would shift from liberalization to management.[89]

Meanwhile, despite Chen's repeated calls for the establishment of the three direct links early in his term, overall progress on opening direct links was limited under his presidency. Some liberalization did occur. In early 2001, Taiwan opened the "mini three links," which allowed direct trade and travel between the offshore islands of Matsu and Jinmen and the Mainland. Though still small, the number of passengers taking advantage of the mini three links has grown quickly (as has the number of cargo ships).[90] In 2003, both China and Taiwan approved applications from several Taiwanese airlines to provide charter flights for Taiwanese businesspeople returning to Taiwan for the Lunar New Year. The flights still were required to stop in Hong Kong or Macau, but the businesspeople did not need to deplane. In 2005, six Taiwanese airliners and six Chinese airliners were allowed to offer direct charter service for businesspeople returning to Taiwan for the Lunar New Year. This time, the flights only had to pass through Hong Kong airspace on the flights to and from Taiwan; a total of forty-eight such flights were offered. A similar arrangement was put in place for the 2006 Lunar New Year, with seventy-two flights scheduled; charter flights were also allowed during three other holidays in 2006.[91] Yet more substantial progress on the direct links issue was hamstrung by differences between Beijing and Taipei concerning how to negotiate an agreement.

Specifically, the Chen administration demanded that direct links across the Taiwan Strait must be realized through negotiations based on "the principles of mutual respect for sovereignty, parity and dignity"[92]; Taiwanese officials rejected Beijing's suggestion that direct links could be negotiated by the private sector.[93] However, Beijing had boycotted the quasi-official SEF-ARATS negotiation channel since 1999, when Lee Teng-hui announced his "two states" formula, and the Mainland made Taiwanese acceptance of a one-China principle a prerequisite for resuming talks (e.g. Chao 2004, 699). Chen, meanwhile, predicted (wrongly, it turned out) that China would relent if he were to win re-election,[94] and he consistently refused to accept a one-China principle as a prerequisite for negotiations.[95] In the end, direct links were not realized during the Chen administration.

In summary, through at least the first half of 2002 the general trend in the Chen administration's economic policies toward Mainland China was liberalizing. After that, the direction of policy change became more ambiguous. Some policy liberalization continued, but Chen's government also signaled a greater willingness to crack down on illegal investments in China, and the government did not announce any major liberalization initiatives after 2002. In the remainder of this section, I seek to account for these changes, focusing in particular on the political influence of Taiwan's business community.

Political Changes and Business Influence

The presidential election in 2000 appeared to signal a new political environment, in which internationalist business interests would hold more leverage vis-à-vis politicians than during the Lee Teng-hui era. In the months before the election, business interests articulated a desire for the candidates to commit to changing Taiwanese cross-Strait economic policy if elected.[96] Taiwan's major industrial organizations advocated liberalizing cross-Strait commercial restrictions (my interviews), and the National Federation of Industry openly predicted that regardless of who won the election, cross-Strait economic policies would be adjusted.[97] Not surprisingly, organizations of Taiwanese businesses on the Mainland were particularly vocal in their support of an improved cross-Strait economic environment, and they asked candidates to promise to liberalize cross-Strait investment and to open up direct links. Associations representing local Taiwanese businesses have formed in most places in Mainland China where a sizable number of Taiwanese businesses have invested, and they aim to improve the business climate within those regions for Taiwanese businesses. Senior officials from these organizations also participate in an organization (the Union of Presidents of Associations of Taiwanese Businesses on the Mainland—*Dalu Taishang Xiehui Huizhang Lianyihui*) that issues statements on behalf of Taiwanese businesses on the Mainland in general.[98] In a close three-way presidential race, all three candidates—Chen Shui-bian of the DPP, Lien Chan of the KMT, and independent James Soong—paid attention to these recommendations. Soong openly called for removing restrictions on the dollar value of individual investments, while Lien suggested it would be possible to achieve direct links with the Mainland after the two sides entered the World Trade Organization. Even Chen emphasized that it was necessary to remove "provisional and passive [*xiaojixing*] cross-Strait economic policies," an indirect reference to Go Slow, Be Patient.[99]

Chen Shui-bian emerged victorious in the election, an accomplishment that would have been regarded as highly improbable only a year earlier. Making his victory possible was a split in the KMT, in which Soong broke away and mounted an independent bid against Chen and Lien. Soong drew 37 percent of the vote, the bulk of which otherwise most likely would have gone to the KMT candidate. As a result, Chen was able to win with only 39 percent of the popular vote. The legislature remained firmly in opposition control: the KMT held a majority of the seats, while the DPP controlled only about one-third of the seats.

Chen's political position after the election was tenuous. Within a few months of the election, an opposition alliance—composed of the KMT, the New Party, and Soong's newly formed People First Party—had formed in the legislature; the alliance controlled nearly two-thirds of the legislature's seats. Moreover, the opposition squarely advocated improving the cross-Strait economic environment, meaning that businesses disenchanted with cross-Strait economic policy had a clear alternative to Chen and the DPP. Chen took several steps to stabilize his position, including appointing Tang Fei of the KMT as premier,[100] and making clear that he would not declare independence or do anything drastic that might spark a crisis with China. But it was also clear that if Chen hoped to have any chance of achieving re-election in 2004, he would need to expand his base of support: it would be overly optimistic to think that he would face a divided opposition again the next time around. Further, there is reason to believe that this environment gave business interests considerably more bargaining leverage over Chen than they had had vis-à-vis Lee regarding cross-Strait economic issues. There are at least three reasons for this.

First, several high-profile tycoons and business associations became increasingly vocal in their criticisms of cross-Strait economic policies. Such criticism had the potential to influence the public's confidence in Chen's handling of economic affairs. Taiwan's most well-known businessman, Y. C. Wang, was particularly critical of continued restrictions on cross-Strait commerce, arguing bluntly that if Taiwanese leaders did not develop more competent economic policies, the island would "be finished" (wandan).[101] Shortly after a high-profile meeting with Chen to exchange views on the economy in December 2000, Wang blasted the president for his unwillingness to accept the one-China principle and to improve the cross-Strait economic environment: "Although I have communicated with President Chen regarding [cross-Strait economic] issues, if you look at the new government's policies and methods, President Chen obviously has not internalized what I have said."[102] In November 2000, Wang organized a meeting with several of Taiwan's top business magnates to discuss Taiwan's economic and political situation, and to pressure the government to adjust the Go Slow, Be Patient policy. Others at the meeting, such as Taiwan Semiconductor chairman Morris Chang and Quanta Computer chairman Barry Lam,[103] echoed Wang's concerns about cross-Strait commerce. Chang and Lam noted that if the government didn't relax restrictions on high-tech investments in China, Taiwan's high-tech industry "would not be able to survive."[104]

The president was quite sensitive to such high-profile criticism, especially given his tenuous support base on assuming office and the deteriorating state of the island's economy (which I will discuss in more detail in the next subsection). Since magnates like Wang and Chang were not extremely close to the KMT,[105] their criticism did not ring with partisanship; rather, voters might well view such business leaders as endorsers on economic affairs.[106] Furthermore, the opposition pan-blue alliance in the legislature came out in favor of relaxing restrictions on cross-Strait commerce,[107] presenting voters with a clear alternative to the continuing status quo of Go Slow, Be Patient. Interviewees in the government and in the different parties generally agreed that Chen felt enormous pressure to liberalize cross-Strait commercial policies in this environment.

A second factor that made Chen particularly attentive to business concerns was that the DPP had for years had an "antibusiness" image (an image confirmed to many in the business community by Chen's effort to halt construction of the fourth nuclear power plant[108]), and both Chen and then DPP chairman Frank Hsieh wished to change this.[109] Again, their desire to improve this image arose in large part from Chen's tenuous political position and a belief that being tainted as antibusiness would not be conducive to attaining the support of the median voter in future elections (my interviews).[110] In February 2001, Hsieh delivered a speech to a business conference in which he emphasized that the DPP in fact was not antibusiness but rather was opposed to special relationships between government and business that make it difficult for truly competitive firms to prosper. Furthermore, he highlighted the government's decision to open the "mini three links"—which allowed direct transit between Taiwan's offshore islands and the Mainland beginning in January 2001—as a signal that the government was moving in the right policy direction as far as businesses were concerned.[111] A desire to change the image of the party naturally made the president more susceptible to pressures from the business community to actually implement policy changes, including with regard to cross-Strait commerce.

Finally, Chen and the DPP did not possess financial assets on anywhere near the scale of the KMT's financial empire. Furthermore, the DPP's links with business groups were not as extensive as in the KMT—particularly vis-à-vis big businesses.[112] The DPP's relatively limited financial capacity certainly increased the potential leverage of key financial contributors. Of course, there are many large businesses that contribute to all major parties and presidential candidates; their aim in doing so is to preserve reasonably good relations with all key power brokers. Such gifts generally lack even an implicit quid pro quo.[113] Nevertheless, Chen did receive the open support of several prominent business magnates prior to the election, including Stan Shih of Acer, Chang Rung-fa of Evergreen, and Hsu Wen-lung of Chi Mei (see, e.g., Rigger 2001, 140). These three businessmen in particular had substantial business operations on the Mainland, and had at times indicated publicly a desire for a relaxation of cross-Strait economic restrictions.[114] Undoubtedly their support for Chen derived from several factors (including, perhaps, a desire to see less corruption in Taiwanese political-business relations), and it is clear that businesses in Taiwan tend to view their relationships with politicians from a long-term perspective.[115] But at the same time, Chen had reason to be particularly attentive to their opinions given his tenuous political position.

These factors suggest that Chen was responding, at least in part, to internationalist business pressure when he made the decision to relax the Go Slow, Be Patient policy in 2001. Indeed, business was very heavily represented at the Economic Development Advisory Conference that Chen convened in the summer of 2001 to make recommendations concerning Taiwan's economic policies and whose recommendations formed the basis for Chen's replacement of Go Slow, Be Patient. While the largest bloc of delegates was composed of government or party officials, roughly 34 percent were representatives of the business community (including both industrialists and representatives from business organizations). Most of the remaining delegates held positions in think tanks or universities; only a handful of delegates represented labor (which might be expected to take a somewhat more protectionist stand).[116] In other words, business interests clearly had a very strong hand in shaping the policy recommendations on which Chen acted. While it is hard, of course, to find a "smoking gun" that clearly links Chen's liberalization decision to business pressure, this evidence is nonetheless suggestive.

Economic Troubles

Taiwan's economic outlook began to dim shortly after Chen became president, and by 2001 the economy was in its worst recession in half a century. In a competitive democracy, presiding over such a disastrous reversal in economic fortunes is obviously a major political liability, and Chen's administration clearly wished to improve the economic climate. Voices from both inside and outside the DPP were emphasizing that cross-Strait integration was central to the island's long-term economic prospects. While business leaders like Y. C. Wang warned repeatedly that the health of their enterprises depended on the ability to move production facilities to the Mainland, economic analysts stressed that Taiwan's efforts to increase investment in the domestic market (both from abroad and from domestic sources) would be thwarted by the lack of direct links across the Taiwan Strait. Warnings to this effect by the U.S. Chamber of Commerce in Taiwan and the Taipei European Business Association were particularly high-profile.[117] Given the continued growth of the Mainland market, investors would clearly view inconveniences in cross-Strait interaction as a major drawback to investing in Taiwan.

Meanwhile, foreign businesses and analysts warned that Taiwanese efforts to turn the island into a regional operations hub, a place where companies with Asian operations might want to locate their headquarters, would be hampered by the lack of direct links to China.[118] Max Fang, chairman of the Taipei International Procurement Management Association, stressed in a 2001 interview that Taiwan's inability to open direct links with the Mainland has "considerably hindered Taipei from developing itself into a regional center in Asia Pacific." Moreover, he noted that though many companies have had their international procurement office in Taiwan serve as their regional procurement headquarters, "with all of the difficulties [relating to lack of direct links with the Mainland], for Taiwan [to retain that] position is becoming very questionable."[119] And in the summer of 2001, executives from Dell Computers and IBM threatened to move their Asia Pacific regional purchasing headquarters to Hong Kong if Taiwan did not open direct links with the Mainland.[120] At the same time, the opposition parties endorsed opening cross-Strait commercial ties as a means of remedying the deteriorating economic situation, and suggested that economic restrictions on cross-Strait ties were partly to blame for Taiwan's economic difficulties. Director-general of the KMT's Mainland Affairs Department Chang Jung-kung noted in 2002, for example, that "foreign businessmen are still greatly bewildered by Chen's waffling cross-Strait policies, while people in Taiwan simply care more about when direct voyages across the Strait will be permitted in order to boost economic development."[121]

In short, the political pressures to relax restrictions on cross-Strait commerce were likely magnified by the poor economic situation. This was true because economic experts, business leaders, and the opposition parties argued alike that restrictions on cross-Strait economic ties were a major barrier to the island's economic recovery, and that continued poor economic performance would be a major political liability to Chen in the next presidential election. Indeed, an official in one opposition party told me in early 2001 that he thought Chen might relax the Go Slow, Be Patient policy before the year-end legislative elections precisely because he hoped to demonstrate to the voters that he and the DPP cared about Taiwan's economic troubles and were capable of doing something about them.

The Limits of Liberalization

Nevertheless, as discussed earlier, the decision to lift the Go Slow policy did not usher in a new era of liberalization in Taiwan's cross-Strait economic policies. Rather, after the 2002 lifting of the ban on semiconductor investment in China, Taiwan did not for the remainder of the Chen presidency undertake any new broad liberalization initiatives in investment policy, and little progress was made on the issue of the three direct links. Indeed, the Chen administration was quite frank about its desire to place more emphasis on "effective management" and less on "aggressive liberalization" in its cross-Strait economic policies. The crackdown on UMC in particular highlights this general shift. Why did liberalization stall after the Chen administration appeared initially to embrace it?

I have argued in this section that Chen advocated and ultimately achieved liberalization in Taiwan's cross-Strait economic policies in part because he was in a weak position politically and was courting support (or at least hoping to temper criticism) from the island's business community. But it is clear that from the very beginning liberalization provoked some backlash within the DPP. For example, officials both in the DPP and in opposition parties whom I interviewed in early 2001 suggested that the DPP's New Tide Faction was concerned about the implications of cross-Strait economic integration (as economic dependence on China could undermine Taiwanese sovereignty over the long run). While most DPP factions were pragmatic and highly concerned with electoral performance, the New Tide Faction was more ideologically driven (e.g. Rigger 2001, 74). Furthermore, before the 2001 legislative election, New Tide was probably the single most influential faction within the party. It was certainly the most highly organized faction within the DPP and through 2001 controlled the largest bloc of DPP seats in the legislature (my interviews).[122] Moreover, New Tide members tended to take more rigid ideological positions. As faction leader Wu Nai-jen argued (quoted in Rigger 2001, 74), "[The New Tide's] function within the DPP is . . . to bring to the party a consideration of the long-term view. Our feeling is most factions just think about the next election, about their own interests." The faction's internal clout within the DPP made it a significant constraint on Chen's ability to liberalize cross-Strait economic restrictions at a quicker pace.[123] Furthermore, relatively protectionist economic interests form an important part of Chen's pan-green coalition. The DPP's primary support base is in Taiwan's south, and southern Taiwan sectors, especially agriculture, tend to be less competitive in world markets. In short, even early in his administration, when he frequently indicated his desire to liberalize cross-Strait economic policy and when he courted the support of the island's business community, Chen found it difficult to pursue a liberalizing agenda because he faced significant constraints from within his own coalition. In large measure because of this, it took over a year and a half before his government scrapped the Go Slow policy.

By the end of 2001 Chen's political calculus had changed. On the one hand, his political position became somewhat less precarious following the Legislative Yuan elections in December 2001. The DPP became the largest party in the legislature after the elections, holding 87 seats in the 225-member body.[124] On the other hand, the formation of the TSU (Taiwan Solidarity Union) in 2001 and its surprisingly strong showing in the 2001 elections (it collected 13 seats[125]), presented Chen with a new constraint. With Lee Teng-hui as its symbolic leader, the TSU took a hard-line position on the issue of Taiwanese sovereignty. And, as National Taiwan University professor Phillip Yang emphasized, the TSU—and Lee—opposed further economic openings to China: "While Chen has softened his stance by . . . relaxing restrictions on business investment in China, Lee remains a hard-liner."[126] The establishment of the TSU meant that adopting centrist cross-Strait policies could potentially cause "deep green" DPP supporters—those most committed to Taiwanese independence—to defect to the TSU. Consider remarks made in early 2002 by DPP lawmaker Lin Chong-mo: "Though controversial, all TSU proposals have been able to strike sympathy with a sizable number of people. The phenomenon suggests the DPP should adhere to its founding platform in addressing such thorny issues as cross-strait ties."[127] Furthermore, though Lee Teng-hui announced his support early on for the DPP candidate in the 2004 presidential election, it was clear that the TSU would not cooperate unconditionally with the DPP. The TSU's legislative whip emphasized in 2003, for example, that the TSU would try to prevent the Chen administration from "compromis[ing] national interests," noting in particular that his party would not yield in its opposition to liberalization of cross-Strait economic policy.[128]

In this environment, the political benefits for Chen associated with further liberalization of cross-Strait economic policy were less clear-cut than they had been at the start of his term. While continued liberalization had the potential to help solidify Chen's support among moderates and within the business community, it might also have driven some of his supporters to the TSU. Faced with this dilemma, Chen chose to solidify his base, and in so doing he pursued a re-election strategy that differed greatly from his approach to the 2000 election. Rather than appeal to business in order to establish credibility among moderates concerning his economic policies, he instead tried to make Taiwan's sovereign status and cross-Strait relations the primary issue in the 2004 election. He kicked off his re-election campaign by reasserting his previous remark that "each side of the Taiwan Strait is a separate country,"[129] and for the remainder of his campaign he sought to rally support by emphasizing that he was the candidate who would "protect Taiwan."[130] The strategy clearly cost him support within the business community, and some of the prominent magnates who had supported him in 2000 did not do so in 2004.[131]

Broadly speaking, Chen's policy choices are consistent with my core argument. Early in his administration, he was in a weak political position and sought to improve his standing among moderate voters. To do so, he appealed to the business community and sought endorsements within that community during the 2000 campaign, and again as the economy soured in late 2000 and 2001. His political weakness, and his desire to increase his support among centrists, meant that the preferences of the island's business community could not be ignored. He was under enormous pressure to liberalize, at least to some extent, Taiwanese economic policies toward Mainland China. However, by the end of 2001, Chen's own political position was less tenuous; at the same time, the political leverage within his coalition of those opposing further liberalization of cross-Strait economic ties increased with the establishment of the TSU and its early success. The relative political leverage of internationalist business interests thus declined somewhat, and liberalization likewise stalled after 2002.

Nonetheless, Chen's experience also makes clear that the political clout of internationalist economic interests is not a fully fixed, exogenous variable, at least in this case. Rather, that internationalist businesses had less influence over policy after 2002 was in large measure a consequence of a choice made by Chen: to make the issue of Taiwan's sovereign status his primary focus as the 2004 election approached. If he could succeed in making the sovereignty issue the primary focus of the 2004 campaign, a loss of support within the business community would not necessarily be that damaging to him; while voters might view business as a reliable endorser on the economy, it is far from clear that they would see business leaders as endorsers on the sovereignty issue.

To put it differently, if the economy were the primary issue in the campaign, Chen arguably would have needed to continue pursuing liberalization of cross-Strait policies in order to capture the support of the median voter; otherwise, obtaining endorsements from the business community would have been difficult. This would have been especially problematic for Chen because his credibility among the electorate on economic issues was already low given the island's poor economic performance in his first term. The problem for Chen was that pursuing liberalization of cross-Strait economic ties risked splintering his own coalition. Once the TSU was established, "deep green" DPP supporters had a viable "exit option" and might defect if Chen pursued moderation on cross-Strait economic policies. By making the Taiwanese sovereignty issue the dominant issue in the campaign, Chen was able to avoid this dilemma and find an alternative path to victory. Chen, in essence, was gambling that the median voter would vote for the pan-green ticket over the pan-blue ticket if his or her vote were based solely on the issue of Taiwan's sovereign status. (And, of course, Chen's choice may well have been made easier by the simple reality that an emphasis on Taiwanese sovereignty appears to correspond to his own sincere preferences.) In short, after 2002, internationalist business interests had less leverage over Taiwan's governing coalition in large measure because Chen chose to build an alternative winning coalition centered on the sovereignty issue.

6. Conclusions

Taiwanese restrictions on cross-Strait economic integration during the Lee Teng-hui and Chen Shui-bian administrations were motivated primarily by security concerns. Yet Taipei's economic policies toward Mainland China in fact varied considerably over the course of these two presidencies. Some of this variation reflected changes in the severity of conflict across the Taiwan Strait. For example, Lee's adoption of the Go Slow, Be Patient policy in 1996–97 in part grew out of a more conflictual cross-Strait political environment—triggered in part by Lee's own efforts to increase Taiwan's stature in world affairs. But changes in the level of conflict are not sufficient to account for changes in Taiwan's economic policies vis-à-vis the Mainland. For example, Chen Shui-bian's decision to relax the Go Slow, Be Patient policy was made despite the absence of any significant détente in the relationship between Beijing and Taipei. Applying the theoretical argument developed in Chapter 2, however, offers some more leverage in understanding shifts in Taiwanese policy over time. That is, the effects of cross-Strait political conflict on Taipei's economic policies toward the PRC have been conditioned by the domestic political influence of internationalist economic interests in Taiwan; in that regard the case is broadly consistent with hypothesis 2.

Of course, all theoretical models simplify reality to some extent, and this chapter has shown that other factors too have conditioned conflict's effects on Taiwan's cross-Strait economic policies. For example, we saw that the extent to which economic ties with the PRC entailed negative security externalities for Taiwan itself varied over time. As a case in point, official acquiescence to the initial wave of Taiwanese investment in the PRC was driven in part by the reality that these were small-scale producers, whose investments did not generate substantial security externalities for Taiwan. New president Ma Ying-jeou's more relaxed view toward cross-Strait economic exchange suggests, moreover, that different leaders can reach different conclusions about the security consequences of trade. Finally, it is clear that the political influence of internationalist interests is sometimes endogenous to specific choices made by leaders. Chen's decision to focus on sovereignty issues in the 2004 campaign effectively meant that endorsements from prominent business actors would be less important than if he had chosen instead to focus on economic issues. Nevertheless, thinking in terms of interactions between cross-Strait political conflict and the configuration of domestic political interests within Taiwan does help to provide a more complete—if still imperfect—account of Taiwan's economic policies toward the PRC than would otherwise be possible. The theoretical framework developed in Chapter 2, in short, provides important "empirical value-added" for this case. The next chapter considers policy motivations on the other side of the Strait.

Making Commitments Credible
PRC Policy Toward Taiwan

1. Introduction

Recall the theoretical arguments developed in Chapter 2, which pointed toward two general puzzles associated with cross-Strait commerce. The first, which was addressed in the previous chapter, concerned security externalities: given that the security externalities of cross-Strait economic integration are generally negative for Taiwan, why does the island not do more to restrain economic ties with the Mainland? This first puzzle was resolved, in part, by focusing on domestic politics in Taipei and the political costs leaders there would have to pay were they to crack down on cross-Strait economic flows more forcefully. The second puzzle concerns the behavior of the Taiwanese firms that are willing to trade with and invest heavily in the Mainland market. Given that political conflict sometimes escalates into actions like economic sanctions (or, in the extreme, wars), which can harm economic ties, why does cross-Strait political conflict not deter Taiwanese firms from investing in China? How can the PRC make credible commitments to protect the interests of Taiwanese firms that invest in the Mainland? The present chapter considers this second puzzle through an examination of PRC policy toward Taiwan.

2. The Problem for Mainland China: Credible Commitments, Credible Threats

The overview of cross-Strait political conflict presented in Chapter 3 suggests that it is useful to think of the China-Taiwan relationship as a bargaining game where the key issue to be resolved is Taiwanese sovereignty. Chinese leaders prefer reunification, and at a minimum wish to block the formalization of Taiwan's de facto independence. However, the extent to which they are able to obtain these goals hinges on the commitment they are willing to demonstrate to Taiwan. That is, in order to discourage Taiwanese leaders from pursuing policies designed to consolidate the island's sovereignty, Chinese leaders must be willing to impose costs on Taiwan—and doing so is generally costly to China as well. A willingness to impose costs not only discourages the specific Taiwanese behavior that has led China to respond, but it sends a signal that bolder moves toward independence *might* be met with yet sterner responses. Chinese leaders must be concerned that the response they choose is sufficiently resolute; too soft a response, and Taiwanese leaders could well conclude that China is not highly committed to the issue, effectively giving them the green light to move more boldly on the sovereignty issue.

When signaling commitment to the issue of Taiwanese sovereignty, Chinese leaders have a portfolio of potential responses from which to choose. Some options would be damaging to cross-Strait commercial ties—either directly or indirectly—while others would have little or no immediate effect on cross-Strait commerce. The former set of options includes economic sanctions, embargo, or military attack. The latter includes military build-ups (which are costly to China today but reduce the costs of a future attack), military exercises, less cooperative behavior vis-à-vis countries that recognize greater Taiwanese sovereignty, and brinkmanship (or risky behavior that raises the probability of war).

It seems wildly implausible that Taiwanese firms would be willing to invest so heavily in Mainland China—thereby exposing themselves to substantial risk in a relationship characterized by serious conflict—unless they felt that the first set of options was highly unlikely. But it is hardly obvious why they would come to feel this way. Certainly Mainland Chinese leaders have been quite willing from time to time—through their missile tests near the Taiwanese coast in 1996, their harshly worded 2000 white paper, their bellicose language in 2004—to signal their resolve on the Taiwan issue. And, as we will see, while Mainland Chinese officials have certainly *said* that they would protect Taiwanese firms, why Taiwanese firms would take them on their word in this regard is even less obvious. Yet the fact that Taiwanese firms are investing heavily in China suggests, strongly, that these assurances are credible. The task of this chapter is to explore the sources for this credibility.

The next section examines in more detail Chinese signaling behavior toward Taiwan. Broadly speaking, while Beijing has at times sent costly signals to demonstrate its resolve on the issue of Taiwan's sovereign status, it has been extremely reluctant to do so in a way that would harm bilateral economic interactions.

Section 4 seeks to explain Beijing's efforts to separate economics from politics in its signaling behavior toward Taiwan, and develops two causal arguments in this regard. The first follows broadly from the theoretical argument developed in Chapter 2: the PRC is governed by an increasingly internationalist coalition that would pay high political and economic costs for signaling in a way that is detrimental to cross-Strait economic ties. As such, Beijing signals in other ways, saving actions that could seriously undermine bilateral commercial relations as a last resort when other signaling mechanisms have failed to stave off Taiwanese efforts to consolidate the island's sovereign status. The second argument is a straightforward realist account, whereby PRC officials recognize that cross-Strait economic exchange generates security externalities that are positive for Beijing. As such, the PRC protects and encourages the cross-Strait economic relationship because doing so advances Beijing's political goals concerning Taiwan. Evidence suggests that both causal logics are at play in this case. Section 5 concludes by noting that the cross-Strait case generally confirms hypothesis 2, but that the case also suggests some refinements to the theoretical argument developed in Chapter 2.

3. Examining Chinese Signaling Behavior Toward Taiwan: Separating Economics from Politics

As we saw in Chapter 3, the issue of Taiwan's sovereign status has been a source of serious conflict in cross-Strait relations. Taiwanese presidents Lee Teng-hui and Chen Shui-bian have aimed to redefine Taiwan's status in ways unacceptable to Beijing, and PRC leaders have sought to convince Taiwanese (and U.S.) officials that they are willing to pay very high costs—including fighting a war—to prevent the island from formalizing its de facto independence or effectively precluding unification as a possible future option. But even if PRC leaders are resolved to fight a war to prevent formal Taiwanese independence, they would be much better off if they could signal this resolve effectively without fighting, since a cross-Strait war would be extremely costly for all involved. Chinese leaders thus have an incentive to send costly (and hence credible) signals of their resolve when challenged on the sovereignty issue. To the extent the PRC can credibly signal its resolve on the issue of Taiwan's status, Taiwanese leaders should be less willing to adopt highly revisionist policies that could potentially trigger a military conflict.

In fact, Beijing has been willing to send costly signals of resolve—particularly when Taiwanese leaders have pursued policies that the PRC considers to be provocative. But PRC officials have been careful to signal resolve in ways that have relatively limited effect on the bilateral economic relationship. That is, they have generally avoided signaling mechanisms—such as economic sanctions—that would undermine cross-Strait commerce. To the contrary, Chinese leaders have usually tried hard to reassure Taiwanese businesses during periods of high tensions across the Strait.

Lee's Cornell Visit and China's Response: 1995–1996

Consider first how China responded to Taiwanese president Lee Teng-hui's visit to the United States in 1995. A visit by a sitting president to the United States, from China's perspective, implied a much larger world role for Taiwan than was acceptable to Beijing. Lee's remarks at Cornell University, moreover, were seen by Chinese leaders as especially provocative. The Chinese response was two staged.

Chinese leaders responded to the issuance of Lee's visa in an angry but restrained manner. China recalled its ambassador to Washington and halted all military-to-military contacts with the United States. Earlier in the year, Taiwan and the Mainland had agreed to a new round of semiofficial cross-Strait talks for that summer. Mainland officials did *not* call off these talks after the announcement in May that Lee had obtained a visa to visit the United States; in fact, ARATS vice chairman Tang Shubei was allowed to travel to Taiwan in late May as part of the preparations for the new round (Sheng 2001, 27; Swaine 2001, 323). Swaine (2001, 323) speculates that Chinese leaders wished to signal disapproval but still held out hope that Lee would either not travel to the United States or would offer a conciliatory speech.

However, when Lee went ahead with the trip and delivered a speech—considered provocative by Beijing—in which he emphasized the existence of the Republic of China on Taiwan (Chen 1999), Chinese leaders decided a tougher response was necessary to signal resolve on the issue of Taiwanese sovereignty.[1] In the summer of 1995 China undertook missile tests in the sea north of Taiwan, and in August and November staged two large-scale military exercises. Two more sets of military exercises followed in early 1996, along with missile tests as close as 35 kilometers off the Taiwanese coast (Swaine 2001; Sheng 2001). The exercises marked the most serious escalation in cross-Strait tensions since the 1950s and raised fears in Taiwan that war was imminent (Zhao 1999a).

China's strong response to Lee's efforts to raise Taiwan's international profile was meant to demonstrate resolve on the issue of Taiwanese sovereignty. Though the signal was firm, Chinese leaders clearly made a concerted effort to avoid spillover into cross-Strait commercial relations. Throughout the second half of 1995, China tried to assure Taiwanese investors that their rights and interests on the Mainland would not be influenced by worsening cross-Strait political relations. For example, ARATS president Wang Daohan told Taiwanese investors that "although political relations across the Taiwan Straits are strained, economic and trade cooperation ... are not strained and are still developing."[2] Tang Shubei similarly noted that despite tensions, "Taiwan investors' rights and interests on the Mainland are not affected in any way."[3] Chen Yunlin, then executive deputy director of the Taiwan Affairs Office, provided similar assurances.[4] Local officials, meanwhile, continued to welcome Taiwanese investors despite the crisis. Tianjin official Wang Guanghao, for example, made it clear that his city still hoped to attract Taiwanese investors, noting that "despite the tension, Taiwanese investment will grow in this city."[5] And shortly after the crisis, Jiang Zemin emphasized that "political differences should not be allowed to affect and interfere with economic cooperation between the two sides."[6]

This is not to suggest that the spike in tensions had no effect on the behavior of Taiwanese investors. Growth in cross-Strait trade stagnated in 1996 (see Figure 2 in Chapter 3), and Taiwanese surveys of Mainland investors found them to be deeply concerned over the crisis. One survey found that 84 percent of Taiwanese investors believed that a worsening of relations across the Strait increased the risk associated with future investments.[7] Other companies noted that they were adopting a more conservative attitude regarding Chinese investments until tensions eased,[8] and some investors expressed concern that the spike in tension was leading some Mainlanders to form "anti-Taiwan sentiments" (*choutai qingxu*).[9] Still, no Taiwanese firms announced plans to cancel or scale back Mainland investments—and indeed, as Figure 3 (in Chapter 3) shows, investment continued to pour into China during the crisis.[10] In short, although Taiwanese firms expressed concern about deteriorating cross-Strait relations, the sharpest spike in tension in over thirty years was not enough to cause a significant change in their patterns of Mainland investment. Mainland officials made a determined effort at the time to keep tensions from affecting cross-Strait commerce, and that effort appears to have worked quite well.

Lee's "Two-States" Theory and Beijing's Response: 1999–2000

A similar pattern emerged in 1999 during the next serious spike in cross-Strait political tensions. In July of that year, Lee Teng-hui declared that cross-Strait relations were in fact "special state-to-state relations," which to Chinese leaders suggested a sharp move by the island in the direction of independence. At the time, Wang Daohan was planning a trip to Taipei in the fall as part of a renewed dialogue between the two sides; after Lee's announcement, Beijing angrily canceled Wang's trip (Swaine 2001, 330). The PRC bitterly denounced Lee's formulation, and Mainland scholars and commentators suggested that war could be imminent (Sheng 2001, 222).[11] Meanwhile, the two military leaders who sat on the Politburo—Chi Haotian and Zhang Wannian—emphasized that the army would prepare for a war in the Taiwan Strait.[12] Chinese president Jiang Zemin argued that Lee's formulation was a dangerous new path, and during a summit with Bill Clinton warned that "if it becomes apparent that [Taiwanese leaders] are playing with Taiwanese independence . . . we absolutely will not sit and watch without taking action."[13] In early 2000, shortly before Taiwan's second presidential election (which took place in March) and several months after Lee announced his "two states" theory, Beijing released a white paper that bitterly accused Lee Teng-hui of promoting Taiwanese independence. More importantly, the report indicated that indefinite delay by Taiwanese authorities on negotiations over unification would constitute legitimate reason to use military force against the island, a condition that was not underscored in government pronouncements previously.[14] In short, China's response to Lee's pronouncement was, again, stern—although the Mainland did not undertake another round of risky missile tests immediately off the coast of Taiwan.

Once again, however, Mainland officials did their best to provide assurances to Taiwanese investors during the crisis. In September, deputy director of the Taiwan Affairs Office Li Bingcai stressed that "no matter what happens to cross-Straits relations . . . we will continue our unremitting efforts to promote the development of cross-Straits economic relations."[15] Noted another official, "We'll stick to what President Jiang Zemin said, that economic exchanges across the Straits should not be affected by any differences."[16] An official radio commentary directed at Taiwan likewise emphasized that "the two-state theory has seriously damaged the interests of people on both sides of the strait, but the mainland will not obstruct cross-strait economic cooperation because of political differences." Lee's theory, the commentary noted, "cannot obstruct the development of cross-Strait economic and trade exchanges."[17] Officials at the local level were also reassuring: for example, the party secretary of Fujian Province, Chen Mingyi, stated that "Fujian province will, as always, welcome Taiwan compatriots to come for sightseeing and invest in business ventures."[18] In early December of that year, moreover, the State Council enacted a set of rules designed to protect Taiwanese investors. The Chinese government had spent several years drafting the rules, which were meant to be guidelines for implementation of an earlier law protecting Taiwanese businesses.[19] The guidelines reaffirmed that Taiwanese businesses would be given preferential treatment in the Mainland market, and that "the state does not nationalize or requisition investments by Taiwan compatriot investors." The new rules also guaranteed access to schools for children of Taiwanese investors and their employees, while guaranteeing Taiwanese businesses access to machinery, inputs, and services on par with other Chinese companies.[20] High-level officials, including the minister of trade and economic cooperation Shi Guangsheng and the director of the Taiwan

Affairs Office Chen Yunlin, argued that the new guidelines underscored Beijing's commitment to protecting the interests of Taiwanese investors in China.[21]

In short, though Mainland officials reacted strongly and negatively to Lee's "special state-to-state" formula, they tried—as they had in 1995–96—to signal resolve in a way that would not damage the cross-Strait economic relationship. Indeed, Beijing appeared to be doing its best to reassure Taiwanese businesses that their interests would be protected regardless of the course of cross-Strait political relations.

Chinese Signaling During the Chen Shui-bian Administration: 2000–Present

After his election as Taiwanese president in 2000, Chen Shui-bian initially emphasized stability in cross-Strait relations, as evidenced, for example, by the "5 No's," which he announced in his inaugural speech. Meanwhile, despite obvious displeasure that Chen of the officially pro-independence DPP had been elected, Beijing's rhetoric was generally mild in the first years of his presidency. Blunt warnings to voters delivered on the eve of Taiwan's election had failed to persuade voters to abandon Chen; indeed, the harsh rhetoric may have contributed to Chen's victory (e.g. Mulvenon 2004a). However, four years later, as the 2004 Taiwanese presidential elections approached, Chen increasingly took policy stances that were viewed with alarm in Beijing. As early as 2002 he had declared each side of the Taiwan Strait to be a separate country (*yi bian yi guo*), and in the summer of 2003 he began to push for the use of referenda to decide controversial issues in Taiwanese politics.[22] In the fall Chen began to push for a new constitution, which he believed should be drafted in 2006 and submitted to Taiwanese voters in a referendum.[23] Mainland Chinese officials feared that direct referenda and the drafting of a new constitution could help to establish legal independence for Taiwan, and they warned against adopting a referendum law—especially one that failed to prohibit votes on issues like Taiwan's official name or its flag.[24] Under pressure from Chen, who was successfully using the referendum issue to boost his political standing, the legislature passed a referendum bill in November 2003. Though the bill that passed placed strict limits on the use of referenda—no votes on changing the flag or the Republic of China name; no vote on a completely new constitution; and high hurdles for votes on constitutional amendments[25]—Chen soon seized on an apparent loophole in the law, which granted the president the power to hold a "defensive referendum" were Taiwan to face an imminent security threat. Chen argued that the hundreds of Chinese missiles capable of striking Taiwan and deployed in Fujian Province constituted just such a threat, and announced his intention to hold a referendum at the same time as the 2004 presidential election.[26]

Beijing's initial response, at least rhetorically, was quite stern. Military officials warned that Chen was "playing with fire," and one official said of Taipei, "If they refuse to come to their senses and continue to use referenda as an excuse to seek Taiwan independence, they will push Taiwan compatriots into the abyss of war."[27] Premier Wen Jiabao warned that Chinese people would "safeguard the unity of their motherland at all costs" (Mulvenon 2004b). Chinese leaders also tried to leverage improved U.S.-China relations into obtaining the United States' help in pressuring Chen to backtrack (Mulvenon 2004a). The effort was somewhat successful: President Bush, in a December meeting in Washington with Wen, clearly indicated that he opposed Chen's referendum proposal. Though Chen went ahead with the referendum, the questions asked were fairly innocuous (and certainly less provocative than possibilities being tossed about in early December).[28] As such, and perhaps also in recognition that shrill rhetoric prior to the 1996 and 2000 elections had been counterproductive, Beijing's tone was notably less harsh in the immediate run-up to the March 2004 election (Suettinger 2004).

However, Chinese leaders became deeply pessimistic after Chen's narrow (and disputed) electoral victory (Christensen 2005), and their signaling behavior changed in turn. As I noted in Chapter 3, Chen remained uncompromising on the issue of Taiwan's sovereign status; indeed, his position appeared to harden.[29] He also intensified his push for a new constitution for Taiwan.[30] Furthermore, as the December 2004 Legislative Yuan elections approached, Chen's rhetoric became even more alarming to Beijing as he sought to increase pan-green support by playing up the sovereignty issue (Christensen 2005). In response to Chen's apparently uncompromising position, Beijing began to ratchet up its rhetoric on the Taiwan issue. Hoping to debunk suggestions that China would be constrained by deepening cross-Strait economic ties—or a possible international boycott of the 2008 Olympic Games scheduled for Beijing—from fighting a war to prevent Taiwanese independence, Chinese officials began to reemphasize Wen Jiabao's "pay any price to prevent Taiwan independence" formulation.[31] Wen himself referred to unification as "more important than our lives."[32] And Chinese minister of defense Cao Gangchuan warned that "the People's Liberation Army has the determination and capability to resolutely smash any 'Taiwan independence' splittist conspiracy."[33] Meanwhile, in July 2004, China undertook well-publicized military drills at Dongshan Island in Fujian Province. Though the exercises have typically occurred on an annual basis, this time China emphasized a new objective: "striving for air supremacy over the Taiwan Strait."[34]

Chinese officials also began to suggest in 2004 that China might pass a "unification law" to signal the importance of the Taiwanese sovereignty issue—and, presumably, to tie the hands of future policymakers in this regard. In a visit to England in May, Wen Jiabao promised to "seriously consider" such a law when he was asked about it in a meeting.[35] Chen Shui-bian, meanwhile, began in the summer of 2004 to warn that the passage of such a law would serve as a "mandate" for a Chinese invasion.[36] In December, Beijing announced that the proposed legislation would take the form of an "antisecession" law rather than a "unification" law.[37] The law was ultimately adopted by the National People's Congress in March 2005. Though the law writes that the "state shall do its utmost with maximum sincerity to achieve a peaceful reunification," it also warns, "In the event that the 'Taiwan independence' secessionist forces should act under any name or by any means to cause the fact of Taiwan's secession from China, or that major incidents entailing Taiwan's secession from China should occur, or that possibilities for a peaceful reunification should be completely exhausted, the state shall employ non-peaceful means and other necessary measures to protect China's sovereignty and territorial integrity."[38] Though Chinese leaders undoubtedly believed before that they had the authority to use "non-peaceful means" to prevent Taiwanese independence, the passage of the law can nonetheless be viewed as a costly "hands-tying" signal, as it legally obligates future Chinese leaders to respond forcefully to "major incidents entailing Taiwan's secession from China." In short, as seen in the 1990s, China during the 2000s has used a diversified portfolio of signaling mechanisms to demonstrate its resolve on the issue of Taiwan's status.

Since Chen's victory in the 2000 election, however, Beijing has been more willing to politicize the cross-Strait economic relationship than it had been in the 1990s. As before, PRC officials have on several occasions appeared to go out of their way to reassure Taiwanese investors during times of increased cross-Strait tensions. In the fall of 2004, for example, top CCP (Chinese Communist Party) officials like Jia Qinglin emphasized the need for continued cross-Strait cooperation and called on officials to protect the interests of Taiwanese investors.[39] But PRC officials have also been more willing to harass one particular category of Taiwanese investors: those that express support for the DPP or for Taiwanese independence, often referred to as "green" Taiwanese businesses because of their association with the pan-green camp in Taiwan. After the 2000 election, for example, Chinese officials announced that the Mainland would no longer welcome the investments of pro-independence businessmen, saying it didn't want these types of businesses to benefit from investing in China—as they might use their earnings to advocate independence back home.[40] In early 2001, moreover, rumors swirled that the Mainland operations of Hsu Wen-lung, a prominent Taiwanese tycoon who supported Chen, were ordered shut down by Beijing.[41] Though those rumors appear to have been unsubstantiated, Beijing did explicitly single out Hsu by name after the 2004 Taiwanese presidential election: while criticizing

Hsu in particular, Mainland officials repeated warnings from 2000 that pro-DPP Taiwanese investors would not be welcome in China.[42] To date, the PRC appears to have limited its actions against green Taiwanese businesses to harassment, such as through increased audits and inspections. But the willingness to threaten high-profile Taiwanese businesses nonetheless marks a significant shift in PRC policy toward Taiwan. This shift is explored at greater length in the following section.

Summary

Since the mid-1990s, in response to efforts by Taiwanese leaders to consolidate the island's sovereign status and raise its profile on the world stage, Chinese leaders have tried to signal that they both oppose Taiwanese independence (or moves in that direction) and are resolved to prevent it—using force if necessary. But with a few important exceptions, the PRC has generally tried to avoid signaling resolve in a way that would harm the cross-Strait economic relationship. The next section considers why the PRC has signaled in this way.

4. Explaining Patterns in Chinese Signaling Behavior Toward Taiwan

Beijing's apparent efforts to keep politics and economics on separate tracks when signaling resolve on the issue of Taiwanese sovereignty appear to be a consequence of two broad causal factors explored in turn in this section. First, signaling resolve toward Taiwan in a way that is harmful to bilateral economic flows would entail enormous political and economic costs for CCP leaders. China is governed by a relatively internationalist coalition, which has strong incentive to avoid signaling in such a way if at all possible. Though the high costs of economic sanctions, or in an extreme case war, do not preclude the possibility that the PRC would resort to such measures in handling the Taiwan issue, they do suggest that CCP leaders would prefer to save such measures for a worst-case scenario. Second, just as leaders in Taiwan view the security externalities of cross-Strait economic exchange as being overwhelmingly negative, leaders in Beijing see these externalities as broadly positive. Beijing thus encourages cross-Strait economic integration, viewing it as conducive to broader PRC goals in the Taiwan Strait. In other words, CCP leaders have straightforward realist reasons for avoiding harming bilateral economic relations when signaling resolve toward Taiwan. This section concludes with a closer look at the case of the PRC's harassment of green Taiwanese businesses, which I argue offers a window into the relative explanatory weight of these two causal factors.

*China's Internationalist Governing Coalition and the Separation
of Economics from Politics*

Part of the reason China signals the way it does on the Taiwan issue follows
directly from the theoretical argument outlined in Chapter 2. China is governed
by an increasingly internationalist coalition in which internationalist economic
interests hold a significant amount of political influence. As a result, signaling
resolve over the Taiwan issue in a way that is detrimental to cross-Strait economic
ties would prove very costly to PRC leaders. Such behavior could undercut their
development strategy (both because Taiwan is a major source of foreign investment and because signaling resolve to Taiwan in a way detrimental to commerce
sends a dangerous signal to private firms from other countries—like the United
States—whose political relations with China involve some friction), and it could
lead to a loss of support from domestic internationalist economic interests.

China's development strategy. Since the early 1980s, economic development has
been the primary goal of the Chinese leadership. In a 1982 speech, Deng Xiaoping
argued that China faced three major tasks in the 1980s (including socialist modern-
ization, reunification of the motherland, and opposition to global hegemonism),
but he emphasized as well that "economic construction is at the core of these
tasks; it is the basis for the solution [to China's] external and internal problems."[43]
The emphasis on economic development continued under Jiang Zemin's leadership. In his report delivered at the opening of the Sixteenth Chinese Communist
Party (CCP) Congress in November 2002, Jiang stressed that China "must persist
in taking economic construction as the central task," that "development is the last
word," and that China "must seize all opportunities to speed up development."[44]
The leadership's decision to admit capitalists into the CCP under Jiang's "Three
Represents" theory—formally announced in a July 2001 speech[45]—underscored
its commitment to economic reform. The theory, which holds that the party
should represent society's most productive forces and most advanced culture (that
is, elites), arguably makes the CCP's market-oriented reforms more credible, since
it opens the door to party membership for the key benefactors of such reform.
The theory was enshrined into the CCP's constitution in the fall of 2002, further suggesting that economic reformers and modernizers continued to hold the
upper hand within the party.[46] There is little to indicate that the current leadership under Hu Jintao will deviate from this emphasis on development. Though
Hu, in his speeches, often points to problems like the growing rural-urban gap, he
nonetheless continues to highlight the importance of economic development and
continuing the opening of China's economy to the outside world.[47]

   While leaders in Beijing clearly view economic development as a primary goal, equally important is the strategy they have pursued to attain that objective. Specifically, China's development strategy has been one of economic reform and integration into the world economy. Since 1992, when the Fourteenth Party Congress proclaimed that China would become a "socialist market economy"—indicating that the transition to market had become official policy[48]—China has been the largest recipient of foreign direct investment (FDI) among developing countries (Moore 2002, 3). In 2003 China even temporarily surpassed the United States to become the *world's* largest recipient of FDI.[49] Between 1977 and 2000, China's share of international trade grew sixfold from 0.6 percent to 3.7 percent (Lardy 2002, 4, 178), and by 2004 China had become the world's third-largest trading nation after the United States and Germany.[50] By 2000, moreover, foreign-invested firms accounted for nearly half of China's exports (Lardy 2002, 5). Clearly, the Chinese economy has come to depend quite heavily on integration into the world economy.

To some extent, these numbers might overstate China's openness to the world economy and its dependence on it. In particular, about half of the country's trade consists of imports processed into exports; such trade tends to have a smaller effect on the domestic economy than "normal" trade. Imports not intended to be reprocessed into exports typically face greater protectionist hurdles as well (World Bank 1997, 85; Naughton 2000). Still, Lardy (2002) argues that Chinese integration into world markets proceeded rapidly during the 1990s. He notes that between 1995 and 2000, China's "ordinary imports" grew much more rapidly than imports of parts and components used in export processing and imports of capital goods used by foreign firms—suggesting an opening of China's domestic market (Lardy 2002, 9). Furthermore, Chinese barriers to trade dropped sharply after the 1980s. Tariffs, high by international standards in the early 1990s, dropped sharply over the course of the decade: in 2000, the weighted mean tariff in China stood at 14.7 percent, similar to tariff levels in Brazil and Mexico (World Bank 2002). Moreover, customs revenues suggest that this number overstates China's true level of tariff protection: by 1994, tariff revenues were equal to only 3 percent of the value of all imports, which Lardy notes was "almost certainly the lowest rate of tariff collection of any developing country." Crackdowns on smuggling later in the decade increased tariff collections, but in 2000 tariff revenues were equal to only 4 percent of imports (Lardy 2002, 37–38). Lardy (2002, 39–45) argues as well that China's nontariff barriers to trade also dropped substantially during the 1990s. Finally, China's decision to enter the World Trade Organization (WTO)—under conditions stricter than those normally imposed on new members (Lardy 2002)—suggests a commitment to continue the policy of opening to the world economy.

Given China's development goals, and its strategy for obtaining those goals,

Chinese leaders would undoubtedly view policies that are detrimental to the country's foreign economic ties as being quite costly. From this perspective, when signaling resolve on the issue of Taiwan's sovereign status, PRC officials should view those signals that would be detrimental to cross-Strait economic flows—such as economic sanctions—as being especially costly. They would be costly in part because of their likely impact on the cross-Strait economic relationship, from which the PRC benefits greatly. It is hard to imagine that such signals would have anything other than a chilling effect on cross-Strait economic flows, as Taiwanese investors came to view investments in China as a highly risky endeavor.

PRC signals that were harmful to cross-Strait economic flows could also threaten Beijing's foreign economic ties more generally. On the one hand, such signals might give investors from other countries pause—especially those from countries (like Japan) that have had significant friction with China in recent years. On the other hand, as Leng (1998a; 1998b; 2002) has written, Taiwanese investment in China has itself become increasingly globalized. Though many early Taiwanese investments in China took the form of sole proprietorship enterprises focused on exports (Wei and Zhu 1995, 118), as the Mainland has opened its domestic market to foreign investors Taiwanese firms have increasingly joined alliances with firms from other countries to enter the Mainland market. These sorts of alliances are typically entered into for economic reasons: Taiwanese firms benefit by gaining greater access to capital from multinational corporations (MNCs), while MNCs benefit from Taiwanese firms' natural linguistic and cultural advantages in navigating the Mainland market (Leng 1998b, 148). For example, earlier this decade Taiwan's President Group (*Tongyi*) entered into a joint venture with Starbucks International and a local Shanghai company to bring Starbucks coffee shops to Shanghai (Leng 2002, 271). Furthermore, in trying to evade Taiwanese government restrictions on investing in China, many Taiwanese companies have raised capital abroad to invest in China; Leng (1998b, 146) notes, for instance, that when Formosa Plastics announced its plans to build a major power plant in China in 1996, much of the proposed funding for the plan was to come from Japanese and German banks. As Leng (1998b, 147) writes, this globalization of Taiwanese investment in China means that the "'target' of attacking such investment becomes ambiguous." Sanctions directed against Taiwanese firms would also directly harm firms from other countries; as such, sanctions are far more costly than would be the case if Taiwanese firms did not ally with MNCs when investing in China.

In sum, since China's ruling coalition has pursued a development strategy that depends heavily on integration into global markets, signaling resolve on the Taiwan issue in a way that harmed cross-Strait economic exchange would entail high economic costs for the PRC.

Political influence of internationalist economic interests. While it is difficult to observe leadership accountability directly within China's nondemocratic political system, there is reason to believe that PRC leaders depend at least somewhat on the support of internationalist economic interests. Local officials along China's coast have benefited heavily from foreign investment; policies that undermine those investment flows are unlikely to be popular among these officials. Moreover, the Chinese Communist Party's system of reciprocal accountability appears to give provincial officials from these regions an important voice in leadership selection (Shirk 1993). To the extent that internationalist economic interests do exercise political clout in the PRC, signaling resolve on the Taiwan issue in a way that harms cross-Strait economic flows would not only be harmful to the governing coalition's development strategy but could also entail significant domestic political costs.

Local officials in China tend to benefit from foreign investment for several reasons.[51] Most obviously, foreign investment is conducive to local economic growth. It can provide jobs and expand the local tax base (Wang 1994; Hsing 1998; Shirk 1993; Li 1998; Tian 1999; Zweig 2002). Though the fiscal recentralization program introduced in 1994 ended the fiscal contracting system, which had helped spur reforms during the 1980s, the new system continued to provide local officials with strong incentives to pursue growth-oriented policies. Specifically, after 1994 China's tax system resembled a Western-style federal system, where some taxes are collected by local governments, some by the central government, and some are shared between the two. Meanwhile, local governments continue to have substantial fiscal responsibilities (Montinola et al. 1995, 72; Chung 2001, 56–57; Zheng 2000, 225; Huang 2001, 22). Growth also gives local governments the opportunity to expand their own administrative payrolls (Wang 1994), and the influx of foreign capital obviously means more opportunities for officials to pursue personal enrichment through corruption (Shirk 1994, 33). Finally, high growth rates are generally conducive to the career goals of local officials; that is, promotion becomes more likely, since growth typically indicates successful management of local affairs. It is such career incentives that have likely motivated some local officials to "cook the books" (Rawski 2000) when growth falls short of the central government's expectations.[52]

Given these incentives, local officials have been aggressive in trying to attract foreign investment.[53] As Tian (2006, 149) writes, local officials are often more willing than higher-level officials to grant favorable terms to foreign investors—such as lower tax rates or less stringent inspections or restrictions on imported materials. Hsing (1998, 130) quotes one Taiwanese investor as describing PRC policies designed to attract foreign investment—such as three-year tax holidays—as "made for fools": far better terms could be negotiated by dealing with local governments directly. And Taiwanese investors—given their shared language and culture—have been well-positioned to develop the connections with local officials that make it possible to forge such special arrangements. Indeed, Taiwanese businesses have been skillful at developing close personal relationships with local officials throughout southeastern China (e.g. Hsing 1998; Tian 1999; Tian 2006), and such relationships are mutually beneficial. For Taiwanese investors, these relationships reduce the risks associated with investing in an environment where local officials have substantial de facto discretion in enforcing regulations and imposing fees and other penalties on foreign investors.[54] Local officials, in turn, reap the benefits of greater levels of Taiwanese investment than would otherwise be possible. More broadly, the close relationships between Taiwanese investors and local Chinese officials serve to reinforce the stake that local officials have in stable cross-Strait economic relations.

Clearly, key strategic decisions relating to Taiwan are made at the top of the Chinese political system, meaning that local officials have little direct influence over those decisions. Swaine's (2001, 293–94) research has led him to conclude that, under the previous leadership, key decisions relating to Taiwan were made by Jiang Zemin in consultation with several senior associates and advisors, including Li Peng, Qian Qichen, Wang Daohan, and Zeng Qinghong. Nonetheless, an inability to influence policy toward Taiwan directly does not imply that the interests of coastal provincial officials are not considered at all in the formulation of that policy. While the right to appoint provincial governors and party secretaries rests with high-level officials within the Politburo and the Standing Committee (Huang 2001), those same provincial-level officials are part of a broader "selectorate" that ultimately chooses who sits in the party's highest organs (Shirk 1993).

Most of the compromising and maneuvering related to the composition of the CCP's top collective organs take place behind the scenes: witness the speculation prior to the Seventeenth Party Congress that took place in October 2007. But the decisions reached must be ratified by the party's Central Committee, which Shirk argues is "becoming the key group in the selectorate in China." Notes Shirk (1993, 81), "The body is not merely a rubber stamp; the leader chosen must reflect the preferences of the committee." The composition of the Central Committee has become quite institutionalized in recent years, and currently each province is assigned two full membership seats. Other important constituencies include the military and central government officials—particularly from various ministries (Shirk 1993; Li 2001). Because of the broad range of representation within the Central Committee, leadership contenders generally must build broad bases of support if they are to attain high political office; top leaders should thus be reluctant to impose policies that are unpopular with important segments of the selectorate—such as local officials (Shirk 1993; Li 2001).

I do not wish to overstate my case on this point. It is unlikely, for example, that if the interests of coastal provincial officials were to conflict directly with the interests of another key constituency—such as the military—on an issue like Taiwan over which local officials have little direct influence, then the interests of coastal provincial officials would prevail. As Yang (1996, 437) writes, it is far from clear that the size of a particular bloc's representation in the Central Committee correlates directly with that bloc's actual influence over leadership selection decisions. Fewer Central Committee seats may be devoted to the military than to provincial officials, but military "votes" might count more. Indeed, Shirk (2007) notes that bureaucracies responsible for maintaining order and CCP control over society—which she refers to as a "control cartel"—have disproportionate clout within the CCP. What's more, the extent of local provincial officials' political power within the Chinese political system remains controversial. Sheng (2005) shows, for example, that provincial officials' share of Central Committee full membership positions has declined considerably over the course of the reform era. Sheng also emphasizes the continued "institutional powers vested in the Party center . . . to monopolize top provincial personnel control" (2005, 353–54; see also Huang 1996, ch. 4). Furthermore, Yang (1997) notes that it is difficult for local officials to form a united front when bargaining with central officials. In short, though enacting policies that fundamentally undercut the interests of local officials in China would entail significant political costs for PRC leaders, those costs should not be exaggerated.

To summarize, local officials in China—especially those in coastal regions—have strong incentives to attract foreign investment, and as such can be thought of as internationalist economic interests. Indeed, it is the close relationships local officials have formed with Taiwanese businesses that have helped to make the PRC market an attractive one for Taiwanese firms in the first place. And, though their political clout should not be overstated, local officials are nonetheless influential actors within China's political system. While top leaders certainly have the authority to make policy decisions (especially those involving a key foreign-affairs issue like Taiwan) and to make personnel decisions, there can be little doubt that, at the margins at least, they "generally prefer not to impose unpopular" policies on important members of the selectorate like coastal provincial officials (Shirk 1994, 73).[55] Perhaps even more fundamentally, the close relationships that local officials have formed with Taiwanese firms could potentially complicate efforts by Beijing to use economic sanctions or harassment as a way to signal resolve or exercise leverage over Taiwan. Local officials have long used liberal interpretations of PRC investment regulations as a way to attract and benefit from Taiwanese investment; it is hard to imagine that they wouldn't try to circumvent policies designed to undercut such investment.[56]

Implications. The governing coalition in the PRC can be thought of as internationalist because the CCP pursues a development strategy based on integration into global markets, and because internationalist economic interests—especially local officials in coastal provinces—have significant political clout. That the PRC is governed by a relatively internationalist coalition should, in turn, have important consequences for China's cross-Strait signaling: leaders should view signals that harm cross-Strait economic interactions as being especially costly and should try to avoid them if possible. Obviously, any other signals must be costly as well; otherwise they would be useless. Deploying missiles in Fujian Province, for example, involves costs. But the more internationalist China's governing coalition is, the more likely leaders are to view those costs as lower than, say, a trade sanction. Mainland leaders should view actions with the potential to undermine cross-Strait economic relations as a last resort, hence their efforts to separate politics and economics when signaling resolve on the issue of Taiwanese sovereignty.

It is possible to imagine a scenario that is quite different, one in which leaders in China pursue a development strategy based on domestic protectionism and in which they do not depend at all on the political support of provincial leaders. In such a scenario, the costs of imposing economic sanctions would be much lower, and leaders would be much less reluctant to resort to this type of tactic to signal resolve on the Taiwan issue. Of course, part of the reason that the Mainland is an attractive site to investors in the first place is that it isn't the type of environment suggested in this alternative scenario: a development strategy centered on protectionism would probably not welcome foreign investors. In this alternative scenario, firms from Taiwan that nonetheless tried to do business in China would face greater risk than businesses from elsewhere, precisely because of cross-Strait political tensions and the danger of sanctions or other damaging signals from Beijing. In the real world, the presence of an internationalist coalition in China obviously makes the Mainland a much more attractive site for Taiwanese firms to do business, and it also gives these firms more confidence that cross-Strait political tensions will not affect the commercial relationship.

This is not to suggest that Chinese leaders would never utilize sanctions or an embargo or even a military strike when bargaining with Taiwan, or that an outbreak of war is any less likely in the Taiwan Strait than in other dyads characterized by a high level of conflict. While economic development is clearly a core goal of China, it is not clear where Taiwan's status stands relative to that goal. Chinese leaders have suggested that they would be willing to sacrifice anything, including development, in order to prevent Taiwan's independence. Unfortunately, it is difficult to know in advance how credible this position is in a world where antagonists have a clear incentive to overstate their own resolve (e.g. Fearon 1995). It is conceivable, in other words, that Chinese leaders could be highly committed to economic development and reform but view Taiwan as so important that they would be willing to risk the country's development program in order to prevent Taiwan's independence. It is also conceivable that Taiwanese leaders would doubt this, knowing that Chinese leaders would have every incentive to *say* they would do anything to check Taiwanese independence whether they meant it or not. As such, cross-Strait commerce still involves some political risk. As much as Mainland leaders hope to prevent cross-Strait political conflict from affecting cross-Strait commerce, if Taiwan moved sharply toward independence and other signaling mechanisms failed to convince Taiwanese leaders to back down, Chinese leaders—if truly resolved—might well resort to economic sanctions or military action. In contrast, if Chinese leaders are saving such measures for a worst-case scenario, the likelihood that cross-Strait political tensions might seriously undermine the cross-Strait economic relationship is relatively low.

In summary, Chinese signaling behavior toward Taiwan appears broadly consistent with hypothesis 2 and with the theoretical argument developed in Chapter 2. The PRC is governed by an increasingly internationalist coalition; signaling resolve on the issue of Taiwanese sovereignty in a way that harmed cross-Strait economic ties would be politically and economically costly to PRC officials. As such, Beijing has generally tried to signal in a way that doesn't harm bilateral economic relations. But it remains unclear how much causal weight can be attributed to the constraining effect of an internationalist coalition when trying to explain PRC signaling behavior. Indeed, Chinese officials are undoubtedly motivated as well by straightforward realist reasons to avoid undercutting cross-Strait economic linkages when signaling resolve on the Taiwan issue. A discussion of this sort of realist logic is thus warranted.

Achieving Unification Through Economic Integration?

Chapter 4 showed that the security externalities generated by cross-Strait economic exchange are generally positive for Mainland China and negative for Taiwan. Leaders in Taiwan have been cognizant of these negative externalities and have thus tried, generally unsuccessfully, to slow economic integration across the Taiwan Strait. But leaders in Beijing—not surprisingly—clearly recognize these externalities as well, and there can be little doubt that Mainland China's efforts to reassure Taiwanese investors arise in part because Beijing hopes to benefit politically.

Indeed, Chinese officials have been quite frank in this regard. Li Lanqing, vice premier at the time, noted in 1996 that even if the Mainland suffers some losses in providing preferential treatment to Taiwanese businesses, "the purpose [of such a policy] is to give absolute guarantees to the interests of Taiwanese businesses in China, so that they can develop confidence in the long-term development of their Mainland investments. This policy originates out of [China's] broad national interests."[57] Jiang Zemin in 1994 argued that "enhancing cross-strait economic exchanges and cooperation ... will be useful in boosting the development of cross-Strait relations and national reunification."[58] A slogan commonly used to describe the strategy is to "peddle politics through business, to influence government through the people" (*yi shang cu zheng, yi min cu guan*; Zhao 1999a, 27).[59] My own interviews with scholars and officials in Beijing and Shanghai indicated a fairly widespread belief that cross-Strait economic integration at a minimum makes it more difficult for Taiwan to declare independence (by raising the costs of conflict).

Consistent with a realist logic, Beijing since the early 1980s has officially and consistently promoted economic integration with Taiwan. Beginning in 1980, for example, Taiwanese manufacturers were allowed to enter China duty-free (Naughton 1997, 84). In 1988, Beijing went further in announcing the Regulations on Encouraging the Investment of Taiwan Compatriots, which gave special incentives to Taiwanese businesses to invest in China, such as tax holidays and property transfer provisions; the regulations also prohibit nationalization of Taiwanese firms absent compensation (La Croix and Xu 1995, 126–28). The 1994 Law on Protecting Investment of Taiwan Compatriots reiterated the protections against nationalization and also guaranteed Taiwanese investors the rights to remit profits to Taiwan and to transfer and inherit assets in China. The ability to transfer profits back to Taiwan in particular was seen as a major breakthrough by Taiwanese businesses.[60] And the rules on the implementation of the 1994 law, passed in 1999 and described in the previous section, provided further protections and incentives to Taiwanese businesses. Finally, major Chinese policy initiatives relating to Taiwan since the late 1970s—including the 1979 "Message to Taiwan Compatriots," Ye's 1981 nine-points proposal, Jiang's 1995 eight-points proposal, and even the 2005 antisecession law—have tended to emphasize the desirability of increasing cross-Strait economic exchanges.

That the PRC has been willing to offer Taiwanese investors special incentives that are not enjoyed by investors from other areas strongly suggests political—rather than just economic—motivations for these policies. It is difficult to see why the PRC would adopt policies specifically targeted toward Taiwanese investors if the goal of such policies were simply to attract more foreign investment. Clearly,

Beijing has aimed not simply to increase inflows of foreign direct investment more generally but also to attract more Taiwanese investment in particular. These sorts of Taiwan-specific policies, combined with the frank statements issued by PRC officials concerning the political motivations of such policies, suggest that there can be little doubt that China pushes for cross-Strait economic integration in part because leaders in Beijing view this as conducive to China's political goals vis-à-vis Taiwan.[61] Given these realist motivations for the PRC's efforts to increase Taiwan's economic integration with the Mainland, Beijing's reluctance to signal resolve in a way that is damaging to cross-Strait commerce may derive (at least in part) from a belief that signals of this sort would not only be politically and economically costly but counterproductive to Beijing's long-term goal of political unification with Taiwan as well.[62]

The Case of "Green" Taiwanese Businesses in China

The discussion to this point suggests that Beijing's signaling behavior toward Taiwan—and, in particular, its general effort to avoid signaling in a way harmful to cross-Strait economic ties—is driven by at least two broad causal logics. On the one hand, Beijing's behavior is generally consistent with hypothesis 2 (H2): the PRC is governed by an increasingly internationalist coalition that would pay substantial political and economic costs for implementing policies that undermined the cross-Strait economic relationship. As such, PRC officials have aimed to signal resolve in ways that limit damage to bilateral economic ties while simultaneously seeking to reassure Taiwanese investors that their interests will be protected regardless of the progression of cross-Strait political relations. On the other hand, the PRC reaps positive security externalities from the cross-Strait economic relationship. Officials in Beijing believe that cross-Strait economic ties further their political goals vis-à-vis Taiwan, and as such, for straightforward realist reasons, it would be counterproductive to undercut economic ties with Taiwan. It is quite likely, of course, that both logics are at work here and help to explain PRC signaling on the issue of Taiwanese sovereignty. But is it possible to determine which of these logics carries more explanatory weight?

Sorting out the relative importance of these two causal processes is difficult because the two logics yield similar predictions: in both cases, PRC officials should be reluctant to act in ways harmful to cross-Strait economic ties. An especially useful opportunity, then, is the case of Mainland China's harassment of "green" Taiwanese firms—those that are supportive of the DPP or sympathetic to Taiwanese independence—since 2000. Recall that the PRC's signaling behavior on the issue of Taiwanese sovereignty shifted somewhat after Chen's victory in the 2000 Taiwanese election. Prior to the election, Beijing appeared to bend over backwards to reassure Taiwanese investors that their interests would be protected even during times of tense cross-Strait political relations. After the election, PRC officials were more willing than before to single out green Taiwanese businesses for harassment during times of tension. Importantly, the realist logic and the domestic political constraints logic offer different expectations concerning how PRC officials would be expected to treat green businesses.

The reason is straightforward: green Taiwanese businesses do not generate the same positive political externalities that other Taiwanese firms operating in China generate for Beijing. In general, firms that invest in China have a vested interest in stable cross-Strait relations; Beijing hopes, by encouraging more Taiwanese firms to invest in China, to foster the development of a powerful coalition that would naturally tend to oppose goals, such as Taiwanese independence, that could spark instability in cross-Strait relations (Lam 2001; Leng 1998b, 150–52; Bolt 2001, 83). But this reasoning breaks down for pro-DPP firms. From the PRC's perspective, allowing these firms to profit from the Mainland market essentially means they will have more resources with which to back candidates viewed as unacceptable in Beijing. That is, the political externalities associated with investments by green Taiwanese firms might be negative for Mainland China. Thus, PRC signaling behavior would be more consistent with the realist logic to the extent that Beijing is willing to target and sanction green businesses—but only green businesses—when signaling resolve on the sovereignty issue. This would indicate that PRC officials seek to insulate the cross-Strait economic relationship from harm only when there are security-related payoffs for doing so. By contrast, the extent that Beijing is unwilling to carry out threats against even green businesses suggests that something more than a security externalities logic is driving China's unwillingness to sanction Taiwanese firms, and points more squarely in the direction of large economic and domestic political costs of doing so.

Mainland Chinese authorities were quite clear in announcing—after both the 2000 and 2004 Taiwanese presidential elections—that "green" Taiwanese businesses would no longer be welcome in China. That Chinese officials were willing to target these businesses at all suggests at least some willingness to interfere with cross-Strait economic ties when doing so complements Beijing's political objectives vis-à-vis Taiwan. Furthermore, Mainland officials were willing to do more than simply criticize businesspeople who had supported Chen Shui-bian: after Chen's 2000 election, several prominent supporters of his faced increased harassment by Mainland bureaucrats in the form of unexpected audits and surprise inspections.[63] As a result, some businesspeople, such as Acer's Stan Shih, who had supported Chen openly renounced pro-independence leanings.[64] Others averred in private to Mainland authorities that they supported Chen only because he opposed corruption and not because of his party's stance on the independence issue.[65] As I noted in the previous chapter, several high-profile Chen supporters in 2000 who had large-scale investments on the Mainland adopted a lower profile in Taiwanese politics after 2000.[66] One prominent supporter in 2000, Chang Rung-fa of Evergreen, became more distant from Chen over time and tacitly endorsed Chen's challenger, Lien Chan, in 2004.[67]

One tycoon with extensive investments in China who, after 2000, did not adopt a lower profile in Taiwan—or distance himself from Chen—was Hsu Wen-lung of the Chi Mei corporation. According to a high-level Taiwanese party and government official, who was said in a *China Times* (*Zhongguo Shibao*)[68] article to have a close relationship with Hsu, after Hsu supported Chen in 2000 and became one of his advisors, he was labeled a "green" Taiwanese businessman by Mainland officials. Other companies in China were warned not to buy Chi Mei products, costing the company millions of dollars in profits. After Chen's re-election in 2004, Mainland Chinese officials stepped up their harassment of Chi Mei operations in China; the official noted, for example, that in the months after Chen's win, Chi Mei's Zhenjiang plant would "constantly have dozens of tax inspectors barging in."[69] Hsu became the target of especially scathing attacks from the Chinese government and the official PRC press.[70] In 2005, as the Chi Mei corporation was preparing to announce additional investments in China, Hsu released a retirement statement in which he declared that "Taiwan and the Mainland belong to one China."[71] Given the context, and Hsu's previous support of the DPP (and indeed of Taiwanese independence), it appears likely that he was bowing to PRC pressure in order to protect Chi Mei's investments in China.[72]

Clearly, that Beijing would harass green firms at all runs counter to the logic of the domestic constraints explanation for Beijing's signaling behavior. From the standpoint of internationalist economic interests in Mainland China, sanctions against green businesses should be just as costly as sanctions against other Taiwanese firms. Indeed, Beijing's willingness to harass green Taiwanese businesses during periods of tension since 2000 provides some indirect support instead for the realist explanation for Beijing's signaling behavior. PRC officials have continued to protect Taiwanese businesses whose investments generate positive security-related externalities for Beijing, while singling out only those whose benefits (from the PRC perspective) in this regard are less clear cut.

In contrast, other details concerning Beijing's harassment of green Taiwanese businesses are somewhat less consistent with the realist explanation and more in line with the domestic constraints explanation. First, it appears that Beijing has targeted only a few very prominent supporters of the DPP; there is little evidence that Beijing has planned a more extensive crackdown on green Taiwanese businesses in general.[73] Chinese leaders appeared to recognize in 2000 that politicizing cross-Strait commerce in this way could have a chilling effect on Taiwanese investment flows into China, as they quickly ordered the media to give only low-key coverage to "opposing pro-Taiwan-independence Taiwan businessmen investing in China."[74] Likewise, rumors circulating in 2001 about Chi Mei's closure on the Mainland were quickly denied by Beijing authorities, and some have alleged that the rumors in fact started in Taiwan.[75] In 2004, Taiwanese businesses generally denied that they faced increased harassment after Beijing's warnings directed at green Taiwanese investors.[76] This opinion was echoed by the chairman of Taiwan's Mainland Affairs Council, Joseph Wu, who emphasized in June 2004 that Beijing had "done little to harass" pro-DPP Taiwanese businesses in China.[77] Even the Chi Mei corporation stressed that its operations were running normally in Mainland China.[78]

Certainly Beijing gave no indication that its harassment of Chen's prominent supporters was a harbinger of a greater willingness to sanction Taiwanese investors in order to signal resolve. To the contrary, in response to some media reports that broader sanctions might be considered, Taiwan Affairs Office spokesman Zhang Mingqing commented, "We have heard absolutely nothing about that. Nor do we know how such a rumor could have started."[79] Moreover, top Mainland officials in the fall of 2004 redoubled their efforts to reassure Taiwanese businesses operating in China. Politburo Standing Committee member Jia Qinglin visited Taiwanese factories in Fujian Province and encouraged local officials to protect the rights of those investors. The director of the Taiwan Affairs Office, Chen Yun-lin, likewise emphasized the importance of cross-Strait economic ties: "We must step up co-operation to create better conditions for Taiwanese investment in the motherland."[80] Vice Premier Wu Yi expressed similar sentiments in her own trip to Fujian Province in September.[81]

Furthermore, some statements by local officials in areas that attract large amounts of Taiwanese investment suggest that they might passively resist efforts by Beijing to pursue a more widespread crackdown on pro-DPP Taiwanese businesses in China. For example, when asked in 2000 whether any of the (at least 200,000) Taiwanese businessmen currently living around Shanghai supported independence, the deputy secretary-general of the municipality, Huang Qifen, replied, "Not that I am aware of."[82] Likewise, in response to the rumors in 2001 concerning Chi Mei's closure, several prominent local officials[83] pointed out that politics should not interfere with China's economic development and that they would not ask too many questions about the political orientation of Taiwanese investors.[84] Although local officials are highly unlikely to criticize Taiwanese policy openly and directly, these sorts of statements do tacitly suggest that a wider crackdown on green Taiwanese businesses would be unwelcome.

The green Taiwanese business episode underscores the complexity of the cross-Strait case. On the one hand, it suggests that the domestic political constraints explanation, which follows from the theoretical argument developed in Chapter 2, is incomplete. If Beijing's restraint in dealing with Taiwanese businesses during crisis bargaining with Taiwan were solely derived from the economic and domestic political costs associated with interfering in cross-Strait economic ties, then it seems highly unlikely that Mainland officials would single out such a well-defined class of Taiwanese businesspeople—those that support the DPP or Taiwanese independence—for harassment. Rather, it is far more likely that these firms were targeted because, unlike most Taiwanese investments in China, the security externalities of green Taiwanese investments on the Mainland are not clearly positive for Beijing. As such, Mainland China's restraint appears to derive, at least in part, from the straightforward realist logic I have outlined. The PRC reaps positive security externalities from most cross-Strait economic interactions and as such seeks to protect and encourage such ties; but in those cases where Beijing does not reap positive security externalities from Taiwanese investments, PRC policy has been decidedly less encouraging.

On the other hand, even though Beijing has singled out green businesses for harassment, it has generally exhibited substantial restraint even in this endeavor. During 2004, relations across the Taiwan Strait were extremely tense; in Beijing, the mood was one of deep pessimism as many believed that a war might be inevitable. Mainland Chinese leaders tried hard to signal the seriousness with which they took the sovereignty issue and that they were willing to "pay any price" to check Taiwan's independence; this culminated in the passing of the antisecession law in 2005. Yet Mainland leaders continued to exercise extreme caution in their dealings with Taiwanese investors. Taiwan Affairs Office officials emphasized that the "overwhelming majority" (*jue da duo shu*) of Taiwanese investors in China were patriotic and devoted to business, and continued to be warmly welcomed in China.[85] Only one investor, Hsu Wen-lung, was publicly denounced by Chinese officials, and there is little evidence that the Mainland undertook a more general crackdown. Indeed, even Hsu's Chi Mei corporation continued to operate in China, though Hsu appears to have been pressured into issuing a statement in support of the one-China principle. By the fall of 2004, top Chinese officials were again voicing high-profile appeals and reassurances to Taiwanese businesses while making little noise about the political orientation of those businesses.[86]

5. Economic Interdependence, Security Externalities, and Political Coalitions: A Synthesis

Even as cross-Strait political conflict has intensified since the early 1990s, the PRC has generally tried to avoid harming bilateral economic flows when signaling resolve on the issue of Taiwanese sovereignty. To the contrary, Beijing has welcomed Taiwanese investors, and Mainland Chinese officials have tried hard to reassure Taiwanese businesses that their interests would be protected despite cross-Strait political frictions. Both the theoretical argument developed in Chapter 2 and a straightforward realist argument provide some leverage in explaining PRC signaling behavior toward Taiwan. In the first argument, the PRC is governed by an increasingly internationalist coalition. For leaders in Beijing, sanctions against Taiwanese firms would be both politically costly and damaging to the development strategy they have selected. In the second argument, the security externalities of bilateral economic exchange are generally positive for the Mainland. As such, protecting the flourishing cross-Strait economic relationship, in addition to being in the domestic political and economic interests of the CCP, is also conducive to Beijing's political goals vis-à-vis Taiwan.

China's treatment of "green" Taiwanese businesses offers a window into the relative importance of these alternative explanations. If Beijing's efforts to keep its signals of resolve on the sovereignty issue from harming cross-Strait economic exchange are primarily driven by a realist logic, then there is little reason for Beijing to be restrained in dealing with green Taiwanese investors. Indeed, sanctions directed against these investors would offer Beijing a useful way to demonstrate a high level of resolve on the Taiwanese sovereignty issue. In the end, it appears that both causal logics are probably at work: Beijing's willingness to harass pro-DPP businesses supports the realist argument, but its restraint in doing so—and the thinly veiled opposition by some provincial officials to such a course—is more supportive of a constraints-based explanation. If we return to the puzzle presented at the start of this chapter, PRC commitments to Taiwanese firms are credible both because Beijing reaps security benefits from cross-Strait economic ties and because undercutting those ties would be politically and economically costly to an increasingly internationalist governing coalition in the PRC.

More generally, the theoretical argument presented in Chapter 2 has been proven useful in understanding the political economy of cross-Strait relations. The two mechanisms described in Chapter 2 through which conflict could harm economic flows have each been relevant in this case. Taiwanese leaders have at times sought to limit cross-Strait economic exchange because of concerns over that exchange's security-related externalities. And PRC leaders have been keenly aware that their efforts to signal resolve on the issue of Taiwan's status have the potential to harm the broader cross-Strait economic relationship. More importantly, the salience of each mechanism has been contingent, at least in part, on the political strength of internationalist economic interests in the two polities.

Some qualifications are of course in order. It is clear that other factors have also conditioned the impact of cross-Strait political conflict on the economic relations between Taiwan and the PRC. For example, the extent to which leaders in Taiwan worried about the security externalities of Taiwanese investments in the PRC was partly contingent on the extent to which those investments involved relation-specific assets. And, as the present chapter emphasizes, PRC leaders have tried to limit the economic effects of their signals of resolve in part for straightforward realist reasons.

Perhaps more fundamentally, it seems that the security externalities of cross-Strait economic exchange interact with domestic political dynamics in both Taiwan and China in ways that are not fully captured by the theoretical arguments developed in Chapter 2. To see what I mean here, begin by noting that there are significant differences in patterns of interest alignments in Taiwan versus China on issues relating to cross-Strait economic flows. One theme that emerged in Chapter 4 was a tension in Taiwan between internationalist economic interests, especially business, wanting easy access to the Chinese market on the one hand and those trying to advance Taiwan's sovereign status on the other. Lee Teng-hui in particular has been very suspicious of cross-Strait economic ties, and Chen Shui-bian's skepticism has grown over time. Their views in this regard have often left them at odds with Taiwan's business community, which understandably would like to see further liberalization in the island's economic policies toward Mainland China. In Beijing, by contrast, there appears to be no similar conflict between those advocating a hard line on the issue of Taiwanese sovereignty and those desiring and benefiting from economic integration with the island. Leaders could be both resolute on Taiwanese separatism and supportive of cross-Strait economic links. This basic asymmetry in how interests align with each other on the two sides of the Taiwan Strait, in turn, has had important consequences for patterns in the cross-Strait economic relationship, and thus deserves further consideration.

That cross-Strait economic ties have different security-related effects for the two sides is what ultimately drives these asymmetries in interest alignments. Recall that cross-Strait economic exchange entails several types of security externalities, which are generally positive for Mainland China and negative for Taiwan; furthermore, leaders on both sides of the Taiwan Strait have tended to perceive these externalities in this way. To consider how these externalities bear on coalition formation on the two sides of the Strait, it is useful to simplify each side's polity into three ideal types of actors (drawing on the discussion in this chapter and the previous chapter). The first type might be termed *nationalists*, and includes those who care primarily about the issue of Taiwanese sovereignty and only secondarily about economic considerations. Much of the independence movement in Taiwan clearly falls under this category; the PLA on the Mainland probably does as well. The second type can be termed *internationalists*. These actors are primarily concerned with economic issues and benefit from cross-Strait economic integration. Much of the business community in Taiwan falls into this category, as do many local officials (and probably workers) in Mainland China. Finally, the third type represents *protectionists*, actors who care primarily about economic issues but who are threatened by cross-Strait economic integration. In Taiwan, this group includes many unskilled laborers and farmers; in China, it may include capital-intensive industries and related bureaucracies, though this is less clear-cut given the potential for joint ventures involving Taiwanese capital.

The preferences of the internationalists and the protectionists regarding cross-Strait economic integration are obvious. If it were not for bilateral political conflict over the issue of Taiwan's sovereignty, the level of cross-Strait economic integration would ultimately reflect, in large measure, the relative political clout of these two groups in their respective polities. But, in fact, nationalists are also prominent on both sides of the Strait: indeed, cross-Strait political conflict itself is ultimately rooted in the fact that people in both Taiwan and Mainland China care deeply about the issue of Taiwanese sovereignty. Moreover, because cross-Strait economic exchange has security externalities, nationalists have preferences regarding economic integration. In Taiwan, nationalists should naturally be inclined to join with protectionists in an alliance that resembles the "statist-nationalist-confessional" coalitions described by Solingen (1998). But because nationalists on the Mainland likely see some benefit from cross-Strait economic integration, Solingen's ideal-typical distinction between internationalist and statist-nationalist-confessional coalitions breaks down, at least to some extent, in China.[87] Though this depiction of polities in Beijing and Taipei is obviously a grossly simplified version of reality, it helps to explain why tension exists between the business community and those advocating Taiwan's sovereignty in Taipei, while no obvious corresponding conflict occurs between hard-liners on the Taiwan issue and supporters of an open economic policy in Beijing.

That the security externalities of cross-Strait economic relations can influence the logic of coalition formation in the two polities has important implications for my second hypothesis (H2). Recall that H2 was meant to apply at the margins: the impact of conflict on economic exchange should decline as leaders become more accountable to internationalist economic interests. The discussion to this point, however, suggests that the threshold level of strength that internationalist economic interests need to attain in order to block conflict's deleterious effects on commerce varies depending on the nature of trade's security externalities. In Taiwan, the threshold appears to be quite high since both those who care deeply about Taiwanese sovereignty and protectionist economic interests have reason to oppose cross-Strait economic integration. Yet my findings in Chapter 4 suggest that internationalist economic interests in Taiwan have nonetheless, by and large, been able to clear that threshold. Even though Chen Shui-bian increasingly pushed the issue of Taiwan's sovereignty and expressed growing skepticism about the desirability of deepening cross-Strait economic integration, he did little to slow that integration: at most, he dragged his feet on further liberalization.

For Mainland China, the threshold appears to be substantially lower because no natural alliance exists between actors who care deeply about the Taiwanese sovereignty issue and those with protectionist economic interests. Rather, the nature of cross-Strait trade's security externalities makes a coalition between nationalists on the Taiwan issue and internationalist economic interests more feasible; the ruling coalition in Beijing is thus able to incorporate both those who are most deeply committed to the Taiwan issue (such as the PLA) and those who benefit from economic ties with Taiwan (such as coastal provincial officials) without being torn by internal contradictions. Both groups can agree that economic ties with Taiwan are beneficial and that sanctions—or other signals of resolve that harm those economic ties—would be costly. In other words, for China to make a credible commitment to Taiwan's business community that it won't signal resolve in a way that hurts Taiwanese investors, it is not necessary for internationalist economic interests to be stronger than protectionist and nationalist interests combined. Rather, they must be strong enough only so that a *coalition* between nationalists and internationalists can be a ruling one.

Again, I wish to emphasize that my characterization here simplifies reality greatly and is meant only as a conceptual model through which to view the dynamics of cross-Strait interactions. Indeed, even thinking of internationalists and nationalists as two distinct groups is problematic in the Chinese context because most of the leadership in China over the past twenty years appears to have cared very deeply about the Taiwan issue and at the same time has been clearly intent on pursuing a development strategy based on integration into global markets. Moreover, the harmony that currently appears to exist in China between nationalism on the Taiwan issue and internationalist economic objectives could break down if a crisis ever emerges in the Taiwan Strait that escalates to a very high level. Backing down in such an instance could signal weakness to Taiwan and encourage independence advocates there—the worst possible outcome for those in Beijing who care most about the Taiwan issue. But staying resolute could result in a war with devastating consequences for China's efforts at economic development—the worst possible outcome for internationalists. Since leaders in China seem to hold both goals dear, they have every incentive to manage the Taiwan issue in a way that minimizes the likelihood that they would ever be faced with such a choice.[88]

To summarize, the political strength of internationalist economic interests appears to be an important variable in this case, though its operation across the Taiwan Strait has been somewhat more nuanced than suggested in the theoretical discussion in Chapter 2. On the one hand, it is difficult to imagine that commerce would flourish across the Strait if internationalist economic interests were significantly weaker in either Beijing or Taipei. It does not appear that Beijing's restraint in handling Taiwanese businesses derives from security interests alone; otherwise, we would have expected to see more aggressive actions taken against green Taiwanese firms, which do not provide clear positive security externalities for the Mainland. In Taiwan, leaders have security-related reasons to limit economic exchange; if internationalist economic interests were weak in Taiwan, there can be little doubt that the Lee and Chen administrations would have clamped down far harder on cross-Strait exchange than they were able to ultimately.

On the other hand, it is also hard to imagine that cross-Strait commerce would flourish to the extent it does today if the security externalities of cross-Strait economic ties were reversed—if they were positive, that is, for Taiwan, and negative for the Mainland. Certainly, the Taiwanese government would then welcome cross-Strait economic ties. Such a reversal would unite nationalists and internationalists there, which given the strength of internationalists would almost certainly be an overwhelming political coalition. Yet if in China those who cared most about the Taiwan issue had clear reasons to oppose economic integration with the island, it is far from obvious that Taiwanese businesses would feel as comfortable investing there as they do now. Here again the experience of green Taiwanese businesses is instructive, since national security interests do not run parallel with internationalist economic interests regarding policy toward this class of Taiwanese firms. While China's failure to carry out aggressive sanctions against these firms indicates that internationalists hold substantial clout, that Beijing chose to target these firms at all, and harass some of them, indicates that a broader coalition between nationalists and protectionists on the issue of Taiwan could spell trouble for Taiwanese firms. Just as green Taiwanese firms must feel somewhat insecure today about the protections afforded by the Mainland market, other Taiwanese firms would have less reason to feel confident in their Mainland investments if the security externalities of cross-Strait exchange were more broadly negative for China.

In short, the strength of internationalist economic interests in both Beijing and Taipei is an important reason that cross-Strait economic ties have flourished despite cross-Strait political conflict, but it is not clear that those ties would still flourish if the security externalities of cross-Strait economic exchange were not positive for China. The case is thus consistent with and supportive of H2, while also pointing toward a more complicated interaction between domestic political interests and the security implications of economic exchange than suggested in Chapter 2. Having focused on how economic integration has been able to develop despite conflict in PRC-Taiwan relations, the analysis offered in this chapter and the previous chapter does beg an important follow-up question: Now that economic ties have come to flourish across the Taiwan Strait, what are the political implications for relations between Beijing and Taipei? In particular, does increased economic interdependence between the PRC and Taiwan help to reduce the danger of a cross-Strait military confrontation? The next chapter takes up this important question.

6

Completing the Circle
Economic Interdependence and the Prospects for Peace Across the Taiwan Strait and Beyond

1. Introduction

The previous chapters have considered how it is that economic ties have come to flourish in the Taiwan Strait despite intense and persistent political conflict, showing that the theoretical argument developed in chapter 2 offers some useful analytical leverage in this regard. But that the PRC and Taiwan now share a robust economic relationship despite their political differences does beg an important question: are close economic ties reshaping (or will they in the future reshape) the cross-Strait political relationship? This chapter considers one dimension of this question, whether deepening economic integration across the Taiwan Strait effectively reduces the danger of a cross-Strait military confrontation. In the process, the chapter also considers some of the broader implications the Taiwan Strait case might have for theories linking economic ties to peace more generally.

Deepening economic ties across the Taiwan Strait are widely believed by analysts and scholars to be a stabilizing force in cross-Strait political relations (e.g. Chen and Chu 2001; Sutter 2002; Clark 2002; Bolt 2001; Zhao 2005, 238; Mastel 2001; Wang 2000).[1] The logic behind this view is straightforward. By raising the costs of military conflict, economic exchange potentially encourages restraint in Beijing and Taipei (e.g. Bolt 2001; Chen and Chu 2001). Over the longer term, increased contacts generated by growing economic linkages may also lay an "important foundation for political community" across the Taiwan Strait (Clark 2002; also Wang 2000). Official United States policy is to encourage cross-Strait economic integration for these reasons.[2]

While many studies have found that economic integration tends to reduce the likelihood of military conflict more generally, applying these findings to a particular case can be problematic—the case, of course, could be an outlier. In the Taiwan Strait case, we would be more confident that growing economic linkages do indeed reduce the likelihood of a cross-Strait military confrontation if we could observe the causal mechanisms underlying a pacific effect operating there. Existing studies in the international relations literature have derived at least three broad causal mechanisms through which growing bilateral economic ties can generate a reduced probability of military conflict between states. *Constraint* arguments emphasize the increased costs of military conflict in the presence of economic integration; these costs deter states from settling disputes using military force, or from engaging in provocative behavior that might invite military retaliation. *Information* arguments posit that economic interdependence facilitates nonviolent settling of disputes by enabling states to signal their true level of resolve more efficiently. Finally, *transformation* arguments suggest that economic integration can help to harmonize the foreign policy goals pursued by states. These three causal mechanisms are not mutually exclusive; rather, it may be that economic interdependence promotes peace through multiple channels.

Each of these casual mechanisms specifies a process, with observable implications, through which growing economic ties yield a reduced likelihood of military violence. In order to assess whether growing economic ties across the Taiwan Strait make military conflict less likely, I evaluate the extent to which these causal processes are operating in this case. My conclusions in this regard suggest that caution is warranted when considering the impact of economic integration on the prospects for cross-Strait peace. While I do not rule out the possibility that economic integration across the Strait makes a military confrontation less likely, I do show that the evidence in support of such a proposition remains ambiguous.

As noted, I also aim in this chapter to consider what (if any) implications the cross-Strait experience might have for arguments linking economic interdependence to peace. In particular, I endeavor to use the cross-Strait case to generate additional hypotheses concerning when and how economic interdependence might yield a reduced likelihood of military violence. Though a growing number of exceptions exist, most efforts to test the relationship between economic interdependence and military conflict remain quantitative in nature. These studies have yielded important findings and have made it possible to examine the effects of commercial integration on conflict across different time periods, to compare results using different operationalizations of the key independent and dependent variables, and to control for a broad range of other factors likely to contribute to international conflict. But as Ripsman and Blanchard (2003) note, similarly rigorous qualitative studies have the potential to further refine our understanding of the relationship between commerce and conflict. In particular, carefully selected cases provide an opportunity to trace the processes through which economic ties between countries actually affect (or fail to influence) the decision to use military force. The use of case studies, therefore, may be especially helpful in establishing a causal relationship between commercial integration and the propensity for conflict, and for assessing the validity of different theories that seek to identify the microfoundations underlying any such relationship.

The following section sets forth in more detail the logic of the three different causal mechanisms linking economic interdependence to peace, and comments briefly on the appropriateness of cross-Strait relations as a case study for exploring these different causal processes. Sections 3–5 then assess the extent to which these causal processes are operating across the Taiwan Strait and consider the broader implications of the cross-Strait experience for each of these arguments. Section 6 concludes.

2. Economic Interdependence, Military Conflict, and Causal Mechanisms

The liberal argument that trade promotes peace has a long history, and a series of recent works by Oneal and Russett have confirmed statistically that trade, along with democracy and international organizations (the "Kantian tripod"), is correlated with a reduced likelihood of military violence between countries (Oneal and Russett 1997; 1999a; 2001; Russett and Oneal 2001). But the idea that economic ties facilitate peace remains controversial. Realist scholars sometimes note, for example, that bilateral economic ties typically represent only a small fraction of any two countries' economies; this is especially the case with great powers, which typically have large internal markets and a wide array of trading partners. Economic ties may thus be less likely to have much of an impact on state behavior, particularly when great powers compete over important issues (Mearsheimer 2001, 371).[3] Others argue that economic interdependence can actually provoke conflict because economic ties cause new frictions to develop between countries (Waltz 1979), and still others suggest that economic patterns are more likely a reflection of existing political relations than an important determinant of those relations (e.g. Gowa 1994). Meanwhile, some recent quantitative studies (Barbieri 1996; 2002; Keshk et al. 2004; Kim and Rousseau 2005) and qualitative studies (e.g. Ripsman and Blanchard 1996/97) call into question on empirical grounds the commercial liberal argument.[4]

As Mansfield and Pollins (2003) write, a growing number of studies are advancing the debate by focusing more squarely on the conditions under which economic ties have an effect. That is, they ask not if economic interdependence leads to peace but rather when it does, and thus focus on the variables that might intervene in the relationship between economic ties and conflict.[5] This focus on boundary conditions serves to highlight the probability that economic integration does not always lead to pacific political relations. Given that the effect is not universal, if we are to have any ability to predict whether economic ties will have a pacific effect in a particular case—like the relationship across the Taiwan Strait—it becomes imperative to have a clear understanding of the microfoundations underlying any relationship that might exist between commerce and conflict. In other words, simply knowing that strong economic ties are present in a particular case should not convince us that the likelihood of a military confrontation is therefore reduced in that case. Rather, it would be better to be able to observe whether or not the causal processes that link economic interdependence to a reduction in military violence are operating there. Existing studies have identified at least three non–mutually exclusive causal mechanisms through which economic interdependence can yield a reduced probability of military conflict.

Constraint Arguments

Perhaps the most widely accepted theoretical link between commercial integration and a reduced danger of military violence centers on the constraining effects of economic ties. The argument is straightforward: military conflict has the potential to disrupt commerce between countries. Such disruptions could generate economic shocks by causing firms to lose assets specific to a particular relationship (such as factories abroad that might be seized or destroyed),[6] while forcing firms in both countries to find the next best market with which to interact. Because commercial disruptions are costly, leaders should be less likely to risk military violence with countries with which their home state is integrated economically.[7] Some have argued that these sorts of constraining effects are most likely to happen in democracies, which provide actors who benefit from trade clear paths through which to influence the political process (Papayoanou 1996; Gelpi and Grieco 2003; Russett and Oneal 2001).

Information Arguments

A second causal argument is relatively new, and focuses on information. The argument is an effort to deduce a causal link between commerce and military conflict in a way that is consistent with bargaining models of war (e.g. Fearon 1995; Gartzke 1999; Powell 2002). In these models, disputes sometimes escalate to military confrontations because it is difficult for the states involved to know how committed the other side is to the issues at hand. As such, each side has an incentive to overstate its commitment (or resolve) in the hope that the other side will concede more than it otherwise might; in other words, both sides have an incentive to bluff. Wars can occur when one state believes the other to be bluffing when in fact the other state is highly resolved. The previous chapter suggested that such a scenario could unfold in the Taiwan Strait if Taiwanese leaders push too hard on the issue of Taiwan's sovereign status, underestimating the PRC's true (but to some degree unobservable) resolve on the issue.

Previous chapters have also shown that to overcome these sorts of problems, states that are truly resolute try to signal their resolve by demonstrating a willingness to pay costs in order to achieve a favorable outcome. By sending costly signals, states convey information: since states that lack resolve are by definition unwilling to pay costs to achieve a favorable bargaining outcome, a willingness to send costly signals increases the likelihood that a country will be perceived as resolute rather than as bluffing. We saw that Chinese leaders have been willing to use a variety of instruments—including military build-ups and exercises, issuing public threats that could make backing down in a crisis situation difficult, and passing an antisecession law—to signal their commitment to the Taiwan issue.

Information arguments linking economic interdependence to peace suggest that high levels of economic integration make it easier for countries to send costly signals that allow them to communicate resolve credibly. Absent economic integration, nonmilitary signals are relatively uninformative because verbal threats or economic sanctions are cheap, meaning that a state that is bluffing could issue such signals at relatively little cost. As economic integration deepens on a bilateral level, however, it becomes possible for a country to impose economic sanctions that are costly. Integration into global markets more generally means that a country's tough talk is no longer cheap, because it scares international investors away. Economic integration, then, gives states more ways to demonstrate their true level of resolve in a credible fashion without having to resort to military action, thus reducing the likelihood that a war would arise because one state has miscalculated the resolve of another (Gartzke and Li 2003a; Gartzke 2003; Gartzke et al. 2001; Morrow 1999; 2003; Stein 2003).[8]

Transformation Arguments

A third causal argument focuses on the transformative impact of commercial integration. Here, economic integration harmonizes the goals that states pursue. One version is sociological: when two states have a high level of economic integration, actors within their respective societies will come into greater contact with each other and will interact on a much larger scale. In this environment, they may come to view their interests as shared, and to see prior goals as less important than before. In the aftermath of the Second World War, for example, some American policymakers believed that integrating Germany's economy with the rest of Western Europe would help ensure a transformed German foreign policy: George Kennan wrote that such integration would lead German citizens "to see things in larger terms, to have interests elsewhere in Europe and elsewhere in the world, and to learn to think of themselves as world citizens and not just Germans."[9] A second type of transformation argument centers on the vested interests that economic interdependence creates. As economies become intertwined, those actors associated with the most integrated sectors will begin to view bilateral cooperation as more essential than before economic linkages were established (e.g. Haas 1958). Economic interdependence thus generates new coalitions with different international goals than those held by preexisting coalitions. If economic integration is extensive, these pro-international coalitions will grow large, and will have the ability to influence state goals and perhaps effect a change in the make-up of the governing coalition itself.[10] In this way, leaders who hold the goals at the root of international conflict (territorial conquest, for example) can be replaced by other rulers who do not share such goals. Military conflict becomes less likely, not necessarily because it is more costly but rather because new governing coalitions in both countries no longer place emphasis on the clashing goals that had threatened to lead to war to begin with.[11]

Each of these three causal pathways linking economic interdependence to peace suggests a mechanism through which growing economic interaction across the Taiwan Strait could reduce the likelihood of a cross-Strait military confrontation. But is there any evidence that one or more of these causal processes are actually at work in Mainland China–Taiwan relations? If so, then we might feel more confident that growing economic integration is indeed a stabilizing force in the cross-Strait relationship. However, if such evidence is lacking, then a more cautious attitude would be warranted. The remainder of this chapter addresses this question systematically while also considering what implications trends in cross-Strait relations might have for the three different causal mechanisms more generally.

For two basic reasons, cross-Strait relations represent a useful case study through which to explore the general relationship between economic interdependence and military conflict. First, because Mainland China–Taiwan relations are characterized by serious political conflict and repeated threats of war (as discussed in Chapter 3), the relationship resembles in some respects a least likely test case (George and Bennett 2005). If commercial integration can be shown to influence the likelihood of war even here, where tensions are very high, then commerce is likely to have important effects elsewhere too.[12] Second, the coexistence of a high level of tension and extensive commercial integration in Mainland China–Taiwan relations helps to minimize endogeneity problems. Most of this book has focused on how it is possible for economic integration to flourish even in the presence of political conflict; more generally, that political conflict can undermine commerce suggests that the causal link between economic interdependence and peace might be spurious. That is, the relationship between trade and peace could arise because countries with nonconflictual political relations are both more likely to trade with each other and less likely to fight wars with each other. Because trade and investment flows flourish across the Taiwan Strait even in the presence of serious tension and an underlying threat of war, it is possible to set aside this issue of reverse causality here.

Of course, some of the same problems that arose in Chapters 3–5 are present here as well. For example, efforts to generalize based on this one case may be biased by factors specific to the cross-Strait relationship, such as the idiosyncratic nature of the cross-Strait sovereignty dispute. The unique qualities of the cross-Strait political relationship raise the possibility that economic integration will have an impact on the political relationship in idiosyncratic ways: I am thus cautious about making any sweeping generalizations based on this one case. Rather than present the case as a rigorous scientific test for the different causal arguments outlined above, I instead treat it as an opportunity to derive additional hypotheses concerning those different causal mechanisms, while exploring whether those processes are currently operating in China-Taiwan relations.

3. The Constraint Argument and Cross-Strait Relations

The constraint argument suggests that as economic integration across the Taiwan Strait deepens, leaders in both Beijing and Taipei should become more hesitant in pursuing policies that might trigger a strong response from the other side, because they become more sensitive to the economic consequences of conflict. The logic of the constraint argument suggests that growing economic ties should have an especially large effect on Taiwanese policy: because China's economy is much larger than Taiwan's, cross-Strait trade represents a much larger share of Taiwan's economy than it does the Mainland's. Moreover, while Taiwan's approved direct investments in China now represent more than two-thirds of the island's total outward direct investment flows, those same investments represent less than 15 percent of the foreign direct investment flowing into China.[13] Finally, Taiwan's democratic institutions should make leaders there especially sensitive to the costs of disrupting cross-Strait economic flows because of the negative electoral consequences such shocks would potentially entail (Papayoanou 1996; Gelpi and Grieco 2003; Russett and Oneal 2001). In short, if cross-Strait economic integration does indeed act as a constraint in cross-Strait political relations, the constraining effects should be especially evident in Taiwanese policy.

As we saw in Chapter 3, however, rapidly expanding cross-Strait economic ties did not correspond with a more cautious Taiwanese foreign policy under the Lee Teng-hui and Chen Shui-bian administrations. To the contrary, Taipei's policies toward the Mainland became more provocative (from the PRC perspective) despite burgeoning economic links. Lee Teng-hui pursued a very assertive foreign policy, culminating in 1999 in his description of the cross-Strait relationship as one of "special state-to-state relations." And though Chen Shui-bian initially appeared set to pursue a relatively moderate cross-Strait policy, his policies toward China grew more provocative over time, even as bilateral economic ties expanded extremely rapidly after 2001. In 2002, for example, Chen suggested a formula for cross-Strait relations—one country on each side of the Strait (*yi bian, yi guo*)—which closely paralleled Lee's state-to-state argument, which had enraged Beijing in 1999. Chen's decision to hold a referendum on issues relating to Taiwan's national security at the same time as the 2004 Taiwanese presidential election, his announced intention to revise the ROC constitution, and his scrapping of Taiwan's National Unification Council likewise were viewed by Beijing as highly provocative. It is quite clear, in short, that Taipei's policies toward Mainland China became more rather than less provocative even as economic ties across the Taiwan Strait grew rapidly after the early 1990s.

At first blush, Taiwan's policies appear to confirm the realist argument about the unimportance of economic relations as a constraint on state behavior: the possibility that commerce might be disrupted is not likely to deter Taiwan's leaders from pursuing other, more significant goals. It is important to proceed cautiously, however, in drawing inference from the broad trends described in the previous paragraph. On the one hand, it is possible that Taiwan's policies are more consistent with the constraint argument than they appear at first glance. It is conceivable, for example, that a newly democratic Taiwan would have been even more forceful in asserting its sovereignty had it not been for the constraining influence of economic integration with China. Time lags may also be at play: the new Ma Ying-jeou administration appears set to pursue more conciliatory cross-Strait policies than those pursued by his predecessors. On the other hand, it may be that economic integration has the effect of making Taiwan's policies *more* provocative, from Beijing's standpoint, than would otherwise be the case: since economic integration raises the costs of military conflict for both Taiwan and Mainland China, Taiwanese leaders know that Beijing will be less willing to resort to force, and as such the island can get away with more. These very different possibilities, of course, implicitly reference a counterfactual about which we can only speculate:

how political relations would have evolved in the absence of extensive economic linkages. It would thus be useful to see some sort of evidence that Taiwan's leaders have tempered their policies toward Beijing out of worry that a cross-Strait confrontation would be detrimental to the cross-Strait economic relationship—or, alternatively, that they have completely disregarded such concerns. I focus here on one episode from 1999: Lee Teng-hui's characterization of cross-Strait relations as "special state-to-state."

Recall from the previous chapter that Chinese officials viewed Lee's unexpected policy shift, announced in an interview with a German radio station in July 1999,[14] as highly provocative. Mainland Chinese officials emphasized repeatedly that Lee was "playing with fire,"[15] and took a number of steps to signal resolve on the issue of Taiwanese sovereignty. China put its ground forces on heightened combat readiness beginning July 13; at the same time Mainland fighters began conducting more frequent air exercises near the Taiwan Strait. The Chinese navy also conducted exercises during August and September.[16] China clearly hoped to signal to Lee that his new formulation for cross-Strait relations was risking a military confrontation with the Mainland.

I was unable to find any evidence, however, that the burgeoning cross-Strait economic relationship acted as a significant constraint on Lee's willingness to risk confrontation with China. Rather than back down in the face of Beijing's response, Lee stuck with his new formulation. In Lee's public statements there is no indication that he was deterred by the potential economic losses that Taiwan would suffer if the crisis were to escalate to armed conflict. In fact, Lee was openly dismissive of the possibility that his actions would lead to a military conflict.[17] Furthermore, Su Chi, then chairman of Taiwan's Mainland Affairs Council, has written a detailed account of the episode, and he too does not mention the cross-Strait economic relationship as a constraining factor.[18] There is little to suggest, in short, that economic integration acted as a constraint on Taiwanese policy during this episode.

Interestingly, to the extent that Taiwanese officials referenced the economic consequences of a military confrontation with China at all during this crisis, it was to emphasize the economic costs that *China* would pay. For example, Lee highlighted China's economic problems as he downplayed the chances Beijing would "willy-nilly take action against Taiwan."[19] Taiwan's defense minister Tang Fei similarly argued that for the Mainland, "using force would be a last resort, because [China is] concerned about international pressure and economic growth." Tang also suggested that a Chinese embargo was highly unlikely because the Mainland, too, benefits from cross-Strait economic ties.[20] These sorts of comments suggest that increasing cross-Strait economic integration—because it increases the costs of war for China—may actually *encourage* Taiwanese leaders to adopt more revisionist policies than they otherwise might.[21]

To see why, consider a highly simplified portrayal of cross-Strait bargaining over Taiwan's identity. Suppose that Taiwan chooses a level of sovereign status ranging from reunification to formal independence; Beijing, in turn, can either accept that decision or fight a war to try to attain something better. In deciding whether or not to accept Taiwan's offer, Mainland Chinese leaders would compare that offer to the expected outcome of war (minus the costs of fighting a war). Taiwan's leaders, in turn, would be expected to choose a level of sovereign status that Beijing marginally prefers over fighting a war. If cross-Strait economic integration increases the costs of fighting for Mainland China, then Beijing should be willing to tolerate a greater level of Taiwanese sovereignty than before.[22] Appendix A presents a simple model that helps to demonstrate the logic of this result.

Lee's statements clearly suggest that he believed economic factors *did* act as a constraint on the willingness of Chinese leaders to go to war. However, even if Lee was correct in this assessment, the effect on the underlying probability of war remains indeterminate: if Taiwanese leaders are willing to exploit an increased reluctance by China to fight a war by taking a stronger position on Taiwan's sovereign status, then the decrease in China's resolve may be negated by increased dissatisfaction with Taiwan's policies.[23] Lee's public statements suggest that he was willing to exploit perceived increases in China's costs of war by pushing further on the sovereignty issue than he might otherwise have done. This logic, incidentally, is not lost on Beijing: Mainland leaders appear to be quite aware that factors increasing the potential costs of war for China may also make it easier for Taiwan to drift toward independence. As such, they have tried to downplay the costs of war relative to the importance that they place on the Taiwan issue. Indeed, Mainland officials have declared, as noted in the previous chapter, that they are willing to pay "any costs" to check Taiwanese independence (Yan 2004).

I do not wish to overstate my case here. I am not suggesting that growing cross-Strait economic integration is a primary cause of Taiwan's stance on the sovereignty issue. Certainly other factors, like domestic political dynamics in Taiwan, are far more important. Rather, I am simply suggesting that, along the margins, growing economic integration may make it possible for Taiwan to take a stronger stance than it otherwise might. Furthermore, I have presented evidence from only a single episode. It is not at all clear, for example, that Chen Shui-bian shared Lee's views in this regard (I have uncovered no evidence that he did), and it appears unlikely that current president Ma Ying-jeou shares those views. (Later I consider events under Chen more fully in the context of transformation arguments.)

More fundamentally, constraining effects can also arise indirectly in democracies through voters who might punish leaders who have endangered the economy by adopting risky foreign policies. Such an indirect constraint mechanism does not necessarily preclude leaders from occasionally ignoring international economic flows when making foreign policy decisions; rather, it suggests that such leaders are likely to be punished by voters in polls and elections. Over time, such a process should lead, on balance, to a less provocative foreign policy, though not necessarily in a linear fashion in which growing economic ties lead directly to proportionately fewer provocations. There is certainly some evidence that such a process could be underway in Taiwan: most Taiwanese, for example, are opposed to risk taking in relations with the Mainland.[24] Furthermore, voters expressed considerable dissatisfaction with Chen Shui-bian's cross-Strait policies, and dealt the DPP a crushing defeat in the 2008 legislative and presidential elections.[25] Ultimately, to dismiss with any confidence the argument that economic interdependence-induced constraints reduce the probability of a cross-Strait war, it would be necessary to show that Lee's statements in 1999 and after are not an aberration. But Lee's behavior in 1999 does at least provide reason for skepticism.

Broader Implications

From the perspective of recent findings that the constraining effect of economic interdependence is magnified in democracies, Taiwan's transition to democracy during the 1980s and 1990s makes its behavior especially puzzling. The logic behind these findings is straightforward: because democratic governments have a more encompassing interest in a society's overall economic condition, they are less willing to risk a war that could harm the economy (Gelpi and Grieco 2003). Yet Taiwan's experience as a new democracy suggests that this argument may need to be qualified.

On the one hand, democracy has probably increased governmental accountability on economic issues: when the island slipped into a severe recession early in Chen Shui-bian's first term, for example, Chen's support in public opinion polls dropped sharply. And we saw in Chapter 4 that democracy has certainly provided more avenues, like a growing need for campaign finance, through which business groups can influence politics in Taiwan. On the other hand, democracy has allowed independence supporters—repressed under the previous KMT dictatorship—to mobilize and influence the political process; indeed, democratization made it possible for Taiwan to be led by a president representing a party whose platform endorses independence. Democratization, in short, has helped to unleash Taiwanese nationalist sentiments; playing to these sentiments, and at times cultivating them, puts Taiwanese leaders on a collision course with Beijing's insistence that Taiwan is a part of one China.

In this case, then, it is by no means clear that the net effect of democracy in Taiwan has been to magnify the constraining effect of cross-Strait economic integration on Taiwanese policymakers. Perhaps democracy has made leaders more sensitive to economic conditions, but in democratic Taiwan leaders also need to be much more sensitive to Taiwanese nationalist sentiments than was necessary under the previous dictatorship, when such sentiments were repressed. The increased incentives for Taiwan's leaders to take a firm—and from China's standpoint, confrontational—stance on the issue of Taiwan's sovereign status appear, in this case, to overwhelm any positive effect of democracy on economic integration's constraining influence.

More generally, the cross-Strait case suggests that the impact of democracy on economic integration's effects may itself be contingent on the nature of the bilateral political dispute. When the dispute centers on issues that a country's citizens care deeply about, such as issues over territorial sovereignty, democracy can actually undercut any constraining effect of economic ties by creating pressures for leaders to take a relatively uncompromising position. Democracy's weak interactive effect in the present case might also be in part a consequence of the newness of Taiwan's democratic institutions. As Mansfield and Snyder (1995, 29) write, publics in transitional democracies are often susceptible to mass mobilization based on nationalistic appeals: "New participants in the political system may be uncertain where their political interests lie . . . and are thus fertile ground for ideological appeals." Both Lee Teng-hui and Chen Shui-bian tried to mobilize support through nationalist appeals to Taiwan's sovereign status. Perhaps, as democracy becomes more institutionalized on the island, these sorts of appeals will prove less effective. Chen Shui-bian's extremely low standing in public opinion polls late in his term, and the strong showing of the KMT in 2008, may in fact suggest the beginnings of such a trend (e.g. Ross 2006).

4. The Information Argument and Cross-Strait Relations

The information effects of economic interdependence can potentially arise through two distinct processes. First, integration into global capital markets can make threats more costly, and hence more credible, by scaring off international investors. Second, economic interdependence, by making it possible to impose costly economic sanctions, gives policymakers a greater range of signals through which to demonstrate resolve without resorting to war. My focus here is on this second process, since it arises from bilateral economic flows rather than integration into global markets more generally. In the cross-Strait context, the argument suggests economic integration reduces the likelihood of war because Mainland China now has the ability to impose very costly economic sanctions against Taiwan, giving it the capacity to display a high level of resolve; if it were not for extensive cross-Strait economic ties, Mainland China would have to rely on military force to signal a similar level of resolve. The analysis of China's signaling behavior presented in Chapter 5 suggests, however, that there is reason to be skeptical about the likelihood of such a causal sequence occurring in cross-Strait relations.

Recall that Beijing has gone to considerable lengths to avoid signaling resolve toward Taiwan in a way that could harm the cross-Strait economic relationship. Even at times when relations with Taiwan have become very tense, Mainland China has generally sought to reassure Taiwanese businesses operating in China that their interests would be protected regardless of the nature of cross-Strait political relations. The harassment since 2000 of "green" Taiwanese businesses—those that support Chen Shui-bian and the DPP—represents an exception, but even here Beijing has been very cautious. Only a few very high-profile businesses appear to have been targeted, and since the fall of 2004 top Mainland officials have redoubled their efforts to reassure Taiwanese investors. In Chapter 5 I argued that Beijing's reluctance to signal resolve toward Taiwan in a way that harms cross-Strait economic ties is driven by two factors: the high political and economic costs associated with economic sanctions, and the negative security implications such signals could entail for Beijing—cross-Strait economic ties, recall, have security externalities that tend to be positive for Mainland China.

Beijing's repeated assurances to Taiwanese businesses appear, at least initially, to be inconsistent with the information argument. Beijing has continued to rely on signaling instruments like military threats and exercises rather than take advantage of the increased opportunity afforded by economic integration to send credible signals by imposing, or threatening, economic sanctions. Still, as discussed in the previous chapter, it is possible that China views economic sanctions as a last resort, something to be used only when war is imminent. Because economic sanctions would be extremely costly for Beijing, their enactment would be a strong and credible signal of resolve, one that could lead Taiwan to back down in a crisis over the island's sovereign status. Certainly some analysts in China view economic sanctions as a potentially useful coercive device that could be deployed instead of, or prior to, military force. For example, a 2004 *China Daily* report noted that some PRC specialists on cross-Strait issues supported economic sanctions against Taiwan as a means to halt the island's drift toward independence.[26] A 2004 report by an analyst with the Chinese Academy of Social Sciences Institute of Taiwan Studies concluded that full-scale economic sanctions could paralyze Taiwan's economy within two months, and suggested that Beijing could use economic sanctions instead of war as a way of blocking Taiwanese independence.[27] More recently, Hu

Angang, director of the Center for China Studies at Tsinghua University, likewise emphasized Taiwan's vulnerability to a trade embargo while warning that "we have simulated a trade war ... [and] it will be fatal for Taiwan."[28] To the extent Beijing views economic sanctions as a last-resort measure to signal resolve before undertaking a military attack, deepening economic ties make war less likely by making this last-resort signal more credible.

But my analysis in Chapter 5 suggests that an alternative interpretation is also plausible. Because economic integration with Taiwan has security externalities that are favorable for Mainland China, it is not clear that Beijing would utilize economic sanctions as a signal of resolve, even as a last resort before going to war. The logic is straightforward: though economic sanctions directed against Taiwanese businesses would send a strong and credible signal of Beijing's resolve in stopping Taiwanese steps toward independence, sanctions would also most likely be deeply counterproductive to Beijing's longer-term goal of reunification. More specifically, the actors in Taiwan who would be hurt most by economic sanctions—those businesses with a large stake in the Chinese market—also happen to be, on balance, quite pragmatic on the issue of Taiwan's sovereignty.[29] Ultimately, if Beijing is going to achieve its goal of reunification, unless it hopes to conquer the island and rule it through coercion alone (which would be extraordinarily costly), it needs long-term allies there (or, if not allies, at least actors who might acquiesce to Mainland authority). Taiwanese businesses with Mainland investments are the most obvious candidates, because they already have a stake in China.[30] In this regard, Beijing might well do its best to protect Taiwanese investors even if a war were to erupt in the Taiwan Strait.[31]

In short, burgeoning economic ties across the Taiwan Strait certainly give Beijing the option of sending a very strong signal to Taipei, through economic sanctions, without having to resort to military force. Yet it is far from clear that Beijing would ever use this option, even as a last resort. China's past signaling behavior demonstrates an obvious reluctance to signal resolve in a way that hurts Taiwanese businesses operating in China. Moreover, though economic sanctions would demonstrate resolve and as such might help to deter Taiwanese independence, sanctions would also be counterproductive to China's long-term goal of reunification because they would almost certainly alienate key constituencies on the island. There is thus good reason to be skeptical that the causal processes specified in the information argument are likely to operate in a way that reduces the chances of a military conflict in the Taiwan Strait.

I have focused on the bilateral version of the information argument here because I am interested in how bilateral economic integration across the Taiwan Strait influences the likelihood of a cross-Strait military confrontation. Yet a few words are in order concerning the second version of the argument, which focuses on integration into global markets more generally (rather than on bilateral economic relations). The argument is developed by Gartzke and Li (2003a), who theorize that capital market integration makes threats to use military force more costly, and hence more credible, because such threats lead to capital flight.[32] Currently, China maintains substantial capital controls, in large measure to prevent speculative flows of capital that could destabilize the country's financial system. Gartzke and Li's argument suggests that if Beijing were to lift these controls in the future, it would reduce the likelihood of a cross-Strait military confrontation. A China that is more highly integrated into world capital markets would need to be more judicious in directing military threats at Taiwan, since such threats would have greater potential to spark capital flight. At the same time, Chinese threats would become more credible, increasing the likelihood that Taiwan would back down in the event of a crisis and that war would be averted. Chinese leaders, of course, would most likely view this externality of capital account liberalization in a negative light. For a China integrated into global capital markets, PRC threats directed against Taiwan would become more credible because they would impose extra costs on *China* without imposing any obvious additional costs on Taiwan. In this regard, threats directed against Taiwan would actually make a China that is integrated into global capital markets weaker; war would become less likely, but Beijing's capacity both to bluff and to coerce would decline as well.

Broader Implications

More generally, the relationship across the Taiwan Strait suggests that a deeper conundrum may be implicit in the bilateral version of the information argument. On the one hand, as economic ties become more extensive, the potential information that can be imparted through economic sanctions grows as well. Thus, deeper economic ties make it possible to signal, with a greater level of credibility, the resolve to fight a war without actually fighting. On the other hand, imposing economic sanctions most harms the very actors—those engaged directly in commerce—who have a vested interest in stability and who would be expected to oppose national goals that increase tensions with other states. As such, imposing sanctions can also be counterproductive, as the country enacting them risks punishing its most sympathetic audience in the target state, thereby potentially undercutting its influence within that country.

The argument might thus be less applicable in dyads where one state follows what Abdelal and Kirshner call a "Hirschmanesque strategy."[33] When country A hopes that increasing economic integration with state B will give it increased influence over B's foreign policies—by, for example, creating vested interests in

B that favor stability with A—it will view economic sanctions as fundamentally at odds with such a strategy. Abdelal and Kirshner (1999/2000, 120) suggest this dynamic is most likely to be present when economic ties between A and B are both extensive (or at least potentially extensive) and highly asymmetric (such that B's economy is disproportionately dependent). Thus, while deepening economic ties increase the information that could potentially be imparted through economic sanctions, states might become less likely to take advantage of this signaling mechanism when ties are asymmetric. These sorts of dyads are therefore potentially quite dangerous, because the state pursuing the Hirschmanesque strategy may seek to preserve economic linkages even in the event of war; if so, economic ties would have no informative value at all.

5. Transformation Arguments and Mainland China–Taiwan Relations

Transformation arguments suggest that increasing economic integration between Mainland China and Taiwan should facilitate harmonization in the foreign policy objectives of leaders in Beijing and Taipei. Such change might arise through broad public opinion shifts brought on by increasing societal contacts. Alternatively, cross-Strait commerce might empower new coalitions less interested in sovereignty issues and more interested in stability and trade. In this section, I focus on the Taiwanese side for the same basic reasons I did when considering constraint arguments: since cross-Strait commerce represents a bigger portion of Taiwan's economy than the Mainland's, any transformative effects that arise are more likely to materialize in Taiwan first. As with the constraint and information logics described earlier, evidence of transformative effects in cross-Strait relations remains ambiguous.

Growing commercial relations across the Taiwan Strait have certainly led to greatly increased societal contacts between Mainland China and Taiwan; some argue that these contacts lay the basis for future political reconciliation (and perhaps reunification; see Wang 2000). As Chao (2003, 285–86) notes, economic exchanges to some extent "spilled over" into politics during the 1990s: Chao links the formation of Taiwan's SEF and Beijing's ARATS, and their subsequent quasi-official negotiations in the early 1990s, to a need to manage growing cross-Strait exchanges. These sorts of political contacts, over time, can potentially have a transformative effect by facilitating a sense of shared community. Though these talks ended abruptly after Lee Teng-hui issued his "special state-to-state" statement, and remained suspended under Chen Shui-bian's presidency, they have recently restarted under Ma Ying-jeou.

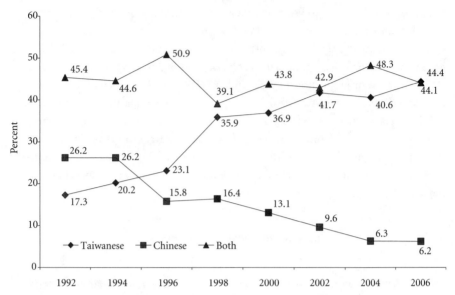

FIG. 4. Changing Taiwanese identity. Source: Data from Election Study Center, N.C.C.U., important political attitude trend distribution. http://esc.nccu.edu.tw/eng/data/data03-2.htm.

Nonetheless, as Chao (2003) emphasizes, growing economic exchanges and personnel flows across the Taiwan Strait clearly have not correlated with increased public support in Taiwan for reunification with the Mainland. For example, most Taiwanese (approximately 61 percent in one poll) favored maintaining the status quo in cross-Strait relations when polled in 1997, and a similar percentage held that position in 2008.[34] At the same time, support for the Mainland's "one country, two systems" formula has remained consistently low. Meanwhile, the percentage of Taiwan's citizens who consider themselves to be Taiwanese, and not Chinese, has grown in recent years. One poll discovered that in 1992, 26 percent of respondents considered themselves "Chinese," 17 percent considered themselves "Taiwanese," and 45 percent "both Chinese and Taiwanese." By 2006, those answering "Chinese" had dropped to 6 percent, while the percentage of those answering "Taiwanese" had risen to a similar level to those answering "both" (44 percent).[35] Figure 4 summarizes these trends.

It is necessary to be cautious, however, in drawing any inference from these broad trends: some argue that burgeoning economic ties across the Taiwan Strait have in fact slowed the development of a separate Taiwanese identity. Yun-han Chu (2004) concludes, for example, that there is little evidence that economic integration is transforming Taiwanese public opinion in a decisive way toward a pro-unification consensus. He argues instead that growing economic integration has acted as a brake on the growth of a separate Taiwanese identity. While support for independence grew sharply in the mid-1990s, it has leveled off considerably since then.[36] At the same time, support for reunification under the right circumstances remained quite stable during the course of the 1990s. According to postelection surveys conducted by the Workshop on Political System Change at National Taiwan University, those supporting unification "if Mainland China and Taiwan become politically, economically, and socially compatible" stood at 57 percent in 1993 and 56 percent in 2000 (Benson and Niou 2005).[37] Obviously, it is extremely difficult to link these survey results to levels of economic integration across the Taiwan Strait. The best that can be said is that economic integration may have prevented Taiwanese public opinion from becoming even more at odds with Beijing's objectives than otherwise might have been the case.

Meanwhile, it is also clear that growing cross-Strait economic ties have generated a growing constituency in Taiwan with a direct stake in the cross-Strait economic relationship, and that this constituency has tended to advocate a relatively pragmatic approach to cross-Strait political issues. The Taiwanese government estimates that roughly one million Taiwanese live in Mainland China; of these, about half are Taiwanese businesspeople, and their families make up much of the rest.[38] A 2004 Ministry of Economic Affairs poll found that nearly 77 percent of Taiwanese manufacturers have investments in Mainland China.[39] A media poll likewise found that a majority of Taiwanese listed and over-the-counter companies surveyed had invested in Mainland China in 2002.[40] The poll found that 80 percent of those surveyed believed economic and political relations across the Taiwan Strait are closely related, and that improved political relations are essential for Taiwan's economy. Meanwhile, 73 percent supported resumption of cross-Strait talks under the rubric of the 1992 consensus.[41]

Anecdotal evidence tells a similar story. Business leaders often emphasize the importance of maintaining good relations with the Mainland. After Chen's 2004 re-election, a spokesman for the General Chamber of Commerce suggested that "empowered by the people's mandate, President Chen should strive for better cross-Strait relations."[42] In the run-up to that election, numerous Taiwanese businesspeople in China expressed dissatisfaction with Chen's confrontational cross-Strait policies: some stressed that Chen's policies caused instability, which was bad for the economic relationship.[43] Noting that many corporations backed Chen in 2000, the secretary-general of the Taiwan Businessmen's Association in Dongguan (a popular investment locale for Taiwanese firms) concluded that "they made a mistake and they see that cross-Strait relations have only got worse in the past four years."[44]

Furthermore, as we saw in Chapter 4, as the constituency with a stake in the cross-Strait economic relationship has grown, politicians in Taiwan have appealed to that group more directly. In the 2000 presidential election campaign, all three main candidates—Chen Shui-bian, Lien Chan, and James Soong—emphasized that they would liberalize cross-Strait investment policies, and strive to open direct links between the two economies.[45] In 2004, the pan-blue ticket of Lien and Soong appealed to this constituency even more directly. They made four broad commitments (each of which carried with it more specific promises): opening direct links across the Taiwan Strait; opening capital flows across the Strait; providing preferential tax treatment to Taiwanese investors (to encourage repatriation of profits); and implementing welfare policies to benefit Taiwanese investors in China (such as helping to build schools so that the children of Taiwanese businesspeople in China would have the same education as children in Taiwan).[46] KMT officials even tried to bypass the Chen administration in negotiating trade liberalization agreements with Beijing, and the party established bureaus on the Mainland "to facilitate communication and the resolution of business disputes" relating to Taiwanese companies (Ross 2006). Ma Ying-jeou emphasized during the 2008 campaign that he wished to liberalize Taiwan's restrictions on cross-Strait economic ties, and he moved quickly to do so after assuming office (Romberg 2008). The DPP's 2008 presidential candidate Frank Hsieh's tough criticism of Ma's cross-Strait economic vision, meanwhile, gained little traction with voters.

Despite these recent trends, it is probably premature to declare that economic interdependence across the Taiwan Strait has already yielded a transformation in Taiwan's foreign policy goals. We also saw in Chapter 4, for example, that although Chen did liberalize investment policy early in his first term, he nonetheless continued to pursue a political agenda clearly at odds with Beijing, despite the opposition to that agenda from those with an economic stake in China. In a 2003 interview, Chen was blunt when asked about business demands for closer ties across the Taiwan Strait: "as for the welfare of some businessmen, or politicians, or individuals, these must absolutely come after the welfare of the overall nation."[47] Recall that Chen's support in the business community was tenuous by 2004, and he ran his re-election campaign without the backing of some prominent magnates who had supported him in 2000.[48] Yet Chen's campaign was still successful; indeed, he increased his vote share from under 40 percent in 2000 to over 50 percent in 2004. Chen succeeded in part because he was able to craft a winning coalition that included both those seeking to build a stronger Taiwanese identity and those threatened, economically, by growing commercial links with Mainland China. The same cross-Strait policies that managed to alienate the business community from Chen likely served to increase his support among protectionist interests (such as farmers and relatively unskilled laborers), who are more concentrated in southern Taiwan (Chen 2004). In sum, though the DPP suffered a crushing defeat in the 2008 elections, Chen's success at constructing a winning nationalist/protectionist coalition in 2004 suggests that a decisive economic interdependence-induced transformation in Taiwan's foreign policy goals has not yet occurred.

Thus, whether economic integration across the Taiwan Strait will effect a broader transformation in Taiwan's foreign policy goals, bringing those objectives into greater harmony with Beijing's own goals, remains uncertain. Growing economic ties have certainly generated a new constituency in Taiwanese politics, which favors foreign policy goals that are less at odds with Beijing than the goals of the Chen administration; this constituency, moreover, has clearly become an important component of the KMT-centered pan-blue coalition. The KMT's own transformation in this regard is quite remarkable: the party that once spurned any contact with the Chinese Communists and that once tried hard—with Lee Teng-hui at its head—to slow economic integration with China now actively courts businesses with an interest in China by emphasizing stability in cross-Strait political relations and progress in cross-Strait economic relations. Whether this constituency can position itself as a key component of *any* winning coalition in Taiwan—and thus influence heavily the determination of the island's broader international and cross-Strait goals over the long term—remains to be seen. As we saw in Chapter 4, Chen Shui-bian's cross-Strait policies after 2002 demonstrated that it is still possible to govern Taiwan while making only limited concessions to actors with a vested interest in China's economy.

Broader Implications

More generally, that the Lee and Chen administrations were able to pursue foreign policy objectives that conflicted sharply with Beijing's goals despite burgeoning cross-Strait economic ties suggests that interdependence-induced transformation of state goals may be difficult to achieve in most cases. Rarely do states with seriously conflicting political objectives exhibit extensive economic linkages as those seen across the Taiwan Strait. If commercial integration even here has been insufficient to effect a transformation in Taiwan's political goals by decisively reshaping the island's domestic political dynamics, then the lesser economic ties found in most other cases of political conflict may be even less likely to transform state goals and the nature of dyadic conflict.

6. Conclusions

On the surface, the relationship between Mainland China and Taiwan appears to confirm the argument that economic interdependence reduces the likelihood of military conflict between states. Since economic ties have blossomed across the Taiwan Strait, Beijing and Taipei have thus far avoided a military clash despite intensely conflicting goals between the two sides. But it has proved to be quite difficult to establish a clear causal link between deepening economic integration and the absence of war in the Taiwan Strait. It may be the case, then, that Beijing and Taipei have avoided a military confrontation, to date, at least, primarily for reasons independent of the burgeoning economic ties between them.

Economic interdependence-induced effects might, of course, become more prevalent and easily observable in the future. Until now, for example, Mainland China has avoided signaling resolve toward Taiwan through economic sanctions. While I have suggested that there are reasons to believe Beijing might never choose to use economic sanctions as a signaling device against Taiwan, it is possible that Mainland officials are simply holding back, viewing sanctions as an option of last resort before fighting. If so, then growing economic ties do act as a stabilizing force in cross-Strait relations, by giving Beijing a way to signal resolve in a very credible way without resorting to war.

Perhaps more likely is the possibility that economic ties will come, over time, to have a transformative effect on the cross-Strait relationship. Citizens on either side of the Taiwan Strait may start to identify more with one another as contacts between the two societies continue to increase. Furthermore, a growing number of Taiwanese businesses and individuals have an economic stake in Mainland China. These actors tend to support foreign policy objectives that are less in conflict with Beijing than those pursued by recent Taiwanese governments. If this new constituency continues to grow, appealing to support from among its members may become critical to building future winning coalitions in Taiwanese politics. In such a scenario, because they would find it difficult to garner support within this constituency, politicians and parties espousing objectives likely to raise tensions in the Taiwan Strait would also find it increasingly difficult to capture the presidency.

Whether or not economic integration across the Taiwan Strait has a clear effect on the prospects for military confrontation between the two sides, I have suggested that the case may have broader implications for arguments linking economic integration to the probability of military conflict. Thus this chapter has aimed not simply to determine whether particular causal mechanisms were operating or not in the cross-Strait case but also to consider why or why not. That is, I have sought to use the case to put forth some broader hypotheses concerning the conditions under which different interdependence effects are likely to materialize.

First, in examining whether economic interdependence has constrained Taiwan's policies toward China, I found that democratization in Taiwan appeared, initially, at least, to mitigate any constraining effects. While democracy has increased the political clout of business actors who gain from economic ties with China, it has also enabled a deeper sense of Taiwanese identity to take root among the island's citizens, encouraging leaders to play to and even cultivate these new sentiments. These latter effects put Taiwan on more of a collision course with Beijing, and appeared to swamp the constraining effects that might have arisen through growing business influence in democratic Taiwan. This finding is counterintuitive and contradicts other studies that have found democracy to enhance the constraining impact of economic integration (e.g. Gelpi and Grieco 2003; Papayoanou 1996). From Taiwan's experience, I hypothesized that the impact of democracy on economic integration's effects is itself contingent on the nature of the bilateral political dispute. When citizens in a country care deeply about an issue at the core of the dispute (Taiwan's sovereign status, in this case), democracy may actually correspond to a reduced, rather than enhanced, constraining impact of economic interdependence.

Second, I found little clear evidence that bilateral economic ties across the Taiwan Strait have improved the efficiency of Mainland China's signaling toward Taiwan. Beijing has gone out of its way to minimize any negative impact cross-Strait political tensions might have on the economic relationship; as such, Chinese leaders have not seized on the opportunity economic links provide to demonstrate a willingness to pay costs in preventing Taiwanese moves toward independence. China's reluctance here may in part reflect a perception in Beijing that economic sanctions against Taiwan would be counterproductive to China's broader goals vis-à-vis the island: while economic sanctions would certainly send a strong message to Taipei, they would also undermine Beijing's standing with the actors—businesses—who tend to be overwhelmingly opposed to Taiwan's independence. I suggested that this sort of conundrum carries over to other cases where economic ties arise in politically conflictual dyads, and hypothesized that the causal mechanism specified in the information argument is more likely to break down in dyads in which economic interdependence is asymmetric and one state pursues a "Hirschmanesque" strategy.

Finally, though there are signs that economic ties across the Taiwan Strait are beginning to exert a transformative impact on Taiwan's politics, these changes do not (yet) appear decisive. Chen Shui-bian was re-elected president in 2004 despite pursuing increasingly confrontational cross-Strait policies and suffering a loss of support in the business community. He did so in part by appealing to actors who are threatened by economic integration with China. Since economic ties across the Taiwan Strait are extensive, Taiwan's experience suggests that the threshold level of economic interdependence needed to generate transformative effects on a state's foreign policy goals is quite high. The Taiwan Strait case, then, might serve as a cautionary tale for states pursuing policies of economic engagement with political rivals—Kim Dae Jung's Sunshine Policy toward North Korea and Bill Clinton's engagement policy toward China come to mind—that seek to achieve a transformative effect.

Generalizing the Empirical Findings
Beyond the Taiwan Strait

1. Introduction

Taken together, the chapters on PRC-Taiwan relations present a narrative that is generally supportive of hypothesis 2, that international political conflict should have a smaller effect on economic ties to the extent that leaders are accountable to internationalist economic interests. Likewise, the theoretical argument advanced in Chapter 2 clearly provides "some empirical 'value-added'" (Lake 1999) in an examination of cross-Strait economic relations. In other words, a focus on the political strength of internationalist economic interests in China and Taiwan allows for a more complete explanation of cross-Strait economic patterns than would otherwise be possible. The previous chapter on the cross-Strait relationship, meanwhile, considered more fully the implications of growing economic linkages between the PRC and Taiwan: while there is little direct evidence that growing cross-Strait ties have had a clear pacifying effect to date, the chapter concluded on a cautiously optimistic note, suggesting that there is some evidence that economic ties may come, over time, to have a transformative impact on cross-Strait political relations. Chapter 6 also considered some broader implications of the cross-Strait case for theories linking economic interdependence to a reduced likelihood of military violence.

The examination of cross-Strait relations presented in the previous four chapters, then, was a useful undertaking from a theory-testing perspective. In particular, the analysis served to bolster confidence in hypothesis 2 while also suggesting some possible addenda or modifications to that hypothesis as outlined in the conclusions to Chapter 5. And for reasons discussed in Chapters 3 and 6, the cross-Strait relationship exhibits some qualities of a crucial case for examining the effects both of conflict on economic flows and of the reverse relationship. In that regard, some generalization is possible on the basis of the study. But because the core puzzle motivating this study is a general one, and because the theory developed to help resolve the puzzle was constructed in general terms, some further consideration of its broader applicability is warranted. That is the task of the present chapter. The chapter begins with a simple quantitative analysis using trade data from a large sample of countries. The analysis provides further tests of the hypotheses presented in Chapter 2. The chapter then develops short case studies of relations between India and Pakistan and between North and South Korea. As will be detailed presently at greater length, the two cases represent good contrasts to the cross-Strait case through which to investigate the core theoretical arguments advanced in Chapter 2.

Before we proceed, however, a few caveats are in order. The primary empirical focus of this book has been the relationship across the Taiwan Strait, and it is simply not feasible to go into a similar level of detail when examining the cases presented in the current chapter. Moreover, key concepts, such as the political strength of internationalist economic interests, are difficult to measure even in a detailed case study. Measuring them in a quantitative analysis involving a large sample of countries over time is even more challenging. The quantitative analysis thus makes use of proxy variables to capture these concepts; the use of such measures deserves close scrutiny. But while it is important to bear these caveats in mind, the analysis in this chapter nonetheless provides evidence that the core argument may generalize quite well to cases beyond the Taiwan Strait. At a minimum, even if these caveats lead the reader to heavily discount the findings presented in this chapter , the findings can be viewed as a plausibility probe that is strongly encouraging about the wider applicability of the general argument.

2. Conflict and Trade Among Seventy-Six Countries: Simple Quantitative Tests

The argument presented in Chapter 2 advances straightforward expectations concerning the relationship between international political conflict, international economic flows, and the political strength of various domestic political interest groups. Broadly speaking, political conflict should lead to reduced economic flows between countries (hypothesis 1). This effect should be especially large when internationalist economic interests have limited influence within the domestic political systems of the countries involved; conversely, the effect of conflict on international economic flows should be muted or non-existent when internationalist economic interests are strong within the countries involved (hypothesis 2). A test of these expectations, in turn, requires suitable measures of the three key variables: economic flows between countries, political conflict between countries, and the political strength of internationalist economic interests within countries. A satisfactory test should also measure and control for other factors likely to influence economic flows between countries.[1]

Measuring Key Variables

Of the three key variables just listed, the most straightforward to quantify is the level of economic integration between countries. The analysis presented here uses bilateral trade flows among pairs of states as its dependent variable. Reliable trade data are available for a large sample of countries over time; data on other economic flows, in particular, foreign direct investment, are more limited on both counts (number of countries and time frame). This study employs *bilateral* trade flows because its primary independent variable, conflict, is itself fundamentally bilateral in nature. The findings reported in this section use bilateral trade data from a sample of seventy-six countries over the years 1960–1992.[2]

Measuring conflict represents more of a challenge. This study defines conflict as the extent to which the political goals, or interests, of two countries diverge; conflict is high in cases where two countries hold important goals that are fundamentally incompatible. Given this definition, to rely on measures that focus solely on observed military confrontations between countries, such as the Militarized Interstate Dispute (MID) data, would be inappropriate. Indeed, as Li and Sacko (2002) have shown, the effect of MIDs on trade often occurs prior to the actual military dispute. Rational economic actors will typically anticipate the possibility of future military conflict and will thus limit exposure in advance; as such, only unexpected MIDs tend to have a directly observable impact on bilateral trade flows.

While using militarized disputes may be inappropriate here, measuring conflict in a way that captures the extent to which states have conflicting goals is clearly no easy task, and any measure is bound to have serious drawbacks. The analyses presented in this section use a measure that captures the similarity of two countries' voting behavior in the United Nations General Assembly. If two countries tend to vote alike, they are coded as having relatively similar interests, and if their votes tend to diverge, they are coded as having relatively dissimilar interests. The measure is coded so that higher numbers represent more dissimilar voting patterns, and is lagged one year (since it may take some time for changes in the level of conflict between countries to influence their trading relations).[3] The obvious caveat here is that any vote in the United Nations may or may not concern issues over which a particular country cares deeply. As such, Appendix B includes robustness tests that consider alternative measures of conflicting interests, such as the similarity/dissimilarity of two countries' alliance portfolios.

As with conflict, coding the political strength of free-trade economic interests within a large sample over an extended period of time is hardly a straightforward task. One possible method is to code individual countries directly by observing the workings of their political systems (e.g. Solingen 1998; Papayoanou and Kastner 1999/2000; Papayoanou 1999). In a large-sample study, however, the consistency across space and time of such a coding scheme would be suspect. The analysis here instead uses a proxy for openness that builds from the following assumption: free-trade interests are relatively strong politically in countries with low protectionist trade barriers and relatively weak in countries with high protectionist trade barriers. The reasoning behind this assumption is straightforward: if the actors who benefit from integration into global markets hold strong political clout domestically, they would be expected to utilize that political clout to break down trade barriers (which, obviously, are contrary to the fundamental economic interests of such actors). Conversely, if protectionist economic interests hold strong political clout, decision makers would find it politically costly to pursue free-trade policies.

Clearly, using trade barriers as a proxy for the political clout of free-trade interests is not without problems. Proxy variables are rarely perfectly collinear with the more difficult-to-measure variables of interest they are meant to represent. In this case, though it is hard to imagine that trade barriers would be high in a country where the actors who benefit most from trade have strong political clout, one can imagine more easily a scenario in which a government that is relatively autonomous from free-trade interests nonetheless chooses a liberal trade policy because doing so is widely believed by economists to be good for the economy. Trade barriers, in short, serve as only a rough proxy for the political strength of pro-trade interests; I later qualify my conclusions accordingly.

A separate problem is that trade barriers are notoriously difficult to measure. Indicators such as average tariffs or revenues from import duties, for example, overlook more difficult-to-quantify nontariff barriers (many of which are hidden). Some measures get around this problem by focusing on outcomes, assessing the divergence between expected trade (based on the predictions of some model) and actual trade. One potential problem here, however, is that trade flows are in part endogenous to conflict. That is, if conflict does in fact damage trade, then the incidence of conflict will lead countries in these sorts of outcome-based measures to appear more protectionist than they really are. The problem is minimized to the extent that conflict's effects do not extend beyond a particular pair of states. However, when conflict between two countries is severe, and especially if it becomes militarized, then it is likely to affect those countries' other trading relations as well. Some recent studies have confirmed these sorts of spillover effects empirically (Glick and Taylor 2005; Kang and Reuveny 2001).

The analysis presented here proceeds using an outcome-based measure developed in Hiscox and Kastner (2002). The measure estimates country-specific trade distortions using a bilateral trade model that controls for the size of each country's economy and the distance between the two countries.[4] Since the tests presented here consider the impact of conflict on bilateral trade flows—meaning that the unit of analysis is the dyad, or pair of states—I use the average level of trade barrier protection across each pair of countries. Given the difficulties associated with measuring trade barriers, Appendix B reports robustness tests using alternative measures.

Now, hypothesis 2 suggests that conflict's independent effects on bilateral trade flows should be contingent on the strength of internationalist economic interests within the two states. In terms of the proxies just described, dissimilar voting patterns in the United Nations should have a bigger negative impact on bilateral trade for pairs of countries with high average trade barriers than is the case for pairs of countries with low average trade barriers. This should be so even after controlling for any independent effects of trade barriers on trade flows. To capture this effect, I include an interactive variable, which is the product of the variable capturing UN voting dissimilarity and the variable capturing average trade barriers in each dyad. This interactive variable takes on its highest values when two countries have high trade barriers and also have highly dissimilar voting patterns in the United Nations. It takes on lower values if UN voting patterns are more similar, or if trade barriers are lower. It takes on its lowest values when countries vote in a similar way in the United Nations and also have low trade barriers. As such, hypothesis 2 yields the expectation that this interactive variable should be negatively correlated with bilateral trade after controlling independently for the effects of conflict and trade barriers. Such a finding would suggest that conflict has a bigger negative effect on bilateral trade when trade barriers are high than when they are low, ceteris paribus.

Control Variables

The model controls for the standard "gravity" model variables of economic size and distance.[5] Here I use the distance between the two countries' major airports (in kilometers) and the product of the two countries' gross domestic products (in real dollars). Other control variables include the product of the two countries' per capita incomes (under the expectation that richer countries on a per capita basis will trade more),[6] the average geographic remoteness of the two countries,[7] the number of countries in each dyad (0, 1, or 2) that are islands, and the number that are landlocked.[8] Countries that are isolated or are landlocked should tend, on average, to trade less than other states, while island countries should tend to trade more than other countries on average.

The model also controls for factor endowment differentials. Variables for the ratio (highest to lowest) of the two countries' per capita arable land and the ratio (highest to lowest) of the two countries' per capita income are included, under the expectation that at least some trade will be driven by differences in factor endowments (in line with the Hecksher-Ohlin trade model).[9] Mansfield and others (2000) find that pairs of democracies tend to trade more with each other than other pairs of states, so I also include a dichotomous variable, equal to 1 if at least one country is a nondemocracy, and 0 otherwise. This variable should be negatively correlated with bilateral trade flows. Finally, to control for temporal dependence in the data, a variable equal to the level of bilateral trade in the previous year is included as an independent variable. All continuous variables are included in their natural log form.[10]

Results

Results are presented in Table 1. The interactive variable is omitted from Model 1, and is added to Model 2. Consider first the model omitting the interactive term. Here, the estimated coefficients on most of the control variables are correlated in the expected direction with bilateral trade flows, though several are not statistically significant (including average remoteness, the number of islands, the dichotomous autocracy variable, and the land ratio variable). Of more interest to the present study, the findings confirm hypothesis 1: the UN dissimilarity variable is negatively correlated with bilateral trade flows and is statistically significant at the 98 percent level of confidence. In substantive terms, however, the effect is relatively small. If all control variables are held constant at their mean value (or median value for dichotomous variables), the model predicts that a shift from similar interests (*UN dissimilarity* is set to its 20th percentile) to dissimilar interests (*UN dissimilarity* is set to its 80th percentile) yields a drop of just 4 percent in bilateral trade. The small size of this substantive effect is not entirely surprising. Hypothesis 2 predicts, after all, that the effects of international political conflict should be more pronounced when internationalist economic interests are weak domestically; as such, the impact of moving from similar to dissimilar interests as measured by *UN dissimilarity* should be somewhat larger than 4 percent in these instances.

Model 2 (Table 1) addresses this possibility more directly because it includes the interactive term, meaning that it serves as a rough test of hypothesis 2. The

TABLE I

The Effect of Conflict on Bilateral Trade,
Ordinary Least Squares Estimates

Independent Variable	Model 1	Model 2
Lag Trade (ln)	.78★	.78★
	(114.35)	(113.43)
GDP Product (ln)	.25★	.25★
	(26.86)	(27.19)
Distance (ln)	−.32★	−.33★
	(−14.71)	(−14.97)
Per Capita Income (ln)	.10★	.11★
	(9.71)	(9.99)
Remoteness	.27	.70
	(.45)	(1.15)
No. Landlocked	−.08★	−.08★
	(−3.49)	(−3.38)
No. Islands	.03	.03
	(1.29)	(1.27)
Autocracy	.01	−.01
	(.51)	(−.48)
Income Ratio	.07★	.07★
	(5.80)	(5.80)
Arable Land Ratio	−.01	−.01
	(−1.25)	(−1.22)
Average Trade Barriers	−.60★	−.27★
	(−13.44)	(−3.33)
UN Voting Dissimilarity	−.12[†]	3.02★
	(−2.31)	(5.04)
Average Trade Barriers★ UN Voting Dissimilarity		−.91★
		(−5.26)
Constant	−1.90★	−3.28★
	(−4.92)	(−6.50)
R-Squared	.8842	.8843
N	60,809	60,809

★ $p < .01$; [†] $p < .02$ (one-tailed tests); T-statistics in parentheses.

findings confirm the hypothesis, as the coefficient on the interactive variable is both negative and highly significant. For a substantive summary of these findings, consider Figure 5 : here, the y-axis represents expected values of bilateral trade, and the x-axis represents different levels of interest dissimilarity. The upper solid line represents a dyad that is composed of countries that are relatively open to trade (*Av trade barriers* is lower than 80 percent of the dyads in the sample), and the lower solid line represents a dyad composed of countries that are relatively closed to trade (*Av trade barriers* is higher than 80 percent of the dyads in the sample). The dotted lines around each of the solid lines represent 95 percent confidence intervals. Not surprisingly, the more protectionist dyad has lower levels of expected trade. But of more interest here is that expected trade drops for the protectionist

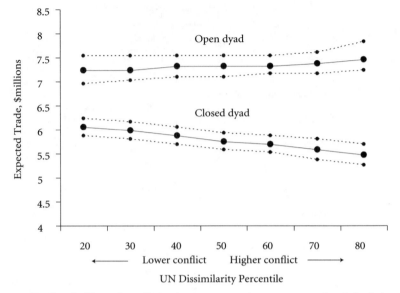

FIG. 5. Predicted effects of conflicting interests on trade: open versus closed dyads, based on Model 2 in Table 1. The open dyad is one in which *trade barriers* (the average level of protectionism in the two countries) is lower than 80 percent of the dyads in the sample. The closed dyad is one in which *trade barriers* is higher than 80 percent of the dyads in the sample. The values reported on the x-axis are percentiles for *UN dissimilarity*: for example, 60 means that the two countries in the dyad have more dissimilar voting patterns in the United Nations than 60 percent of the dyads in the sample.

dyad as interest dissimilarity grows. For the relatively open dyad, in contrast, trade remains relatively steady as interest dissimilarity grows. In general, these findings appear to support hypothesis 2: conflicting interests have a larger negative impact on trade within dyads composed of relatively protectionist countries than they do within dyads composed of more open countries.[11]

Still, the findings do raise a number of issues. First, even for dyads composed of countries relatively closed to trade, the substantive effect of interest dissimilarity is not overwhelming. In the simulation presented in Figure 5, trade in the closed dyad drops from approximately US$6.05 million for a dyad with relatively similar interests (more similar than 80 percent of the dyads in the sample) to US$5.47 million for a dyad with relatively dissimilar interests (more dissimilar than 80 percent of the dyads in the sample). The drop in trade is only about 10 percent. A second issue concerns the effects of interest dissimilarity in the open dyad. Here, trade actually inches up as conflict increases, albeit at an insignificant rate. This is somewhat surprising: while hypothesis 2 predicts that the effects of conflict will be lessened when internationalist economic interests are strong, it does not predict that conflict's effects will disappear entirely—and even turn marginally positive for the most open dyads. It is possible, of course, that these two issues arise because of shortcomings associated with the proxies for conflict and trade barriers. Appendix B reports a series of robustness tests that, in general, tend to provide additional confirmatory evidence in support of hypothesis 2.

Discussion and Qualifications

The findings presented in this section are generally supportive of hypothesis 1 and hypothesis 2. Conflict, as captured by divergence between countries in their UN voting patterns, has a significant, though relatively small, impact on bilateral trade flows, a finding consistent with hypothesis 1. Meanwhile, this independent effect of conflict is significantly larger when trade barriers are relatively high than when they are relatively low, a finding that is consistent with hypothesis 2. The tests reported in Appendix B suggest that these findings are relatively robust to alternative measures of conflict and alternative measures of trade barrier protection. The findings thus provide some evidence that the theoretical argument developed in Chapter 2 applies on a more general scale.

Nonetheless, as I emphasized earlier, considerable qualification is in order. The models estimated in this section used proxy variables to capture two core concepts: the level of conflict between countries, and the domestic political strength of internationalist economic interests. While Appendix B details findings using several alternative measures of conflict that in turn help to allay some of the concerns about the conflict proxies, measuring the domestic political strength of internationalist economic interests proved somewhat more vexing. All alternative measures detailed in the appendix build on the same basic assumption that trade barrier protection represents a reasonably good proxy for the domestic political strength of internationalist economic interests. To the degree that this assumption is justified, the findings presented here are strongly encouraging. However, if the reader is more skeptical of this assumption, then it is perhaps best to view these findings as a plausibility probe into the broader applicability of hypothesis 2, the findings of which are still encouraging and which invite further study.

3. India–Pakistan and North Korea–South Korea Relations: The Logic of Case Selection

The remainder of this chapter further examines hypothesis 2 in the context of two additional case studies: India–Pakistan relations and the relationship between North and South Korea. In comparison with the analysis of the Taiwan Strait case presented earlier, the material presented here is but a brief sketch of each case, meant to further probe the generalizability of the argument presented in Chapter 2. The logic of case selection is quite straightforward. Hypothesis 2 predicts that a domestic political variable—influence of internationalist economic interests in domestic governing coalitions—intervenes in the relationship between international conflict and international economic flows. My strategy here is to hold constant as much as possible the independent variable, conflict, while choosing cases where the intervening variable differs substantially from its values in the cross-Strait case. The expectation, then, is that levels of economic integration should also differ, all else equal, from levels seen in cross-Strait relations, despite similar levels of political hostility. Though these case studies are brief, they nonetheless thus provide an opportunity to probe a bit deeper, not simply into *levels* of economic integration but also into the *processes* through which conflict influences bilateral economic flows—drawing here on the two broad causal mechanisms described in Chapter 2. The remainder of this section describes in some detail the nature of bilateral conflict in each of these two cases before considering the political clout of internationalist economic interests within each of the four countries involved. The section concludes with a brief overview of the expectations hypothesis 2 yields for each case.

Political Conflict in India-Pakistan Relations and Relations on the Korean Peninsula

As with the relationship across the Taiwan Strait, both India-Pakistan relations and North Korea–South Korea relations are characterized by serious conflict and military rivalry. And as in the Taiwan Strait case, both rivalries involve sovereignty-related disputes: the status of Kashmir in the India-Pakistan case and the terms of reunification in the relationship on the Korean Peninsula. The cases, of course, are not perfectly analogous on this score, an issue I will return to in the conclusion to this chapter. But conflict is sufficiently severe in all three cases to suggest that we are, to a considerable extent, holding this variable constant here.

India and Pakistan. The relationship between India and Pakistan has been marred by conflict since British India was divided into the two new independent states in 1947. The two countries fought wars over Kashmir in the late 1940s and again in 1965; they also fought each other during the Bangladesh War of 1971 and have been involved in numerous skirmishes, some with significant casualties, in the years since. Among the key issues at the root of the rivalry between the two countries has been the status of Kashmir, a majority Muslim state in India, which has been claimed as well by Pakistan.

Prior to independence from Britain, the Indian National Congress and the

Muslim League were unable to achieve compromise on a united India. Most broadly, many Muslims were concerned that their interests would not be protected because they would be vastly outnumbered in a unified India. In the end, British India was split into two states: India and Pakistan. The division was based on demographics, with Muslim majority areas going to Pakistan (Ganguly 2001, 15).

At the time, Kashmir was a nominally independent "princely state," one that recognized British rule in the region; after partition, it was expected to choose between India and Pakistan. Kashmir was a particularly difficult case, as it had a Hindu monarch, a Muslim majority population, and it bordered both the presumptive India and the presumptive Pakistan (Ganguly 2001, 15). Maharaja Hari Singh, the state's monarch, initially refused to join either India or Pakistan. But rebellion erupted in southwest Kashmir in October 1947, and Pakistani troops soon moved in to aid the rebels;[12] Singh appealed to India for help. Jawaharlal Nehru, the Indian prime minister, agreed to do so if Kashmir were to join India. Nehru also attached the condition that the leader of a mass-based political party in Kashmir supported by a majority of the Muslim peasantry, Sheikh Abdullah, must also agree that Kashmir should join India, as this would lead the Kashmir population to view the move as more legitimate. After Sheikh Abdullah backed the move, Kashmir joined India, in October 1947, and India sent troops into Kashmir to help put down the Pakistan-supported rebellion. Indian and Pakistani troops were soon fighting the first India-Pakistan war over Kashmir (Ganguly 2001, 16–17). Though a cease-fire was achieved in 1949, Pakistan continued to view the accession of Kashmir to India as illegal and illegitimate (Schofield 1996, 163), and Pakistani leaders retained the goal of gaining control over Kashmir in the future (Ganguly 2001, 31). The first India-Pakistan war over Kashmir ended with Pakistan controlling the western, mountainous part of Kashmir and India controlling the rest. The two sides fought a second war over Kashmir in 1965–66, and in 1971 fought a war that resulted in the secession of East Pakistan and the creation of Bangladesh.

After the conclusion of the Bangladesh War, India-Pakistan relations remained relatively stable for the remainder of the 1970s, but the 1980s brought renewed turbulence to the bilateral relationship. Serious crises erupted on the subcontinent in 1984, in 1986–87, and again in 1990.[13] Bilateral relations later became strained again when India, in 1998, detonated five nuclear devices and Pakistan soon followed suit with tests of its own. In 1999, a new crisis erupted as Pakistan sent troops into northern Kashmir, triggering armed conflict with India, which led to several hundred battlefield deaths. In what became known as the Kargil War, India was able ultimately to repel the attackers. Ganguly suggests that Pakistan may have been motivated in part by the waning insurgency in Kashmir and a desire to force the issue back onto the international agenda (Ganguly 2001, 121–22). Prospects for improved bilateral relations took a further blow when Pervez Musharraf seized power in Pakistan following a coup in October 1999: Musharraf had been the key planner of the Kargil operation (Ganguly 2001, 134). Relations between the two countries again spiraled toward crisis in late 2001 after terrorists attacked the Indian Parliament. India linked the terrorists to a Pakistan-based group, Lashkar-e-Taiba; Indian officials demanded, among other things, that Pakistan ban the group and take action to stem the flow of terrorist insurgents into Kashmir (Ganguly and Hagerty 2005, 168). As tensions escalated, both countries mobilized their militaries and appeared close to fighting another war[14]; the crisis ultimately ended peacefully in late 2002 when India demobilized its military (Ganguly and Hagerty 2005, 168). After 2003 relations between the two countries stabilized considerably. Nonetheless, the core issues that have given rise to tensions and crises in the past remain largely unresolved (e.g. Fair 2005), and the future of the relationship appeared uncertain in the aftermath of the November 2008 terrorist attacks in Mumbai.

North Korea and South Korea. Like Taiwan, Korea was a Japanese colony for most of the first half of the twentieth century, and like conflict in the cross-Strait relationship, conflict between North and South Korea dates to national division after the Second World War. However, while the division between the PRC and the ROC arose from the dynamics of a civil war—and the eventual retreat of ROC forces to Taiwan—the division of the Korean Peninsula on the 38th parallel was a consequence of international factors (e.g. Gu 1995, 135).

The United States had agreed, during the Second World War, that Korea should be independent and unified after Japan's defeat. As the war drew to a close, however, Washington worried that Japanese control on the Korean Peninsula would be replaced by Soviet control. Shortly before Tokyo's surrender, the United States proposed dividing Korea at the 38th parallel into what was supposed to be temporary zones of control; Moscow accepted (Cumings 2005, 187). As relations between the United States and the Soviet Union soured after the Second World War, the division began to look less temporary; the U.S.-backed Republic of Korea (ROK) was declared in August 1948, and the Soviet-backed Democratic People's Republic of Korea (DPRK) was established less than a month later (Oberdorfer 2001, 7). Both Washington and Moscow withdrew troops from the Korean Peninsula by 1949, though both sides continued to provide aid to their respective client states.

North Korea invaded South Korea in 1950 in an effort to reunify the nation; the North's young leader, Kim Il-Sung, had received the backing of both Mao and Stalin prior to the invasion (see, e.g., Oberdorfer 2001, 8). The war, of course, drew in both the United States (under the United Nations banner) and China, and ultimately ended in stalemate in 1953; the final cease-fire line was very near the dividing line at the war's start. South Korea entered into a formal alliance with the United States—U.S. troops remain in South Korea to this day—while North Korea received substantial support from the Soviet Union and from China. Pyongyang signed treaties of Friendship, Cooperation and Mutual Assistance with Moscow and Beijing in 1961 (Oberdorfer 2001, 11).

With the exception of a brief détente during the early 1970s, relations between the two Koreas were in general highly confrontational from the 1960s through the 1980s. The North perpetrated a number of sensationally provocative incidents against the South, including the following: a commando raid on the Blue House (South Korea's presidential residence) aimed at assassinating President Park Chung Hee; an attempted assassination against Park's successor, Chun Doo Hwan (a bomb attack in Burma, which killed several members of Chun's cabinet); and the bombing of a South Korean airliner over Burma in 1987 (which killed over one hundred Korean civilians).[15] The attacks may have aimed to destabilize South Korea; after the 1987 attack, North Korea has largely backed away from these sorts of terrorist activities.

By the late 1980s, increasingly democratic and wealthy South Korea was pursuing improved relations with China and the Soviet Union under President Roh Tae Woo. The policy, *Nordpolitik*, was ultimately successful; Moscow recognized the ROK in 1990, and China followed suit two years later. Seoul's improved relations with the Soviet Union and the PRC also paved the way for the two Koreas to enter the United Nations in 1991 as separate countries. Pyongyang had opposed such a path, insisting instead that the two sides enter the United Nations as a single entity. As relations between Seoul and North Korea's two major patrons improved, however, South Korea was able to gain assurances that neither would veto its entry into the United Nations (see, e.g., Gu 1995, 186; Oberdorfer 2001, chs.9 and 10; Kahler and Kastner 2006). The year 1991 also saw renewed détente in the relationship between North and South Korea. High-level talks were held that autumn in both countries' capitals, culminating in December with the Agreement on Reconciliation, Nonaggression and Exchanges and Cooperation Between the South and the North. In the agreement, the two sides recognized "that their relations, not being a relationship between states, constitute a special interim relationship stemming from the process toward unification" (Oberdorfer 2001, 262). Later that month, the two sides also agreed that neither should possess nuclear weapons, and shortly thereafter Pyongyang reached an agreement with the International Atomic Energy Agency (IAEA), which paved the way for international inspections (Oberdorfer 2001, 263–68).

The improved political climate on the Korean Peninsula in 1991–92 was short lived, however. Inspectors from IAEA found discrepancies that suggested a more expansive program than North Korea had admitted to. A prolonged crisis over Pyongyang's nuclear program ensued, defused only after the United States and North Korea reached the 1994 Agreed Framework. Under the terms of the agreement, North Korea agreed to freeze its nuclear operations at Yongbyon and to allow continuous IAEA inspections. The United States, for its part, agreed to organize an international consortium to provide North Korea with two light water reactors by the early 2000s; in the meantime, North Korea would receive imports of fuel oil to compensate for the loss of electricity-generating power at Yongbyon (Oberdorfer 2001, 357).

The election of Kim Dae Jung as South Korea's president in 1997 yielded a new policy of engagement toward the North; it was dubbed the "Sunshine Policy." The new president emphasized that he would strive for "peaceful coexistence" rather than unification (viewing the latter as, instead, a longer-term goal), and that his administration would aim to reassure the North of Seoul's good intentions (Levin and Han 2002, 23–24). The Sunshine Policy included three core principles: "no toleration of North Korean armed provocations, no South Korean efforts to undermine or absorb the North, and active ROK attempts to promote reconciliation and cooperation between the two Koreas" (Levin and Han 2002, 24). Additionally, the new policy aimed to de-link bilateral economic and political interactions (Kwon and Lim 2006; Levin and Han 2002, 24), a point which will be considered in greater detail further on. In a 2000 speech in Berlin, Kim Dae Jung proposed substantial new South Korean assistance for the North, including investments in North Korean infrastructure and aid to develop the North's agricultural system to help remedy the causes of famine in North Korea (Oberdorfer 2001, 427). Kim's speech was favorably received in Pyongyang and helped pave the way for a direct summit with Kim Jong Il in Pyongyang in the summer of 2000. The summit culminated in the signing of a joint declaration, which included, among other points, a planned return visit to Seoul "at an appropriate time" by Kim Jong Il (Oberdorfer 2001, 431).

In retrospect, the 2000 summit probably represented the apogee of Kim Dae Jung's Sunshine Policy. Kim Jong Il's return summit to Seoul never materialized, and the achievement of the 2000 summit itself was later tarnished by revelations of large-scale cash transfers to the North by the Hyundai company shortly before the meeting; by 2003 many in the South viewed the summit as having been bought.[16] A new crisis emerged on the Korean Peninsula in 2002, when U.S. officials confronted North Korea with evidence that it was developing a uranium enrichment program separate from the Yongbyon facility. The United States declared the North to be in violation of the 1994 Agreed Framework, and arranged for the suspension of fuel aid to the North. In response, North Korea restarted its reprocessing activities at Yongbyon, expelled the IAEA inspectors, and announced its withdrawal from the nuclear Nonproliferation Treaty (NPT) in 2003 (Laney and Shaplen 2003, 18–19). Efforts to find a diplomatic solution through the six-party talks (a series of talks beginning in 2003, which have included China, Russia, Japan, and the United States, in addition to the two Koreas) were initially unsuccessful; in the fall of 2006 North Korea conducted an underground nuclear test. Nonetheless, South Korea proceeded with its engagement policy despite renewed tensions on the Korean Peninsula, and Kim Dae Jung's successor, Roh Moo Hyun, remained committed to the Sunshine Policy even in the wake of Pyongyang's 2006 provocations, including the October nuclear test and the test firing of seven missiles over the summer.[17] Roh's persistence seemed to pay off, as relations on the Korean Peninsula improved dramatically in 2007; the six-party talks yielded a new framework agreement for North Korean denuclearization, and in October Roh himself traveled to Pyongyang for a summit with North Korean leader Kim Jong Il.

Political Coalitions in India, Pakistan, and the Two Koreas

While the level of conflict in India-Pakistan relations and North Korea–South Korea relations is reasonably similar to that seen in the relationship between the PRC and Taiwan, the coalitional patterns in these two cases diverge greatly from the Taiwan Strait case. Though there has been significant variation over time, as detailed in previous chapters, the political influence of internationalist economic interests within the governing coalitions in Taiwan and the PRC has generally grown substantially since the early 1980s. Such interests now represent an important constituency in both polities. By contrast, for the bulk of the postpartition era, India and Pakistan have been governed by highly protectionist coalitions; only recently has this begun to change in India. The two Koreas, in further contrast, have come to represent a mixed dyad; internationalist economic interests hold substantial political clout in the South but remain marginalized in the North. Next I elaborate on each of the four countries.

India. From independence into the early 1990s, the political leverage of internationalist economic interests was extremely limited in India. Since 1991, however, India has entered a reform era during which it has undergone a series of economic liberalizations. Though the reforms were initiated in response to a balance of payments crisis, their persistence suggests that the political clout of internationalist economic interests is growing in India.

Beginning under Nehru in the early 1950s, India pursued an economic strategy that centered on socialism and national self-reliance. To this end, policymakers built large protectionist walls around the domestic economy in order to develop investment goods industries within India (Nayar 2001, 86–90). As Nayar (2001, 92) notes, the political leadership in India at the time of independence "had succeeded to power as a result of its long struggle against colonialism under the aegis of the Congress Party. The core value of the anti-colonial struggle unsurprisingly was nationalism, not simply political but also economic." Pursuing an autarkic economic policy centered on self-sufficiency was thus "naturally attractive to the political leadership as a whole." Greatly facilitating Nehru's efforts to push the Congress Party in the direction of socialism and self-sufficiency was that the party did not depend on the support of (especially big) businesses, which were troubled by the lurch toward socialism and autarky in the 1950s.[18] Rather, the core of Congress Party support came from the middle classes and richer peasants, who were more amenable to Nehru's proposed path than was the business community (Nayar 2001, 81–82).[19] To achieve self-sufficiency, the Indian government under Nehru and the Congress Party adopted a web of protectionist barriers to commerce, including an extensive import licensing system and discriminatory policies against foreign subsidiaries (Desai 1999, 11–13). Tariffs came to be used more extensively beginning in the 1970s, in large part because the number of import licenses issued had come to be too large to be managed effectively by central politicians (Desai 1999, 13). Once the socialist and autarkic program was in place, it created strong vested interests in its continuance, so that attempts at liberalizing reform before the 1990s typically met with failure.

Prime Minister Rajiv Gandhi attempted relatively far-reaching reforms in 1985. He initiated these reforms in the absence of any major economic crisis and was apparently motivated by a desire to see India less marginalized on the world stage (Nayar 2001, 121). As he put it at the time, "Self-reliance does not mean autarky. It means the development of a strong, independent national economy dealing extensively with the world" (quoted in Nayar 2001, 122). But the reforms ultimately failed, primarily because they provoked a wide range of opposition. Unsurprisingly, the Left and labor unions opposed liberalization during the mid-1980s; but core elements of the Congress Party as well came to oppose liberalization for strategic reasons, fearing it would lead the party to be tainted as pro-rich (Nayar 2001, 124; Kohli 1990, 330–33). While businesses tended to be favorably inclined to some liberalization, they typically opposed substantial trade liberalization (though there were some exceptions, of course); most business houses feared the new competition that would arise were India to loosen restrictions on trade and foreign investment (see Kohli 1990, 324–28). In short, reforms were thwarted by strong vested interests favoring a continued large role for the state sector and a high level of external protectionism. Joshi and Little (1996, 63) argue that as of mid-1991 India remained the "most autarkic non-communist country in the world."

In contrast to previous efforts, external reforms introduced during the 1990s exhibited a considerable degree of success. The initial catalyst to reform was a severe balance of payments crisis faced by India in 1991. India turned to the International Monetary Fund, which provided a large loan that was conditioned on India decreasing its fiscal deficits and liberalizing its trade regime (Nayar 2001, 141; Desai 1999, 25). While the initial reforms probably went beyond what was necessary to satisfy the IMF (Nayar 2001), they were nonetheless quite limited. Powerful vested interests, both within the bureaucracy and within the opposition (especially the Left), remained opposed to liberalization.[20] Fearing the danger of riots or strikes, leaders tried to make sure that reforms would not trigger widespread opposition from the middle class or from unions (Nayar 2001, 151; Nayar 1998a, 355). As such, though tariffs were lowered substantially, they remained among the highest in the world, and India continued a "virtual ban" on consumer goods imports (Joshi and Little, 67). By the mid-1990s India would remain as "one of the most highly protected countries in the world" (Joshi and Little, 250). Moreover, since elections were expected in the mid-1990s, the initial reform process slowed sharply after 1993 as the governing Congress Party tried to avoid stirring up too much opposition from more statist, protectionist interests (Dutt 1997; see also Nayar 2001, 150–53).

Reforms started up again after the United Front government replaced the Congress Party in 1996. New external reforms included greater tariff liberalization and the removal of some restrictions on foreign direct investment (Nayar 2001, 211–12). Why did the government restart the reform effort? Nayar (2001, 217–18) argues that the United Front government was under considerable pressure to improve economic performance and living standards because of its tenuous political standing (the government did not command a majority in Parliament, and so had to rely on the support of the Congress Party). He further emphasizes that the initial reforms were giving rise to a number of market pressures because they were only partial: new problems continued to emerge, such as balance of payments issues, which put pressure on the government to proceed with liberalization. When the Bharatiya Janata Party (BJP) came to power under a platform of economic nationalism (*swadeshi*) in 1998, the reforms appeared to be in peril. In fact, however, the government continued to pursue a reform program, and Prime Minister Vajpayee's government was soon pushing for faster removal of quantitative restrictions on imports (Nayar 2001). The reform program also survived the 2004 elections, when a new Congress-led coalition replaced the BJP. In short, since the early 1990s, though "the pace of reform has been faltering ... the direction has never changed."[21]

The initiation and persistence of the reform program suggests that the influence of internationalist economic interests within India's political system has been growing. Indeed, though the reforms were initiated by a small group of central government officials, recognition that the prior development strategy was not working extended well beyond this inner circle; India's middle classes increasingly viewed liberalization as necessary (Nayar 1998a). In diverse and democratic India, governing ultimately requires coalition building, which Nayar (2000) argues leads to a centralizing tendency in Indian politics. In a changing world, where the socialist model appeared to be failing, and where states—like the East Asian newly industrializing countries—that embraced globalization were thriving, and after decades of limited economic growth in India, by the 1990s the centrist position increasingly was one that recognized the need for liberalization. Against this context, even the BJP, which once had opposed liberalizing trade and investment reforms, came to support continued liberalization once it assumed power in the late 1990s (Nayar 2000).[22] As liberalization proceeds, moreover, it is likely to empower new actors with a vested interest in openness, as was seen in the case of Taiwan. In India, though the corporate sector was initially supportive of reforms, by the mid-1990s it was increasingly uneasy about continued lowering of barriers to trade and investment flows, which it worried would lead to increased competition. This unease was articulated by India's peak business associations, including the Confederation of Indian Industry and the Federation of Indian Chambers of Commerce and Industry (FICCI; see Nayar 1998b, 2454). These views may change over time, however, as businesses become more integrated into world markets. Indeed, in 2003 the head of FICCI unambiguously endorsed increased economic ties with none other than Pakistan.[23]

Nonetheless, the influence of internationalist economic interests within India's political system, even during the reform era, should not be overstated. Joshi and Little (1996) stress, for example, that the reforms were initiated by a very small group of central government elites in 1991, and that leaders made little effort to explain the reforms to the electorate or to build a pro-reform constituency (5 and 257; see also Chhibber and Eldersveld 2000, 360). Chhibber and Eldersveld (2000) argue that the central government made no effort to provide local leaders with incentives that would lead them to back reforms. As such, the authors find that local elites in India have a much more negative view of reform than local elites in China (see their table, p. 365). This is especially problematic, for though local elites do not have extensive power to shape economic policy, they do "play a critical role in the implementation of the policies adopted by either the national or state governments," and as such can often "thwart reform" (362). Meanwhile, while support for reforms may be more extensive than it was in the decades after independence (especially among the middle and upper classes), Chhibber and Eldersveld find much more limited support for economic reform among the general population in India than they found in China (2000, 365).

In summary, internationalist economic interests were marginalized in India's political system through the 1980s. More recently, India has undergone a period of liberalization, which has led to increased integration into the global economy. That the reform program has persisted for more than a decade and a half suggests that centrist voters in democratic India do not oppose it; indeed, it appears that India's middle classes increasingly recognized the need for a new direction after years of relatively slow economic growth. However, reforms have been halting, and barriers to trade remain substantial; there is certainly no lobby agitating for increased trade with Pakistan that resembles in any way the large and highly vocal community in Taiwan calling for liberalization of cross-Strait economic links. In this environment, while the political costs that leaders might pay for politicizing or restricting economic ties with Pakistan could rise as reforms continue to deepen, those costs most likely remain relatively low.

Pakistan. Internationalist economic interests have held limited political influence throughout Pakistan's history. Though some governments, most notably the Benazir Bhutto and Nawaz Sharif governments of the 1990s, managed to enact partial liberalization of Pakistan's external commercial regime, a protectionist coalition has generally been ascendant politically since independence.

During the decade after partition, Pakistani politics were dominated by a Punjabi-mahajjir elite, which controlled much of the civil service (*mahajjirs* were refugees from postpartition India; Noman 1990). At the time, the executive branch was the primary power center within Pakistan's political system. The West Pakistani elites who controlled the executive had no interest in seeing a more powerful legislature, as that would shift power to the more populous East Pakistan. Not surprisingly, the government adopted policies that were beneficial to the Punjabi-mahajjir elite, which controlled the executive branch; among these policies was the construction of a highly protectionist foreign trade regime. Leaders aimed to build an industrial base (as the industrial base of colonial India was located outside of postpartition Pakistan) through a high level of protection for infant industries; the trade regime that was put in place was heavily biased in favor of a relatively small group of West Pakistani industrialists (Noman 1990, ch. 1).

A new constitution adopted in 1956 called for national elections to be held in 1959. To prevent the inevitable shift of power to East Pakistan that elections would entail, West Pakistani elites within the civil service asked the military to step in, resulting in a coup in 1958 led by Ayub Khan (Noman 1990, 14–15). Noman (1990, 32–33) argues that the new military regime continued to draw considerable support from the Punjabi/mahajjir elite in West Pakistan, suggesting that the regime remained responsive to protectionist economic interests. Though the Ayub government introduced limited import liberalization during the early 1960s (for example, the government devised a free list, that is, a list of imports that could be imported without licenses), Zaidi argues that as of the mid-1960s, import trade continued to be dominated by a licensing system that was heavily biased toward capital goods imports (Zaidi 1999, 170). Indeed, the free list was drastically scaled back in the late 1960s (Zaidi 1999, 171), suggesting that internationalist economic interests continued to be quite marginalized politically.

Ayub resigned in 1969 in the wake of widespread protests against economic disparities caused by his economic policies; he was replaced by Yahya Khan, who agreed to hold elections in 1970, which ultimately led to civil war and the independence of East Pakistan. The Pakistan People's Party (PPP), which won the elections in the West, took the reins of government after the end of the civil war. Zulfiqar Ali Bhutto, the PPP's leader, became president; he later resigned the presidency to become prime minister when his government in 1973 adopted a new constitution, which established a parliamentary system (Baxter et al. 2002, 187). Bhutto's regime maintained very high barriers to trade.[24] He was deposed in 1977 in a coup led by Zia-ul-Haq, whose authoritarian government drew support to a considerable extent from large landholders and industrialists; unskilled laborers and peasants, probably the two groups hurt most by protectionism, did not support him (Noman 1990, esp. table on 131) and were marginalized politically under his regime. A study by Guisinger and Scully (1991) suggests that the Zia regime pursued limited trade liberalization; Zaidi notes, however, that while Zia reduced tariffs to some extent, tariffs on manufactured goods remained among the highest in the world as of 1986 (1999, 173). In short, the regime's efforts to draw support from pro-protection industrialists, the political marginalization of laborers and peasants, and the continued presence of high protectionist barriers to trade all suggest that the political clout of internationalist economic interests continued to be very low under the Zia dictatorship.

The death of Zia in 1988 brought a return to civilian rule, and the PPP was victorious in elections held later that year. Over the next eleven years, the PPP (headed by Benazir Bhutto, daughter of Zulfiqar Ali Bhutto) and the Islamic Democratic Party (IJI, headed by Nawaz Sharif) alternated in power, with each party governing the country on two separate occasions. The period saw a shift toward a more liberal trade regime, particularly when the IJI held the reins of government (1990–1993 and 1997–1999). Backed by an urban industrial-commercial class, Sharif's governments pursued free-market reforms and sought to expand Pakistan's exports (Ziring 1997, 529); moreover, by the late 1990s average tariffs had fallen to 45 percent (down from 225 percent in 1988; see Pigato et al. 1997).

At the same time, however, Sharif sought to expand capital-intensive industries (Ziring 1997, 533), though Pakistan's comparative advantages clearly lie in labor-intensive industry. Moreover, protectionist barriers to trade remained high. As Husain (1999, 103) writes, "Pakistan [of the 1990s] is still left with a complicated, overly protective, and inefficient trade regime," and though Sharif and Bhutto sought some liberalization, "the policies have been so variable that the period has been characterized as a 'muddle-through' scenario."

Broadly speaking, the story that emerges in Pakistan is one of high protectionist barriers to trade throughout the history of the country, but one where the ruling coalition appeared to be moving slowly in an internationalist direction prior to the Musharraf coup of 1999. The overall influence of internationalist economic interests within the mostly authoritarian political system has been limited, though it appears to have grown during the 1988–1999 period, when a return to democracy forced the two major parties, the PPP and the IJI, to pay more attention to median economic interests. However, the reestablishment of military rule following Musharraf's coup in 1999 could only have undermined the political leverage that internationalist economic interests could exert. As Fair (2005, 10) writes, Pakistan's army "for all intents and purposes . . . dictates Pakistan's foreign policy and is the single most important institution domestically." Far from having vested interests in economic liberalization and stability, the army "gains legitimacy to interfere in the country's domestic affairs in part" from conflict with India over Kashmir (Fair 2005, 10).

North Korea. From its being established North Korea has been governed by highly protectionist coalitions. Indeed, the North Korea that emerged after the Korean War was perhaps the "most autarkic industrial economy in the world" (Cumings 2005, 429). Lying at the heart of North Korea's development strategy was the concept of *juche*, or self-sufficiency.[25] The regime early on favored state control of industry and agriculture while purging opponents of heavy industry and collective agriculture; in the years after the Korean War, Kim Il Sung purged remaining political opponents, "notably those who had opposed heavy industry" (Solingen 1998, 119–221). After the 1958 Korean Workers Party Conference, Kim's dominance of the political system was clear (Buzo 1999, 58); Kim proceeded to redouble economic mobilization efforts centered on the Stalinist command economy model (Buzo 1999, 61). In addition to promoting heavy industry and collective agriculture, the development model gave priority status to military-industrial sectors while establishing "an autarkic economy closed off from the international capitalist economy" (Buzo 1999, 61). Internationalist economic interests were clearly marginalized under Kim Il Sung's leadership.

In response to worsening economic conditions, North Korea in the early 1980s announced some liberalizing economic reforms including an increased willingness to seek trade and investment with capitalist countries and an increased emphasis on promoting the development of light industries. The reforms, however, did not indicate a substantial "shift in paradigm" (Solingen 1998, 234); indeed, when Pyongyang was able in the mid-1980s to secure increased aid from the Soviet Union, it appears that the reforms were largely abandoned (Buzo 1999, 139–42; Solingen 1998, 235). Following the collapse of the Soviet bloc after 1989, Pyongyang again implemented limited economic reforms in response to a sudden decline in economic support from Moscow; however, Buzo (1999, 173) writes that the new economic strategy was "aimed at defending, not reforming, the economic system."[26] Among the key steps taken was the establishment in 1991 of the Rajin-Sunbong Free Economic and Trade Zone in the northeastern part of the DPRK (Buzo 1999, 173; Cumings 2005, 436–37). But the zone has hardly been a glowing success story: Nanto (2006, 126) writes, for example, that "Pyongyang has nearly stifled" the development of the zone with "excessive restrictions and lengthy and complex approval processes."

Following Kim Il Sung's death in 1994, some questioned how strong of a grip his son, Kim Jong Il, would have on power. By the end of the decade, however, it became clear that the younger Kim was in fact strongly in control. When Hwang Jong Yop, a high-level official in North Korea, defected in the late 1990s, he observed, "Who is in charge? No one [else] has real power. . . . Only Kim Jong Il has real power" (quoted in Scobell 2006, 6). Kim's primary power base lies within the military (Kim 2006, 67; Scobell 2006, 24–25); indeed, his most important official position is chairman of the National Defense Commission (Kihl 2006, 7; Scobell 2006, 25). After 1998, Kim's regime underscored the primacy of the military in the DPRK by proclaiming a "military-first politics." Official propaganda justified the emphasis on the military by arguing that "the party's policy of giving priority to military affairs is instrumental in winning a victory in the serious ideological stand-off with imperialism" and "the army-based politics of the Party embodies the *juche* idea" (Kim 2006, 65).

In short, internationalist economic interests are marginalized in North Korea's political structure. The state's relatively autarkic economic policies and command economy ensure that few actors have a vested interest in linkages to the global economy. Certainly many would stand to gain by increased linkages, including, for example, workers and consumers; less clear is whether any within the current selectorate, and in particular within the military, would stand to gain. Indeed, the DPRK regime's efforts to stay in power by controlling the information available to the country's citizens would be thrown in jeopardy by extensive opening to the global economy (e.g. Park 2002).

Still, the future remains uncertain. For example, there is widespread consensus within the North Korean regime that the status quo of continued economic decline must be changed (Mansourov 2006, 47). The experience of China demonstrates, moreover, that a highly autarkic system can move gradually in the direction of greater openness, and in so doing gradually build vested interests in reform and openness (Shirk 1994). Indeed, it is possible that the beginnings of such a process might be underway in Pyongyang: in 2002 the Kim regime appeared to be moving tentatively in the direction of greater openness when it began to implement a new reform program. The reforms included new special economic zones, announced shortly after Kim had himself visited Shanghai to learn more about China's economic reforms (Kim 2006). Though the Sinuiju zone along the Chinese border has been a failure (the Chinese businessman who was to head the project has since been arrested in China), Nanto (2006, 125) argues that the Kaesong zone along the border with South Korea appears to have more potential. For example, thousands of ROK firms bid for the three hundred initial slots at the site (Nanto 2006, 125). The reforms are still in their early stages, and North Korea remains highly isolated from the world economy; but the initiation of new reforms does hint at the possibility that actors with a vested interest in foreign economic ties may become more numerous and more prominent in the future.

South Korea. In the years after the Korean War, internationalist economic interests were also quite marginalized within South Korean politics. Syngman Rhee headed a regime that pursued import-substitution industrialization (ISI) and an overvalued exchange rate, thereby "bolstering the economic rents of privileged importers and speculators in exchange for political financing" (Solingen 1998, 222). Rhee himself drew support from the Liberal Party, the military, the state police, and the bureaucracy; the latter, moreover, was staffed by bureaucrats hostile to free trade (Solingen 1998, 219–20; Haggard and Moon 1993, 60). After his military coup in 1961, Park Chung Hee continued, initially, to pursue ISI policies. However, the economy performed poorly in the early 1960s; as rising inflation and a weakening balance of payments pushed the ROK toward crisis, Park's government began to shift toward an export-oriented economic policy in 1963 (Cheng 1990, 156). Reforms implemented under the new policy included a devaluation of the exchange rate, gradual removal of protectionist trade barriers, and incentives (such as cheap credit) for exporting firms (Solingen 1998, 223; Cheng 1990, 158). The new policy reflected an alliance between the ROK's big businesses, which benefited from the new export orientation, and the military regime. Within this alliance, business is often viewed as a "junior partner" (Cheng 1990, 158–59).[27] However, while open criticism and defiance of government policy by the business community "would have been inconceivable under the Park regime" (Moon 1994, 160), big business was not without leverage in its relationship with the government. To help stay in power, the regime bought support with massive contributions from businesses; as such, Kang (2002) has characterized the state-business relationship under Park as one of mutual hostages.

By the early 1970s, the policies of the Park administration were under attack by what Cheng (1990, 165–66) terms a "distributional coalition" of students, church, and opposition parties increasingly united in their opposition to the government's pro–big business policies. In response, the military in 1972 declared a national emergency and adopted a new constitution (the *Yushin* Constitution), which gave the president (still Park) vast powers, including life tenure and assured majorities in the legislature. More politically secure, Park's regime implemented a "big push" economic strategy in the 1970s, which emphasized rapid development of heavy and chemical industries (Cheng 1990, 167). Big businesses, which were given the task of developing the new industries, were the primary beneficiaries of the new policy.

The state-business relationship changed somewhat after Chun Doo Hwan's military coup in December 1979. Park had been assassinated three months earlier amid growing economic and social turmoil: inflation and bankruptcies were up sharply, and strikes and antigovernment demonstrations were on the rise (Oberdorfer 2001, 111–12). Chun initially targeted the big business community with corruption-related charges, hoping in part to distance his regime from the old one; however, after business leaders pledged their support for his regime, the government in return dropped the corruption charges (Moon 1994, 147). But relations between the Chun administration and big businesses were more contentious than under the Park era. Chun pushed through a number of economic reform measures that aimed to rein in Korea's large business conglomerates (the *chaebols*), such as pushing the conglomerates to sell off non-essential subsidiaries. Though many of Chun's reforms ultimately benefited big business—for example, the *chaebols* were the primary beneficiaries of more liberal foreign investment rules—the capacity of the big business community to shape policy to its liking remained limited (Moon 1994, 148–51).

In the late 1980s South Korea underwent a transition toward democracy. Public dissatisfaction with continued authoritarian rule was growing by 1987. The dissatisfaction spilled over into widespread demonstrations in June when Chun chose an old ally, Roh Tae Woo, as his party's presidential candidate for the election later that year, under rules that heavily favored the ruling party. In the face of mounting pressure, Roh and Chun relented and agreed to a direct presidential election in December 1987. Roh won the direct ballot, and elections to the National Assembly followed in early 1988 (Saxer 2002, ch. 3).

The new and increasingly democratic political environment yielded a different state-business relationship than had existed under the Chun regime. Early in his term, Roh, hoping to increase his support among the middle class, pursued a "tough anti-big-business line" (Moon 1994, 153). Yet in the context of increased democracy, big business was more defiant than it had been under the previous authoritarian regime. The *chaebols* began to direct campaign finance toward candidates sympathetic to business concerns while voicing opposition to Roh's stance; Roh's government, in turn, scaled back efforts to rein in the *chaebols* and in 1990 announced policies, such as a currency depreciation, that were favorable to big business interests (Moon 1994, 154–56). Big business could not by any means dictate policy: for example, in 1991 the government prioritized, as a policy goal, reduced economic concentration, an objective clearly at odds with the interests of the *chaebols* (Moon 1994, 157). But the new political environment certainly increased the ability of business to influence government decisions through such mechanisms as lobbying and campaign contributions. As Kang (2002, 193) writes, "Democratization does not change the business sector's generally high demand for rents, but it does affect the supply. With more politicians competing on the supply side, fewer limits were placed on the behavior of the business sector."

The improved position of the big business community relative to the government persisted after Roh's presidency. The demand for campaign finance grew sharply in the 1990s. For example, while candidates spent an already high US$490 million during the 1987 presidential election, that number grew to an astonishing US$2.7 billion for both the 1992 and the 1997 elections (Kang 2002, 195).[28] In an environment such as this, requiring massive resources to compete politically, Roh's successors Kim Young Sam and even Kim Dae Jung, who had stronger support from labor than his predecessors,[29] were ultimately "no different from previous political elites in their manner of political fundraising and their appetite for it" (Kang 2002, 194). Broadly speaking, then, the transition to democracy increased the political clout of internationalist economic interests in South Korea. Democracy clearly increased the influence of the *chaebols*, who benefited from Korea's integration into world markets.[30] But perhaps equally as important, democracy empowered average citizens, who increasingly benefited from the ROK's integration into world markets. As Solingen (1998, 228) remarks, by the late 1980s "the coalitional base supporting an export-driven strategy was stronger than ever" and included not only *chaebols* but also "the middle and even the working class, who had seen remarkable real wage increases."

Summary and Expectations

As in the case of PRC-Taiwan relations, high levels of conflict exist in both India-Pakistan relations and the relationship on the Korean Peninsula. But the coalitional patterns exhibited in these two cases diverge quite substantially from those seen in the relationship across the Taiwan Strait. Broadly speaking, internationalist economic interests have been marginalized politically in both India and Pakistan; only recently has this started to change in India. In such an environment, hypothesis 2 yields the expectation that conflict should have a large effect on bilateral economic interactions. Both governments should be willing to impose restrictions on commerce when they believe that trade generates negative security externalities, and both governments should be relatively unconcerned about signaling resolve in a way that harms bilateral economic relations while engaged in crisis bargaining. In turn, private economic actors should view bilateral economic exchange as a risky undertaking.

The two Koreas, in contrast, represent a mixed dyad: while the North remains one of the most protectionist regimes in the world, the South has since the 1960s pursued an internationalist development strategy. Since the ROK democratized in the late 1980s, moreover, the political clout of internationalist economic interests has increased substantially in Seoul. Hypothesis 2 is somewhat ambiguous concerning expected levels of commerce in such a mixed dyad characterized by high conflict. Conflict should certainly have a bigger effect on economic exchange than in the cross-Strait case. But whether it would have as big an impact as expected in the India-Pakistan case is less clear; this depends, ultimately, on whether a protectionist North Korea can essentially veto bilateral economic exchange. The theory predicts that to an increasing extent, the South Korean government should be unwilling to impose restrictions on commerce even when it believes such commerce entails security externalities. The South Korean government should also be reluctant to signal resolve in a way that is likely to harm bilateral economic flows. But the North Korean government should be willing both to signal resolve in a way that harms economic exchange and to impose restrictions on commerce when it believes that commerce will be harmful to national security.

4. Conflict and Economic Integration in India-Pakistan Relations

In contrast to the Beijing-Taipei rivalry, political conflict in the Pakistan-India case has nearly completely undermined the bilateral commercial relationship. At the time of partition, when British India was divided into the two newly independent states of India and Pakistan, commercial integration between the two states was substantial. In 1948 (the year after partition), India's imports from Pakistan accounted for 20 percent of its total imports, while Pakistan's imports from India accounted for 45 percent of its import total (Johal 1989, 251). Yet by 1954 the two numbers

TABLE 2

India-Pakistan Trade, Selected Years

Year	Percentage of total imports	
	India from Pakistan	Pakistan from India
1948	20.0%	45.4%
1954	2.9%	4.9%
1965	0.9%	0.6%
1979	0.5 %	0.6 %
1985	0.2 %	0.2 %
1990	0.2 %	0.6 %
1995	0.1 %	0.6 %
2000	0.1 %	1.5 %
2003	0.1 %	1.7 %

Sources: Data from International Monetary Fund (various years); Johal (1989, 251); Sridharan (2005, 328).

had declined precipitously to 3 percent and 5 percent, respectively, and after the 1960s bilateral trade flows typically have represented less than one percent of either country's total trade (Johal 1989, 251; International Monetary Fund, various years). In the early 2000s official bilateral trade flows hovered around a mere US$200 million, though in 2005, as bilateral relations between the two countries warmed to some extent, official flows exceeded the US$1 billion mark.[31] Table 2 summarizes official bilateral trade flows as a percentage of each country's total trade.

Of course, limited trade between India and Pakistan is a function not merely of the political hostilities between the two countries. The two economies certainly do not complement each other to the extent that Taiwan and Mainland China do, for example. There is no corollary to the large number of Taiwanese firms eager to move into the Mainland market. More fundamentally, the two countries for years pursued inward-oriented development strategies, which would have yielded limited commercial integration even in the absence of bilateral rivalry. Despite these caveats, it is widely recognized that political hostilities between the two sides have further undermined trade between the two states. For example, the president of the Federation of Indian Chambers of Commerce and Industry recently asserted that potential annual trade between India and Pakistan may approach US$8 billion.[32] Another recent estimate suggests that trade could approach US$10 billion were relations between the two countries to improve.[33]

Security Externalities and Pakistan's Economic Policy Toward India

Since partition, economic relations between Pakistan and India have been undermined, in part because Pakistan has imposed restrictions on trade with India in particular. That is, while Pakistan and India have each maintained substantial trade barriers vis-à-vis the rest of the world in general, conflict with India has led Pakistan to impose especially severe restrictions on bilateral trade flows. This is partly a reflection of concern among Pakistani leaders that too much economic integration with India could potentially give India a greater degree of political influence over Pakistan. In particular, leaders have worried that trade with India could undermine Pakistan's leverage on the Kashmir issue, in part because trade would create vested interests in stability. As we saw in Chapter 4, this concern parallels certain Taiwanese motivations for imposing restrictions on trade with China.

At the time of partition, the economies of India and Pakistan were joined by a de facto customs union (the Standstill Agreements). As Johal (1989, 38) notes, if this de facto customs union were to have been replaced by a permanent one, there is no reason why the two countries would not have remained highly integrated economically. He emphasizes, however, that political disputes, especially the Kashmir issue, led Pakistan to desire a greater amount of economic independence so as not to be influenced by pressure from India. The agreements, in turn, broke down shortly after partition.

Pakistan later imposed restrictions on the movement of goods between India and Pakistan, which led to a trade war in 1949–50. Bilateral trade in those years declined drastically (Johal 1989, 39). Throughout the 1950s and into the early 1960s, India-Pakistan trade was extremely limited, even though their economies remained complementary. Johal (1989, 77) argues that Pakistan "was reluctant to increase trade with India as long as the Kashmir issue was unresolved, and it sought to insulate East Pakistan from Indian influence." Pakistan sought to increase trade with countries with which it had better relations in order to offset the loss of trade with India. For example, after 1963 China became one of Pakistan's most important buyers of cotton, raw jute, and jute manufactures (Johal 1989, 108). In other words, reluctance to trade with India in particular was not simply a consequence of protectionism but rather reflected a concern too about the nature of security externalities associated with bilateral trade.

After war broke out in 1965, the two countries severed bilateral trade relations. India lifted trade restrictions by 1966, but Pakistan refused to follow suit: it wanted first to see the Kashmir dispute resolved (Johal 1989, 129). The two countries finally agreed to reopen bilateral trade with the signing of a protocol in 1974 (Chopra 1977, 478), though trade flows remained extremely limited, in part because of continued Pakistani concerns about being too dependent on Indian trade (Johal 1989, 172).[34] Such concerns remained salient through the 1980s (Johal 1989, 204).[35] Indeed, protectionists tended to form alliances with "political hawks," who were preoccupied with political relations with India.[36] In other words, it was relatively easy for Pakistan to maintain restrictions on trade with India because protectionists had very prominent and willing domestic political allies; this suggests that the domestic political costs associated with maintaining India-specific restrictions on commerce were probably minimal.

Pakistan did agree in 1997 to expand the list of allowable imports from India, but the change was relatively minor,[37] and Pakistan's commerce minister emphasized in May 1998 that little more would be done to open bilateral trade:"We have not given [India] MFN [most-favored-nation] status, we don't intend to give it."[38] Moreover, the decision to relax restrictions in 1997 sparked strong attacks from the opposition, even though the changes were extremely limited. For example, the president of the Pakistan Democratic Party argued that trade should not be expanded with India absent a settlement of the Kashmir dispute, even if trade were beneficial to Pakistan's economy.[39] During the more recent thaw in bilateral relations, Pakistan has expanded the list of allowable imports from India several times (Sridharan 2005, 327). Nonetheless, by late 2006 the number of products that might be imported from India stood at only 1,077, which is small compared to the over 4,000 products that may be imported into Pakistan from other South Asian economies.[40] As Chawla (2001, 148) notes, moreover, many of the products on the permitted list "do not have real export potential from India."[41]

In summary, while Pakistan's overall trade regime has been highly protectionist since partition, its restrictions on bilateral trade with India have been especially severe. To a large extent, these extra restrictions on trade with India have been motivated by political concerns, and in many ways parallel the worries that Taiwanese officials have expressed regarding economic integration with Mainland China. However, while Taiwanese policymakers have become much less willing over time to maintain restrictions on cross-Strait commerce because the political strength of internationalist economic interests within Taiwan has grown, Pakistani officials have not faced the same constraint. To the contrary, officials probably fear attacks, which might arise from political hawks fixated on the Kashmir issue if they were to relax restrictions on trade with India, much more than they fear the resentment of internationalist economic interests provoked by keeping the restrictions in place.

A Brief Analysis of Crisis Signaling Behavior by Pakistan and India

When relations between India and Pakistan have become tense, both countries have been willing to signal resolve in ways that are damaging to bilateral commercial relations. Such behavior stands in stark contrast to Mainland China's signaling behavior toward Taiwan, and has helped to undermine the bilateral economic relationship. In the case of Mainland China–Taiwan relations, recall, Beijing consistently has sought to reassure Taiwanese investors that it will not signal resolve over the issue of Taiwanese sovereignty in a way that might damage their interests. But in the India–Pakistan case, neither government has made such assurances, which would lack credibility regardless since each country has been governed by a relatively protectionist coalition. To the contrary, at times when relations have become tense in recent years, both governments have been willing to signal commitment by taking actions such as closing the border, halting bilateral transportation, or refusing to issue visas.

Consider, for example, the behavior of both India and Pakistan after the Indian parliament was attacked by terrorists on December 13, 2001. The Indian government blamed two Pakistan-based militant groups for the attack and demanded that Pakistan shut down the groups completely and arrest their leaders.[42] Musharraf's response, that Pakistan would crack down if conclusive evidence were found linking the two groups to the attack on the Indian parliament, was less than satisfactory to New Delhi, which claimed that sufficient evidence already existed.[43] Within days of the attack, the Indian government began to signal just how seriously it took the issue, and started mobilizing troops along its border with Pakistan; Pakistan quickly followed suit.[44] But both sides also signaled resolve in ways directly damaging to bilateral commerce. On December 27, only two weeks after the attack on the parliament, India banned Pakistan's national airline from its airspace in order to protest Pakistan's "inadequate" measures at stopping terrorism; Pakistan replied by banning Indian airliners from flying into Pakistani airspace.[45] Both countries also halted all bus and rail transport across the border starting on January 1, 2002.[46]

The signaling behavior of the two parties after the attack on the Indian parliament was not an isolated case in the history of the Indian-Pakistan relationship. Rather, both countries have over time demonstrated a willingness to politicize the bilateral economic relationship when political relations become tense. Prior to the outbreak of hostilities in 1965, for example, several business houses in both India and Pakistan had significant investments in the other country. But when war erupted, these investments were seized by both governments as enemy property; since then, bilateral direct investment has been "non-existent" (Sridharan 2005, 329). In 1986, as bilateral tensions rose after India accused Pakistan of supporting pro-secession Sikh militants in Punjab, India sealed the border in a number of villages as part of its crackdown; in November of that year New Delhi also temporarily stopped issuing visas to Pakistani nationals.[47] Similarly, Pakistan's persistent refusal to entertain granting India most-favored-nation status absent resolution of the Kashmir issue, while in part stemming from Pakistan's concerns over security externalities (as detailed in the previous subsection), is also a signal to India that Pakistan remains committed to the issue of Kashmir.

The willingness of both New Delhi and Islamabad to politicize bilateral economic relations obviously has a direct, negative impact on economic flows between the two countries, but it also has an indirect effect by increasing the risks for those who might consider trade or investment. As Slater and Pearl write in the *Wall Street Journal*, "One reason trade has faltered [between India and Pakistan] is that both countries fear that increased economic ties could be used as a weapon."[48] Echoing this point, a managing director at one Indian conglomerate argues that "a predictable climate of peaceful relations" is the prerequisite for increased trade between the two countries. "If both governments signal their interest in expanding economic and business links, then the business communities will overcome all other short-term impediments to trade."[49]

Case Study: The Proposed Iran-India Gas Pipeline

A proposed gas pipeline linking Iran and India, and the difficulties it has faced getting started , helps to illustrate how political conflict between India and Pakistan can undermine bilateral economic cooperation. The possibility of constructing a natural gas pipeline from Iran to India was first raised in 1989 by Iran. As relations between New Delhi and Tehran were not particularly friendly at the time, Indian officials were initially cool to the idea. By 1993, however, India had changed its position on the pipeline, recognizing that such a project would help address the country's long-term energy needs (Pandian 2005a, 662; 2005b, 313).

Of course, unless Iran and India choose to pursue a costly deep-sea option, any pipeline connecting the two countries would need to travel through Pakistani territory or waters. During the 1990s Islamabad opposed the idea of a pipeline passing through Pakistan, because officials worried about the potential security externalities associated with such a project. The navy, for example, was concerned that if a pipeline were to travel through Pakistani waters, it would make it easier for India's navy to justify entering Pakistan's exclusive economic zone; as such, Islamabad blocked a 1995 feasibility study into a shallow-water route for the pipeline (Pandian 2005b, 314). Pandian (2005a, 662) points to two other possible security externalities associated with an Iran-India pipeline that concerned Pakistani officials. First, a pipeline would help solve India's long-term energy concerns; in other words, it would facilitate continued growth in India's economy. Second, a pipeline would foster "a long-term relationship between India and Iran, which would obviously challenge Pakistan's stake in the region." Sridharan (2005, 330) notes that Pakistan also "fears being locked into a political relationship with India and thus losing political leverage."

Pakistani officials started to reverse course on the issue when India and Iran began in the late 1990s to consider more seriously a deep-sea route for the pipeline, which would bypass Pakistani–controlled areas entirely. If India would benefit from the pipeline anyway, then it would be better from Pakistan's perspective for it to pass through Pakistani territory so that Islamabad would at least be able to reap some transit fees from the project (Pandian 2005a, 663). But even as Musharraf reversed course, Pakistani hawks on the Kashmir issue continued to oppose the project. Noted the conservative daily newspaper *Rawalpindi Nawa-i-Waqt*, "India will earn huge profit by selling the Iranian gas in the domestic market at very high rates. With this money India will buy more and more arms and ammunition to suppress the people of Kashmir."[50]

More recently, however, resistance to an overland pipeline through Pakistan has come from India, which worries about the security of the pipeline. As Slater and Pearl wrote in 2001, "The sticking point is the route: It would be least expensive to go through Pakistan, but India worries that Islamabad might be tempted to turn off the tap if relations worsened."[51] Indeed, though Pakistan has guaranteed the security of the pipeline (Pandian 2005b, 315), India has good reason to view the credibility of such a commitment with at least some skepticism given Islamabad's past willingness to politicize the bilateral economic relationship during periods of political tensions. Still, as Sridharan (2005, 330) writes, this obstacle is not necessarily insurmountable. For example, international lenders could be brought on board; any effort to disrupt the flow of gas for political reasons would then have more serious costs for Islamabad.

The pipeline project might ultimately succeed; indeed, optimism has been growing as relations between India and Pakistan continue their current warming trend, and the two sides in 2008 agreed in principle to begin construction in 2009.[52] But the difficulties the project has faced help to illustrate how political conflict between India and Pakistan has served to undermine their bilateral economic relationship. Both mechanisms discussed in Chapter 2, which link political conflict between countries to a reduced level of economic exchange, appear to be salient in the case of the pipeline. During the 1990s, Pakistani leaders were reluctant to proceed because of the project's security externalities, which they perceived to be negative, on balance, for Pakistan. Indian officials, meanwhile, have expressed concern about the security of the pipeline in Pakistani territory. The project was viewed as risky because bilateral relations were at times very tense and Pakistan's assurance that it would not tamper with the pipeline in the event of a future crisis was not entirely credible.

Summary

The paltry amount of bilateral commerce in the India-Pakistan relationship stands in sharp contrast to the dynamic economic relationship between Mainland China and Taiwan. In Chapters 4 and 5, we saw that two factors in particular have helped to drive rapid growth in cross-Strait economic relations, effectively mitigating the independent effects of conflict. First, increasing political leverage for internationalist economic interests in Taiwan has stepped up the costs to Taiwanese leaders of maintaining security-motivated restrictions on commerce with the Mainland. In the India-Pakistan case, a similar set of security-related concerns has led Islamabad to impose restrictions on commercial integration with India. But because internationalist economic interests have much more limited political clout in Pakistan, Pakistani leaders have been able to keep these restrictions in place without suffering substantial political costs.

Second, China too is governed by an increasingly internationalist coalition in which the clout of internationalist economic interests is growing and the costs of taking actions detrimental to the country's links to the global economy are on the rise. Partly as a result, Chinese leaders have been extremely reluctant to signal resolve toward Taiwan in a way that undermines the bilateral commercial relationship, as doing so involves costs that they would rather not pay. In other words, Mainland China appears willing to signal commitment on the Taiwan issue in a way that is damaging to commerce only as a last resort; as a result, Taiwanese investors view the risks associated with cross-Strait commerce as limited, even though their Mainland investments often involve assets that are relationally specific once deployed. By contrast, both India and Pakistan have been governed by relatively protectionist coalitions that do not pay such high political or economic costs for taking actions detrimental to foreign commercial ties. As a result, both countries have been willing to signal resolve on the issues that divide them, in ways that directly undermine bilateral economic flows. Such signaling behavior not only has a direct and negative effect on trade flows, but it also discourages forward-looking business actors from investing any assets specific to the bilateral relationship, out of fear that those assets might be lost the next time the two countries become locked in a disagreement.

5. Political Conflict and Economic Ties on the Korean Peninsula

Given the intense political rivalry that has characterized the relationship between Pyongyang and Seoul, it is perhaps not surprising that economic integration on the Korean Peninsula has been relatively limited. Prior to the late 1980s, economic ties were banned by both sides and hence were virtually non-existent. But as South Korea democratized, its economic policies toward the North began to change as well. Seoul lifted its ban on trade with the North in 1989, and by the late 1990s was actively encouraging increased bilateral economic ties witho' strings attached. Though North Korean reluctance has limited the impact of the changed ROK policies—for example, bilateral trade still accounts for a miniscule fraction of South Korea's total trade—economic ties between the two Koreas have nonetheless grown substantially since the late 1980s.

As Levin and Han (2002, 6–7) write, Seoul had expressed interest in improved economic ties with North Korea as early as the 1970s. But it was under Roh Tae Woo that a breakthrough finally occurred: in a July 1988 speech, Roh presented a six-point program for improved relations on the Korean Peninsula, which includ-ed increased trade and personnel exchanges. The proposal was part of a broader *Nordpolitik* strategy that aimed to normalize relations with the Soviet Union and China in a manner that would not be perceived in Pyongyang as threaten-ing (Oberdorfer 2001, 188).[53] Importantly, Roh began the process of building a bureaucracy that could manage linkages with North Korea; for example, the Inter-Korean Exchange and Cooperation Promotion Committee was established during his presidency (Levin and Han 2002, 8). Kim Il Sung, however, reacted skeptically to Roh's speech, suggesting that it "was intended to permanently split the country" (Oberdorfer 2001, 189).

Trade between the two Koreas remained extremely limited in the two years after Roh's speech, though there was an uptick after that: trade flows increased from US\$13 million in 1990 to over US\$100 million in 1991 (see Figure 6). North Korea's position on bilateral exchange also shifted to some extent in 1991. In that year's December Accords, Seoul and Pyongyang agreed to a set of guide-lines that included increased economic and cultural exchanges. The North's will-ingness to negotiate these accords undoubtedly reflected, at least in part, the fun-damental success of the *Nordpolitik* policy. By 1991, Roh had managed to improve relations dramatically with both Moscow (which granted diplomatic recognition to Seoul in 1990) and Beijing; facing a loss of external support, and under pres-sure from Beijing to improve relations with the South, Kim Il Sung decided to negotiate with Seoul (Oberdorfer 2001, 260–62). After the accords, inter-Korean trade increased gradually through the mid-1990s; in 1997 bilateral trade stood at US\$300 million, still quite limited but nonetheless far more substantial than before (Ministry of Unification, ROK, 2005).

By the mid-1990s, the South Korean business community was pushing for further liberalization in Seoul's economic policies toward the North. Roh's deci-sion to legalize inter-Korean trade did not extend to South Korean investment in ᵓrth Korea, which continued to be banned. The *chaebols* in particular hoped to ᵓ ban lifted, believing that substantial investment opportunities existed in the ᵓgainst this backdrop, the Kim Young Sam administration in late 1994 substantial relaxation of the South's investment policy toward North

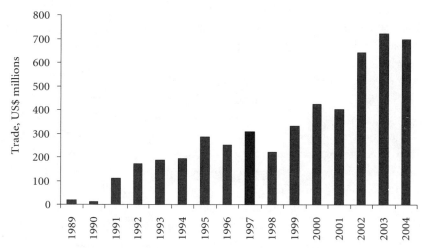

FIG. 6. North Korea–South Korea trade, 1989–2004. Source: Data from Ministry of Unification, ROK, *2005 White Paper on Korean Unification*, 53.

Korea. Several South Korean companies immediately began to explore opportunities in the North (Noland 2000, 110–11). Substantial restrictions remained in place, however, and South Korean firms felt that the initial opening did not go far enough. The new guidelines placed limits on the amount and types of investment acceptable in North Korea, and appeared to favor small- and medium-sized businesses over the *chaebols*.[55] But in the spring of 1995 the Kim Young Sam administration approved two major investment projects in the North (including one by Daewoo)[56]; it announced further liberalization in early 1996, including the scrapping of a US$5 million limit on individual investments (Noland 2000, 111).

Liberalization of Seoul's economic policies toward North Korea during the Roh Tae Woo and Kim Young Sam administrations is clearly consistent with hypothesis 2: the liberalization occurred in an environment where democratization had increased the political influence of internationalist economic interests. But an important caveat is in order. Though the liberalizations introduced by Roh and Kim were substantial, the new policies did not signify a separation of South-North economic interactions from the bilateral political relationship. To the contrary, Roh and Kim hoped to use bilateral economic relations as a means to advance Seoul's political goals vis-à-vis the North. Both administrations adopted a carrot-and-stick approach, liberalizing economic ties to reward cooperative behavior from Pyongyang, and freezing economic cooperation to signal disapproval when North Korea acted provocatively (Kwon and Lim 2006; Noland 2000). For example, Kim Young Sam delayed economic liberalization until after the resolution of the 1993–94 nuclear crisis (Kwon and Lim 2006, 135), and the investment liberalization in 1996 may have been an effort to coax North Korea into talks with Seoul through the South's proposed "four party" framework (Noland 2000, 111). Changes in South Korea's economic policies toward the North, in short, were driven in large measure by the nature of the North-South political relationship during the late 1980s into the mid-1990s.

This does not mean that domestic political processes were irrelevant. Solingen (1998, 235–36) writes that the *chaebols*, which were "increasingly interested in shifting their labor-intensive operations to the North," helped (in conjunction with ROK government and military officials) to conceive of *Nordpolitik*. Furthermore, the link between the North-South political relationship and Seoul's economic policies toward the DPRK was not always ironclad. As a case in point, the Kim Young Sam administration's spring 1995 approval of the two investment projects in North Korea occurred even as the 1994 Agreed Framework appeared to be in jeopardy and tensions on the Korean Peninsula were mounting. At the time, U.S. and DPRK negotiators were deadlocked over details concerning the building of the light water reactors in the North; Oberdorfer (2001, 367) writes that the ROK foreign minister even suggested that Washington deploy aircraft battle groups to the seas on both sides of North Korea in order to increase pressure on Pyongyang.[57] Despite the tense environment, the Kim administration worried that continued delay on investment approval could disadvantage South Korean firms vis-à-vis firms from other countries, such as Japan, that were considering North Korean investments.[58]

South Korea's economic policies toward the North changed more dramatically after Kim Dae Jung assumed the presidency in 1998. The new administration devised a new engagement policy, dubbed the Sunshine Policy, toward the North. The economic component of the new policy was unconditional: unlike policy under the Kim Young Sam administration, the Sunshine Policy explicitly de-linked bilateral economic interactions from the North-South political relationship. Kim Dae Jung's new policy was not a consequence of any clear pressure from the business community but rather reflected a belief that over time, growing economic and social linkages between the two Koreas would help to stabilize the bilateral political relationship, and perhaps eventually promote a transformation of the North Korean regime (e.g. Noland 2000, 113).[59] In other words, the new Kim administration believed that growing economic links with North Korea entailed, over the long run, positive security externalities for the South.

In practical terms, the policy aimed to increase South Korean investment in the North by removing many of the bureaucratic hurdles that might in the past have deterred such investment. Seoul also actively encouraged businesspeople to visit North Korea to explore investment opportunities (e.g. Noland 2000, 113;

Levin and Han 2002, 27–28). The policy yielded some new economic linkages. For example, Hyundai founder Chung Ju Yung visited North Korea several times in the late 1990s (twice delivering herds of cattle as a goodwill gesture). His visits yielded a number of business ventures for Hyundai, including the establishment of a South Korean tourist venture at Mount Kumgang (Noland 2000, 114).[60] Kim Dae Jung proceeded with the Sunshine Policy, and indeed approved the Mount Kumgang project, despite a series of provocative North Korean actions undertaken in 1998, including submarine infiltrations into South Korean waters and the test firing of a long-range ballistic missile (Levin and Han 2002, 92–93). Kim was clearly determined to keep South-North economic relations separate from the bilateral political relationship.

Additional breakthroughs in bilateral economic relations occurred after the 2000 summit meeting between Kim Jong Il and Kim Dae Jung. For example, during ministerial meetings following the summit, the two sides agreed to reconnect inter-Korean rail lines that had been severed since the 1940s (Ministry of Unification, ROK 2005). Meanwhile, Hyundai Asan signed an agreement in August 2000 to develop the Kaesong Industrial Complex in North Korea. The special development zone expected to attract South Korean firms that would benefit from less-costly land and labor in the North. The complex initially would target small- and medium-sized labor-intensive firms in South Korea; in later stages, the development plan called for the construction of a "combined industrial complex of heavy chemical engineering and industrial facilities." A groundbreaking ceremony was held in 2003, and in 2004 fifteen companies were chosen for a pilot complex. The company Living Art began constructing its factory in September of that year and shipped its first load of kitchen pots in December 2004 (Ministry of Unification, ROK 2005, 74–76). By the end of 2006, the project was still moving forward, and twenty-one South Korean firms employed over ten thousand North Korean workers at Kaesong.[61]

In their October 2007 summit meeting, Roh Moo Hyun and Kim Jong Il agreed to expand bilateral economic cooperation. South Korea agreed to build a new special economic zone in Haeju, near the Kaesong Industrial Complex. The two sides also announced plans to develop a joint fishing area in disputed waters to the west of the peninsula.[62] These plans were formalized during talks between the two countries' prime ministers in November. During those prime ministerial talks, the two Koreas also agreed, after years of delay, to begin cross-border freight train service in December.[63] Nonetheless, these tentative steps toward increased economic cooperation came to a halt after conservative Lee Myung-bak assumed the ROK presidency in early 2008. Lee immediately signaled an end to an unconditional engagement policy toward the North: his administration indicated it would not support new joint economic projects with Pyongyang unless the North committed more strongly to abandoning its nuclear weapons program. North Korea responded by expelling from Kaesong several South Korean officials who were helping to manage the complex. Later in the year, North Korea announced that it would halt cross-border freight train service, and that more South Koreans would be expelled from Kaesong—leaving the future of the industrial complex in doubt.[64]

In sum, real progress has certainly been made since the 1980s, especially in the context of Kim Dae Jung's Sunshine Policy (which was also embraced by Kim's successor, Roh Moo Hyun). Nevertheless, progress in bilateral economic relations should not be overstated: broadly speaking, the scale of bilateral economic cooperation remains small. While South Korean firms were enthusiastic about entering the North Korean market in the early 1990s, this enthusiasm soon faded. Opportunities for profit were limited in the still highly autarkic North, and the famine that devastated the country in the mid-1990s further revealed the poor state of the North's economy (Noland 2000, 112). Moreover, for the same reasons that the Kim Dae Jung administration believed that the long-term security externalities of economic integration would be positive for South Korea, officials in North Korea have remained cautious about expanded links. North Korea worries about the "Trojan horse" effects of economic integration, and as such has tried to "fence off" bilateral economic linkages from the rest of the economy (Noland 2000, 115–16, 133). Tourists to Mount Kumgang have little contact with North Korean society, and North Korea's special economic zones are not integrated into the rest of the economy. As Nanto (2006, 126) writes, "Rather than becoming a model of reform for the rest of the economy, Pyongyang seems to view these islands of globalization more as a means to extract funds from South Korean companies."

More fundamentally, Pyongyang has not made a credible commitment to protect and promote the interests of South Korean investors. As such, "the South Korean private sector is cautious and risk averse when it comes to dealings with North Korea" (Levin and Han 2002, 84). The excessive bureaucratic restrictions associated with investing in the autarkic North Korean economy can be stifling (e.g. Nanto 2006). Ventures in the North almost always lose money in the short run, and even over the long term the potential for profit is highly uncertain (Levin and Han 2002, 84); according to one estimate, since the late 1990s more than one thousand South Korean businesses have lost substantial investments or gone bankrupt in North Korea.[65] Furthermore, Pyongyang has been quite willing to politicize economic ties, and an incident in 2005 suggests that its threshold for doing so may be quite low. In this case, North Korea threatened to suspend or scale back Hyundai's extensive business operations in the North, including the

Mount Kumgang tourism venture. The company had earlier dismissed an executive for misappropriating company funds. But because the executive had apparently established a rapport with Kim Jong Il, the incident was considered serious enough in Pyongyang for the regime to consider jeopardizing its relationship with a major South Korean investor.[66]

In summary, though tentative economic linkages in recent years have begun to develop, political conflict on the Korean Peninsula continues to disrupt the economic relationship between South and North Korea. In recent years Seoul and Pyongyang have adopted divergent policies toward bilateral economic cooperation. In South Korea, against a backdrop of democratization and growing political clout for internationalist economic interests, officials gradually liberalized economic policy toward the North; under the Sunshine Policy, economic ties between the two Koreas were actively encouraged. Conversely, North Korea has generally been cool to bilateral economic ties. While happy to accept any financial benefits that South Korean investment in the North might afford, Pyongyang has been careful to guard against any negative security externalities that might arise from bilateral exchange. In this regard North Korea aims to fence off inter-Korean economic and personnel flows from its economy and society at large. The case, then, is largely, but not entirely, consistent with hypothesis 2. In democratic South Korea, where internationalist economic interests are powerful, the government has progressively separated economics from politics in the bilateral relationship (though the new Lee Myung-bak administration appears to be reversing this trend). In contrast, North Korea, governed by a highly autocratic regime in which internationalist economic interests are totally marginalized, has been unable to commit, credibly, to separate bilateral economic interactions from politics. The regime's attitude is such that even South Korean businesses, which might otherwise eye the North Korean market the way Taiwanese firms do the Mainland's, remain largely indifferent to trade and investment opportunities there.

More generally, despite the glimmer of hope offered by the Sunshine Policy, the barriers to a flourishing commercial relationship between the two Koreas may be even more substantial than those existing across the Taiwan Strait prior to the mid-1980s. In China, economic integration with Taiwan since the late 1970s has consistently been viewed as a positive thing for both economic and political reasons. Once China moved in the direction of reform, the economic benefits of Taiwanese trade and investment were obvious. But economic integration was also viewed in Beijing as something that would help to facilitate reunification over the long term because the security externalities of cross-Strait exchange are nearly uniformly positive for the PRC. In this environment, no short-term trade-off exists between the nationalist goal of reunification and the internationalist development strategy. In North Korea, by contrast, inter-Korean economic exchange entails significant negative security externalities. Even moving beyond the simple concerns about the implications of openness for regime stability, were Pyongyang to embrace inter-Korean economic integration the North would certainly be the more dependent partner by far: the South Korean economy is more developed, more diversified, and much larger. In this environment, more hard-line nationalist elements are likely to be far less tolerant of bilateral economic exchange than is the case in Beijing, where a plausible case can be made that cross-Strait economic ties advance the nationalist cause. While this discussion is speculative, it does suggest that a significant coalitional shake-up in Pyongyang is a prerequisite to a flourishing economic relationship on the Korean Peninsula.

6. Conclusions

This chapter has explored the broader applicability of the theoretical argument developed in Chapter 2, and the findings are generally quite encouraging. The quantitative analysis found that the effects of conflict on trade are conditioned on the level of trade barrier protection within the countries involved. This finding turned out to be robust across several different measures of conflict and trade barrier levels. Trade barriers, of course, represent an imperfect proxy for the political strength of internationalist economic interests, and as such it is necessary to proceed cautiously with this finding in drawing broad conclusions concerning the theory developed in Chapter 2. Yet trade barriers should in any event be reasonably well-correlated with the political strength of internationalist economic interests, and so the results of the quantitative analysis are encouraging. At a minimum, they suggest that further research into the broader generalizability of the core argument is warranted.

Meanwhile, the two case studies also generally confirm this study's core hypothesis. The cases offer a sharp contrast to the relationship across the Taiwan Strait. In the India–Pakistan case, internationalist economic interests have been relatively marginalized politically in both countries. In turn, during times of rising bilateral tensions, both countries have been willing to demonstrate resolve in ways detrimental to bilateral economic ties. Their willingness to signal in such ways makes it difficult to commit credibly to long-term economic projects: the proposed Iran–India natural gas pipeline offers a clear illustration along these lines. The Korean Peninsula case, in contrast, represents a mixed dyad: internationalist economic interests wielded growing political clout in the South but were completely marginalized in the North. In turn, while the South has encouraged increased bilateral economic ties, the North has resisted. Though this chapter's treatment of these cases has necessarily been much less detailed than the earlier treatment of the cross-Strait case, at a minimum (as with the large-N analysis) these cases can be viewed as promising plausibility probes into the theoretical argument's broader generalizability.

Of course, important qualifications are in order with the case studies as well. For example, though all three cases are characterized by serious conflict, the nature of the conflict varies to some extent. In both the Taiwan Strait and Korean Peninsula cases, at least one party is strongly committed to unification, which is not the case in India-Pakistan relations. A goal of national unification may increase the likelihood that a country (in these cases, the PRC and South Korea) would try to increase economic ties with the target state in order to achieve "influence" effects (Hirschman 1945; Abdelal and Kirshner 1999/2000). Moreover, the story told in the Korean Peninsula case is somewhat more complicated than that presented in the theoretical chapter. South Korea's embrace of bilateral economic interaction is not simply a consequence of an inability of political leaders to fend off demands from businesses that would benefit from such ties. Indeed, the autarkic and authoritarian North represents a sufficiently unappealing partner, despite its inexpensive labor and shared language and culture, that it has been the South Korean government trying to coax firms into greater engagement rather than the other way around. Nevertheless, while Kim Dae Jung's Sunshine Policy may have been conceived to achieve primarily political/security ends—as a means to transform the political relationship—it is hard to imagine such a policy being implemented in an environment significantly less internationalist than South Korea.

These qualifications aside, the evidence presented in this chapter remains strongly encouraging. The findings presented here suggest that the argument developed in Chapter 2 speaks to cases beyond PRC-Taiwan relations. On a more general level, that is, domestic political dynamics offer a fruitful path through which to explore variation in the relationship between conflict and commerce.

8

Conclusions

1. Overview

This study began with a simple question: why is it that the effects of international political conflict on economic interdependence appear to vary substantially across cases? Or, to put it differently, why is it that economic ties can flourish even in the presence of hostile political relations in some cases but not in others? The core hypothesis developed in Chapter 2 to explain this variation centered on the domestic political influence of internationalist economic interests: when these actors hold strong political clout, the marginal effects of political conflict should be reduced (hypothesis 2). The PRC-Taiwan case study, along with the secondary cases and quantitative tests presented in Chapter 7, were generally confirming of this hypothesis.

The general argument also shed considerable light on the relationship between Mainland China and Taiwan, which in some ways epitomizes the core puzzle. Cross-Strait economic ties continue to expand rapidly despite deep and persistent conflict over the issue of Taiwan's sovereign status. It is hard to make sense of this dichotomy, that is, economic ties in the presence of severe political conflict, without reference to the political strength of internationalist economic interests on both sides of the Taiwan Strait. In Taiwan, the political clout of business interests—which tend to be internationalist, especially with regard to cross-Strait relations—within the governing coalitions has been an important variable shaping the evolution of Taiwan's cross-Strait economic policies. Broadly speaking, the political influence of business grew as Taiwan democratized into the early 1990s; weakened somewhat as Lee Teng-hui consolidated power, especially after he won the 1996 presidential election in a landslide; grew again in the early part of Chen Shui-bian's presidency; and then waned to some extent as the DPP's electoral victory in the December 2001 legislative election left Chen in a less precarious political position (and when the formation of the TSU created more of a protectionist/nationalist counter-weight in the pan-green coalition). These shifts correlate reasonably well with changes in Taiwan's cross-Strait economic policies, though it was clear that many other factors also influenced those policies over time.

Meanwhile, Mainland China has been able to make a credible commitment to protect the interests of Taiwanese investors there, in part because the PRC has been governed by an increasingly internationalist coalition, which would view economic sanctions, or other signals of resolve that harm the bilateral economic relationship, as extremely costly. Indeed, Mainland China has generally been careful to signal resolve toward the island in a way that doesn't harm Taiwanese businesses. Of course, we saw that Beijing's signaling behavior also derives in part from a straightforward realist rationale: the PRC reaps positive security externali-ties from cross-Strait economic ties, meaning that even Mainland nationalists who care most about the Taiwan issue have good reason to promote the expansion of cross-Strait economic ties. The case of "green" (or pro-DPP) Taiwanese businesses suggests that both factors—the presence of an internationalist governing coali-tion and the presence of positive political externalities deriving from cross-Strait exchange—have been important determinants of Beijing's signaling behavior toward Taiwan. These businesses have been the targets of Mainland harassment in part because they do not generate the same sorts of positive political externalities that other Taiwanese businesses do; at the same time, the extent of that harassment appears to be limited (at least to date).

Nonetheless, a number of important caveats are in order. Throughout the empirical analysis it was apparent that numerous other factors also intervene in the relationship between international political conflict and economic inter-dependence. It became clear in Chapter 4, for example, that the *nature* of eco-nomic exchange acts as an important intervening variable. Taiwanese officials became more alarmed about the political implications of cross-Strait economic ties when Taiwan's larger companies became interested in large-scale projects on the Mainland. These investments entailed a higher level of relationship specific-ity—once completed , they could not easily be moved to other locations—than previous Taiwanese investments, meaning that their value hinged in large measure on continued stability in the cross-Strait economic environment. Higher levels of relationship specificity, in turn, potentially entailed more significant negative security externalities for Taiwan (for example, it gave businesses a deeper stake in stable cross-Strait relations and perhaps made them more susceptible to PRC influence). Further exploring these sorts of dynamics—for example, investigating how the structure of bilateral economic ties influences conflict's effects on commerce—might serve as a fruitful avenue for future research.

As I emphasized earlier, it is also important to be cautious in drawing broad generalizations based on the cross-Strait case. Though the relationship exhibits some attributes of a "crucial case," it also has several relatively unique attributes that could influence the relationship between conflict and commerce. For example, it may be that the relationship between conflict and commerce in cases where one or both parties seek reunification is different from the relationship in other dyads.[1] In the cross-Strait case, if the PRC is to achieve its goal of peaceful unification with Taiwan, it ultimately needs political allies on the island; Taiwanese businesses with a strong stake in the Mainland market are perhaps the most likely candidates in this regard.[2] PRC officials might therefore view the political externalities associated with Taiwanese investment as being more strongly positive than they would if unification with the island were not their ultimate goal.

A separate qualification concerns the measurement of key variables used in this study. Measuring two variables in particular, namely, the severity of international political conflict and the domestic political strength of internationalist economic interests, is clearly a difficult undertaking. While it is hard to dispute that conflict is high in the Mainland China–Taiwan relationship, operationalizing conflict over a wide range of countries over time is less straightforward. Assessing the political clout of internationalist economic interests within Taiwan and China also proved difficult, and for the quantitative analyses it was necessary to use a proxy based on the assumption that such interests are strong in countries with low barriers to trade and weak in countries with high barriers to trade. Still, that the quantitative results appeared to be reasonably robust to a range of different measures of trade barrier protection and conflict (including the core findings based on UN voting patterns) is encouraging.

While most of this study has examined when and how conflict affects patterns of commerce between countries, Chapter 6 considered at some length the reverse relationship: whether economic ties, once established in conflictual dyads, can help to reduce the likelihood of military conflict. Based on existing studies, I identified three distinct causal mechanisms through which economic integration could reduce the likelihood of military conflict: economic ties can act as a constraint; they can be a source of information; or they can help spark a transformation of state goals. I examined these different causal processes in the context of cross-Strait relations with two goals in mind. First, I wished to consider whether one or more of these processes are currently operating across the Taiwan Strait. If so, then we might be more confident that growing cross-Strait economic linkages will help to facilitate peace between Mainland China and Taiwan. Second, I asked whether the cross-Strait experience has any broader implications concerning these different causal mechanisms.

While I could not find clear evidence that any of the three causal processes is in fact operating in the Taiwan Strait case, I also found little conclusive evidence that they are not operating. Indeed, there is reason to believe that some of these processes, in particular transformative effects in Taiwan, could appear in the future. In short, my analysis suggests that growing economic linkages across the Taiwan Strait could help to reduce the danger of a cross-Strait war, which would be an unmitigated disaster for all concerned parties: Taiwan, China, and probably the United States as well. But my analysis also suggests that excessive optimism on this score would probably be misplaced. Before we can be certain that growing cross-Strait economic linkages do have a pacific effect, it is crucial that we have a clear understanding of the precise causal mechanism linking those economic ties to peace, and clear evidence that such a mechanism is in fact operating across the Taiwan Strait.

2. Possible Directions for Future Research

This study has shown the utility of incorporating domestic politics more fully into models linking international political conflict to levels of economic interdependence. Throughout, I have focused on one variable in particular: the extent to which leaders are politically accountable to internationalist economic interests. Though I believe that this study represents an important step forward, future inquiry along these lines is likely to prove fruitful.

For example, I have highlighted the tension that can develop when leaders try to pursue foreign policy goals that might conflict with internationalist economic interests, which are likely to be interested less in those goals than in making money . Taiwan is an excellent example in this regard: while Taiwan's presidents have worried about the security externalities associated with cross-Strait trade and investment, Taiwan's business community has been focused instead on gaining access to the Mainland market. In this case, leaders have faced a clear tradeoff between angering an important domestic constituency and pursuing their preferred foreign policy goals.

This way of looking at the case of Taiwan, though clearly a simplification, proved useful, as Taiwan's economic policies toward the Mainland have appeared to be partly contingent on the president's relationship with the business community. But whether trading with an adversary helps or hinders a state's foreign policy objectives is not always obvious. Indeed, Ma Ying-jeou clearly has a very different view of the political consequences of cross-Strait commerce than did his predecessors. More generally, trade, as we saw in Chapter 2, can have contrasting effects. For example, it might make an adversary richer and more militarily powerful (a negative externality) while at the same time making that adversary more dependent and susceptible to the home state's influence (a positive security externality). In such cases, ascertaining whether the security effects of trade are on balance positive or negative can be a difficult and controversial undertaking. In South Korea, the Sunshine Policy is contentious in part for this reason: while the policy's supporters believe that economic integration between the two Koreas will over the long term have net security benefits for the South, its detractors suggest that the policy is making the North stronger and more of a threat than it otherwise would be.

A similar sort of debate emerged in the United States during the 1990s concerning trade with China. Of course, economic effects alone are enough to make trade with China a contentious issue in the United States. For example, members of Congress representing constituencies likely to be harmed by trade with China (such as districts with a high percentage of blue-collar labor) were more likely than other members to vote against granting China permanent normal trading status in 1999 (Xie 2006). Moreover, these sorts of economic considerations undoubtedly spill over into debates concerning the security implications of U.S. trade with China. But clearly such debates are not simply a reflection of competing economic interests. Rather, policymakers and scholars have sincere differences of opinion concerning those implications.[3] A better understanding of the sources of these differences represents a potentially fruitful subject of inquiry, one likely to yield further insight into the domestic politics of trading with an adversary.

For example, in both the U.S. case (with regard to China) and the South Korean case (with regard to North Korea) one contentious issue concerns the likely long-term consequences of increased economic ties. Is economic engagement likely to yield a transformed target state, one that is less hostile and more constrained by a web of economic ties? Or might trade simply make the target state wealthier and perhaps more threatening as a result? Is it possible to generalize on the conditions likely to lead to one conclusion or the other? Likewise, both cases potentially include an important temporal dimension. It may be, for example, that the short-term security externalities of the Sunshine Policy are largely negative for South Korea (the policy makes the North stronger, potentially), but the longer-term benefits are positive (the policy could yield a transformed North Korean state). If so, then how various South Korean decision makers view the security consequences of trading with the North is likely to be contingent on the extent to which they discount the future.

In summary, I have argued in this study that a focus on domestic political variables can be a fruitful way of delving deeper into the relationship between international political conflict and economic interdependence, and I have shown that attention to one variable in particular, that is, leadership accountability to internationalist economic interests, can be especially useful in this regard. But the argument implicitly assumes that leaders can sort out in a relatively straightforward way whether trade with an adversary carries net positive or net negative security externalities. Relaxing this assumption to recognize that trade's security effects are not always obvious, and may in fact vary substantially over time, may open the door to future productive research into the relationship between conflict and commercial integration.

3. Looking to the Future

As I write this conclusion, Taiwan has just completed a new round of elections. Voters dealt the DPP an overwhelming defeat. The KMT and its allies command a three-fourths majority in the new legislature, and Ma Ying-jeou easily defeated DPP candidate Frank Hsieh in the March 2008 presidential election. The elections appear certain to usher in further changes in Taiwan's political and economic policies toward the Mainland. Throughout the campaign Ma clearly advocated a more stable cross-Strait political environment and further liberalization in Taipei's cross-Strait economic policies. His vice president, Vincent Siew, has for years promoted a common market across the Taiwan Strait, a concept vilified, to no avail, as a "one China market" by Frank Hsieh during the campaign. Once in office Ma moved quickly. His willingness to embrace the 1992 consensus facilitated the restarting of the long-frozen dialogue between SEF and ARATS. At the initial meeting held in June 2008, the two sides agreed to establish direct charter flights on weekends, and to open Taiwan to greater numbers of Mainland tourists (Romberg 2008, 10). The two sides agreed to increase the number of direct flights and to open up direct shipping links when ARATS chairman Chen Yunlin visited Taiwan in November 2008.

The new legislature that emerged in 2008, meanwhile, was elected under new rules. The multimember district, single nontransferable vote system, which encouraged party factionalization and enabled relatively extreme candidates to win office with low vote totals, was replaced by a single-member district, two-vote system (in which voters select a candidate and a party, and a portion of the seats in the legislature is then allocated proportionally based on the party votes). The new system (which also cut the size of the legislature in half) is likely to make it more difficult for extreme parties and candidates to win election to the legislature. Should the new electoral system in fact yield more centrist political parties over time, then any future presidents representing the DPP are likely to feel less constrained by hardliners on the sovereignty issue should they pursue more liberal cross-Strait economic policies.

Of course, the future of the cross-Strait relationship remains uncertain. The sovereignty issue in particular is likely to remain highly salient. In his inaugural address, for example, Ma stressed the importance he places on Taiwan's international space: "Only if Taiwan is not isolated in the international community can cross-Strait relations move forward."[4] It is unclear, however, whether PRC officials will be at all accommodating on this issue. And Beijing continues to develop its capacity to punish Taiwan militarily. Recent estimates suggest that the number of Chinese missiles now directed at the island exceeds one thousand, and the overall balance of military power across the Taiwan Strait has been shifting sharply in the PRC's favor. If these trends continue, PRC officials may in the future be tempted to use more coercive mechanisms to achieve unification.[5]

In sum, the apparent paradox of rapidly expanding cross-Strait economic linkages against a backdrop of deeply hostile political relations remains. Yet though the decades-old political conflict remains untransformed, continued growth in bilateral economic flows opens the possibility of a future shift toward a more peaceful equilibrium. Economic ties have grown extremely rapidly even though the past two Taiwanese presidents have tried, though often gingerly, to apply the brakes. As such, economic integration could accelerate if current president Ma Ying-jeou and future Taiwanese presidents prove less willing to stand in the way. If such a scenario unfolds, then the processes described in Chapter 6 are also likely to become more salient. A virtuous cycle could develop in which growing economic ties help strengthen pro-stability and pro-trade domestic coalitions on both sides of the Strait, which in turn would promote even deeper economic integration. Though such a scenario is far from inevitable, it nonetheless remains a viable possibility.

Appendixes

Appendix A

A Simple Model of Cross-Strait Bargaining and the Constraining Impact of Economic Interdependence

Assume Taiwan and China are both utility maximizers bargaining over Taiwan's sovereign status; Taiwan's ideal outcome is independence, and China's ideal outcome is unification. Assume further that Taiwan's sovereign status is continuous and zero-sum: if Taiwan's status shifts toward independence, then the increase in Taiwan's utility is equivalent to the decrease in China's utility. In bargaining with Mainland China, Taiwan chooses a level of sovereign status ranging from reunification to formal independence; Beijing, in turn, can either accept that decision or fight a war to try to attain something better.[1] Assume that both sides know, ex ante, the outcome in fighting a war and the costs both sides would pay in fighting.

For a graphical representation, consider Figure A1. China's payoffs are depicted on the vertical axis and Taiwan's on the horizontal axis. China receives higher payoffs when Taiwan moves closer to unification and lower payoffs as Taiwan moves in the direction of independence; for Taiwan, the payoffs are reversed. Each side's utility for different levels of sovereign status for Taiwan, ranging from reunification to independence, is represented by the downward-sloping diagonal line.

Suppose that if the two sides were to fight a war Taiwan's status at the conclusion of the war would be defined by point A. Taiwan's utility associated with outcome A is AT, and China's utility is AC. Because war is costly, if the two sides fight a war that results in A, their actual utilities associated with that outcome are tempered by the costs they bear in fighting. After those costs are factored in, Taiwan's actual utility for fighting is U, while China's is BC. China' reversion point—the point at which it is indifferent between accepting the bargain proposed by Taiwan

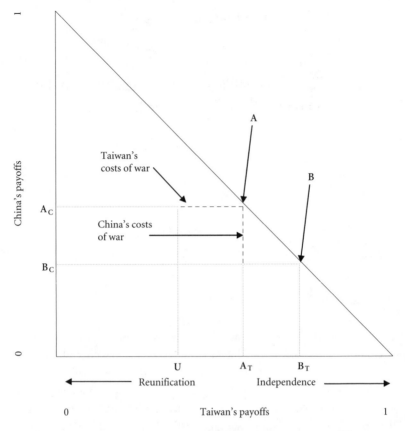

FIG. A1. A simple model of cross-Strait relations. Figures A1 and A2 originally appeared in Kastner (2006a) in Hua, *Reflections on the Triangular Relations of Beijing-Taipei-Washington Since 1995* (New York: Palgrave Macmillan). Reproduced with permission of Palgrave Macmillan.

and fighting a war—thus lies at B. China prefers to fight a war if Taiwan chooses a level of sovereignty to the right of B, but accepts any level chosen to the left of B. Taiwan thus chooses a level of sovereign status just to the left of B: this provides it with the maximum amount of sovereignty that does not provoke a war with Beijing.

How does increasing economic integration affect this equilibrium? Consider Figure A2. Increased economic ties cause the costs of war to increase for both sides. Once the added costs are factored in, Taiwan now favors all bargains to the right of U' over fighting a war with Beijing. However, this shift left in Taiwan's indifference point is not critical because Taiwan effectively sets the status quo. More importantly, Beijing is now willing to accept all bargains to the left of C

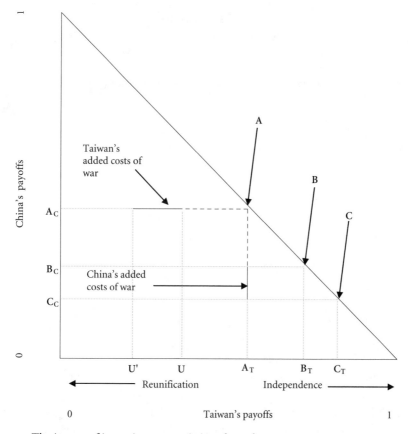

FIG. A2. The impact of increasing economic interdependence.

rather than fight a war with Taiwan. As such, Taiwan can now move all the way to
a point marginally to the left of C on the reunification-independence continuum,
meaning that China's increased costs of war give Taiwan more freedom to move in
the direction of independence than it held prior to cross-Strait economic integration.[2] Notice that this result holds even if Taiwan's costs of war increase more than
Mainland China's do.

Appendix B

Further Details on Quantitative Tests
and Robustness Checks

Sample

The sample of countries used in the analyses is included in Table B1.

Details on Key Explanatory Variables Used

Dissimilarity of voting patterns in the UN: I used Signorino and Ritter's (1999) S measure applied to UN votes, which comes from Gartzke and others' (1999) data. I used the log of Gartzke and others' measure, which I first rescaled so that it ranges from 1 (most similar voting patterns) to 3 (most dissimilar); that is, I multiplied their variable by (-1) and then added 2. Rescaling in this way, so that higher numbers represent more conflict and so that the measure does not span 0, makes it easier to interpret the interactive variable.

Trade barriers: The measure comes from Hiscox and Kastner (2002), who estimated the following equation: $\ln (M_{ijt} / Y_{it}) = a_{it} + \beta_1 \ln Y_{jt} - \beta_2 \ln D_{ij} + e_{ijt}$, where a_{it} is the importing country-year intercept for country i in year t, M_{ijt} represents total trade flow into country i from country j in year t, Y_{it} and Y_{jt} denote national incomes for i and j in year t, D_{ij} is the distance between the major airports of the two countries, β_1 and β_2 are positive parameters, and e_{ijt} is an error term. The a_{it} are taken as proxies for country/time-specific trade policy distortions and are restated as percentage deviations from the most open country in the sample. Here, I averaged across the two countries in each dyad.

Robustness Tests

I estimated the models reported in Table 1 (ch. 7) using several alternative measures of conflict and trade barrier levels.

TABLE B1

Sample of Countries Used in Quantitative Analysis

Argentina	Denmark	Iran	Peru
Australia	Dominican Rep.	Ireland	Philippines
Austria	Ecuador	Israel	Portugal
Belgium	Egypt	Italy	Saudi Arabia
Benin	El Salvador	Japan	Senegal
Bolivia	Ethiopia	Jordan	Somalia
Brazil	Finland	Korea, Rep.	South Africa
Burkina Faso	France	Madagascar	Spain
Cameroon	Gabon	Mali	Sri Lanka
Canada	Germany	Mauritania	Sweden
Cen. African Rep.	Ghana	Mexico	Switzerland
Chad	Greece	Morocco	Thailand
Chile	Guatemala	Netherlands	Togo
China	Guinea	New Zealand	Tunisia
Colombia	Haiti	Nicaragua	Turkey
Congo, Dem. Rep.	Honduras	Nigeria	United Kingdom
Congo, Rep.	Iceland	Norway	United States
Costa Rica	India	Pakistan	Uruguay
Cote d'Ivoire	Indonesia	Paraguay	Venezuela

Alternative measures of conflict include:

Alliance dissimilarity: The extent to which i and j have dissimilar alliance portfolios in time t, again lagged one year. The use of this measure, which comes from Tucker (1999), implies a similar assumption: states with alliance commitments that have relatively little overlap have conflicting interests.[1] Again, because I used interactive variables, I used the log of a rescaled version of Tucker's variable that ranges from 1 (most similar) to 3 (most dissimilar).[2]

Copdab: A measure based on event data found in the Conflict and Peace Data Bank (COPDAB).[3] This dataset codes specific events between countries according to the level of cooperation and conflict suggested by each particular event. I first collapsed these data into a 15-point scale, such that 1 represents extremely high cooperation, 8 is neutral, and 15 represents extremely high conflict, and then took the average across all events for each dyad-year. If no events were coded in a given year, I coded the dyad-year as 8, for neutral relations. Instead of treating this scaled value as a continuous variable, I converted it into a dummy, which equals 1 if the scale averages to greater than 8 for a dyad-year, and which equals 0 if otherwise. The variable is lagged one year.[4]

Rivalry: A measure that attempts to capture whether the relationship between countries i and j is a rivalry, based on data presented in Thompson (2001). Thompson identifies pairs of countries that can be thought of as "strategic" rivals, countries that have a heated relationship with seriously conflicting interests—though not a relationship that *necessarily* becomes militarized. He compares his measure with three other classifications of rivalry that are based on the repeated occurrence of militarized disputes: Diehl and Goertz's (2000) enduring rivalries and two versions of Bennett's interstate rivalries.[5] My measure is coded 1 if any of these four measures codes a relationship as being a rivalry, and 0 otherwise; like the other measures of conflict that I used, it is lagged one year.

Alternative measures of trade barrier levels include:

Sachs Warner: A dummy variable based on a dichotomous measure of trade policy openness developed by Sachs and Warner.[6] The authors code a country as closed to trade if one of five conditions holds: nontariff barriers cover at least 40 percent of trade; average tariffs rates are at least 40 percent; a black market exchange rate is 20 percent or more depreciated relative to the official exchange rate; a socialist economic system is in place; or the state holds a monopoly on major exports (Sachs and Warner 1995, 22). My variable is coded 0 if countries i and j are both open to trade in year t, 1 if one is open and the other is closed, and 2 if both are closed.

Duties: The logged average value, for countries i and j in time t, of import duties as a percentage of the total value of imports.[7] Data for this measure come from the World Bank (2001), and are considerably more limited than the other two measures.

In the analyses presented above, I used the average level of the Hiscox/Kastner measure in each dyad; in robustness tests I also estimated models including instead the maximum or the minimum value of this measure within each dyad.

I first re-estimated the model reported in the first column of Table 1 (ch. 7), substituting in the alternative measures of conflict. As was the case with the UN voting-based measure, each of the other measures was negatively and significantly correlated with bilateral trade flows. These regressions, in other words, further confirm hypothesis 1.

Next, I re-estimated the model reported in the second column of Table 1, substituting in different combinations of the alternative conflict measures and trade barrier measures. All together, this meant estimating a total of twenty models (across the four measures of conflict and five measures of trade barriers). Again, hypothesis 2 yields the expectation that the estimated coefficient on the interactive variable in each of these models will be negative and significant. Table B2 summarizes the sign and significance of the interactive variable's coefficient across the different models. The coefficient on the interactive variable was in the expected direction (negative) in eighteen of the twenty models. In fourteen of the eighteen cases where the effect was in the hypothesized direction, moreover, the significance level exceeded 99 percent. In sum, the interactive effect between

TABLE B2

Robustness Tests, Sign (positive or negative) of the Interactive Variable's Estimated Coefficient

| Conflict measure ⟶ | | | | |
Trade barriers measure ↓	UN dissimilarity	Alliance dissimilarity	Copdab	Rivalry
Average Hiscox/Kastner	−*	−*	−*	−‡
Minimum Hiscox/Kastner	−*	−*	−*	−
Maximum Hiscox/Kastner	−*	−*	−*	−‡
Sachs/Warner	−*	−*	−*	+
Duties	−	−*	−*	+

* $p < .01$; ‡ $p < .15$.

conflict and trade barriers appears to be reasonably robust to alternative measures of conflict and trade barrier protection.

Finally, I re-estimated the model reported in the second column of Table 1 using dyadic fixed effects (Green et al. 2001). Doing so controls for unobserved factors that might influence trade within particular dyads (perhaps, for example, two countries are separated by a mountain range that impedes trade and leads to lower levels than might otherwise be expected). This remedy is not without controversy: Beck and Katz (2001, 492), for example, liken it to "curing a cold with chemotherapy." This is especially the case, they argue, when some independent variables do not vary much from year to year within particular dyads, meaning they will be highly collinear with the fixed effects. Not surprisingly, the magnitude and significance of the interactive coefficient both decline when dyadic fixed effects are added. But the coefficient does continue to be negative and significant at the 95 percent level of confidence.

Notes

Chapter 1

1. For a good discussion of the security consequences of U.S. trade with China, and practical recommendations, see Segal (2004).

2. See, for example, Keshk et al. (2004); Pollins (1989a); Pollins (1989b); Simmons (2005); Li and Sacko (2002).

3. For an excellent summary of the debate and a recent collection of essays on the topic, see Mansfield and Pollins (2003).

4. Kim and Rousseau (2005) find similar results in a sample limited to pairs of countries with disputes that could potentially become militarized. However, Kim (1998), in a sample limited to politically relevant dyads—those comprising either contiguous states or at least one great power—finds the effects of conflict on trade to be much weaker than the effects of trade on conflict.

5. Studies finding that alliances lead to increased trade typically find the effect to be conditioned on some other factor, such as systemic bipolarity (Gowa 1994), whether the alliance involves a formal defense commitment (Long 2003b), and the extent to which trade involves increasing returns to scale goods (Gowa and Mansfield 2004). The effect of alliances on trade does not appear to be universal: recent studies by Keshk et al. (2004) and Oneal et al. (2003), for example, do not confirm a trade-enhancing effect.

6. Levy and Barbieri (2004) and Li and Sacko (2002) represent notable exceptions, though the focus of both of those studies is on military conflict or war rather than on the broader conception of conflict I employ in the present project (see the next section for my precise definition). A growing number of studies has also examined variation in the impact of trade on military conflict. Such studies, for example, have found the effect to be magnified in the presence of democracies (Gelpi and Grieco 2003) or in the presence of preferential trading blocs (Mansfield and Pevehouse 2000).

Chapter 2

1. Morrow (1999). Li and Sacko (2002) find evidence that the possibility of future military conflict affects current levels of trade.

2. This is a general problem for states considering unilateral sanctions. For an interesting (and critical) discussion, see Drezner (2000, 215).

3. On "coercive cooperation," see Martin (1992).

4. A separate but related causal mechanism is identified by Gowa (1994), who observes that countries possessing large internal markets can benefit—at the expense of trading partners—by levying an optimal tariff. Gowa argues that because allies are less likely to fight each other, they can more easily agree to maintain open trade policies because the risks of "defection" are lower.

5. This point is made by Liberman (1996), who argues that relative gains concerns will be more salient among great powers in bipolar systems and less salient in multipolar systems. See also Snidal (1991), who shows that relative gains concerns have a decreasing impact on cooperation as the number of players increases. For a collection of essays that address the "relative gains" debate, see Baldwin (1993).

6. On the problem of "obsolescing bargains" in foreign direct investment, see Vernon (1971, 46–53) and Jensen (2006, 80).

7. Similarly, Gowa and Mansfield (2004, 780) note that individual firms often make "irreversible investments" when choosing to enter a particular export market, such as developing an understanding of the market's legal system. McLaren (1997) shows formally that, given asset immobility across sectors, small countries sometimes prefer autarky to free trade with large countries because free trade will cause domestic investments to shift heavily to the export sector. Once these shifts are made, a cutoff in trade would be ruinous for the small country but not for the large country, which continues to have diversified production. The small country is thus in a weakened bargaining position, which makes it vulnerable to opportunism that could make it worse off than had it never agreed to free trade.

8. Of course, for the larger country, the political externalities of trade are in this instance positive, meaning that it might try to encourage more economic integration with the smaller state (Hirschman 1945).

9. Shirk (1993; 1994) argues that this sort of dynamic in part drove Deng Xiaoping's liberalizing reforms in China.

10. Models of crisis bargaining frequently center on the problem of imperfect information and the difficulty of estimating the resolve of an opponent. In these models, states are typically given the opportunity to send costly signals in order to communicate more effectively their true level of resolve. See, for example, Morrow (1989; 1999); Fearon (1994); Powell (1989); Gartzke (2003); Gartzke et al. (2001); Schelling (1966); Jervis (1970); Schultz (2001).

11. On sanctions as signals, see Baldwin (1985). Both India and Pakistan sometimes close their shared border when relations become tense, as discussed in Chapter 7.

12. For arguments along these lines, see Li and Sacko (2002); Morrow (1999).

13. "In Wake of Strained Sino-U.S. Ties, China Looks to Airbus Instead of Boeing," *China Online News*, May 8, 2001. In LexisNexis.

14. Consider Brazil's decision to start fingerprinting and photographing Americans entering the country in retaliation for similar U.S. policies. See "For Visitors, Fingerprints and Photos," *New York Times*, February 22, 2004: http://query.nytimes.com/gst/fullpage.ht ml?sec=travel&res=9801E2D7173DF931A15751C0A9629C8B63 (accessed June 16, 2008).

15. Though as Solingen (1998, 23) notes, factors like diversification of firm activities

and uncertainty about the likely effects of liberalization mean that identifying preferences over liberalizing reform can be quite complicated.

16. For example, it is significantly more costly for B to obtain those high technology products from elsewhere, and economic losses to A don't exceed any security-related gains associated with not selling to B.

17. Obviously, if states hold military exercises, it may cause commercial actors to flee, but this is because they fear escalation to war, not the exercises per se.

18. On democracy and trade, see also Milner and Kubota (2005).

19. On the impact of different democratic political institutions on trade policy openness, see also Ehrlich (2007).

20. On "liberalization from above," see Solingen (1998, 24).

21. For an analysis that lumps leadership accountability to internationalist economic interests and leadership commitment to an internationally oriented development strategy into a single, broader category, see Papayoanou and Kastner (1999/2000).

Chapter 3

1. Romberg (2003, 14). The two major powers, of course, are China and the United States.

2. The quotations come from Chu (1997).

3. The slogan "liberate Taiwan" dated to the first half of 1949, as it became apparent that the island might become the KMT's last fall-back position. The *Taiwan Wenti Duben* (Reader on the Taiwan Question), a collection of documents relating to Beijing's Taiwan policies compiled by the CCP Central Party School and the Taiwan Affairs Office, dates the slogan to a March 15, 1949, *Xinhua* editorial entitled "Zhongguo Renmin Yidingyao Jiefang Taiwan" (The Chinese People Must Liberate Taiwan) (*Taiwan Wenti Duben*, 39).

4. On the U.S. decision to put the Seventh Fleet in the Taiwan Strait, see Christensen (1996, 133–37). The two most serious crises of the Taiwan Strait during this time period occurred in 1954–55 and in 1958. For a discussion of the 1954–55 Taiwan Strait crisis, see, for example, Benson and Niou (2000). On the 1958 crisis, see Christensen (1996, ch. 6).

5. In a May 1955 speech, Premier Zhou Enlai announced: "The Chinese people can liberate Taiwan via two potential methods: by war or through peaceful means. To the extent possible, the Chinese people are willing to strive to use peaceful means to liberate Taiwan" (*Taiwan Wenti Duben*, 42).

6. For a summary of the key points of both the Message to Taiwan Compatriots and Ye's Nine Points Proposal, see *Taiwan Wenti Duben*, 50–51.

7. Deng Xiaoping first used the "one country, two systems" (*yige guojia, liangzhong zhidu*, usually shortened to *yiguo liangzhi*) slogan in 1982 (*Taiwan Wenti Duben*, 51). Article 31 of the PRC Constitution reads: "The state may establish special administrative regions when necessary. The systems to be instituted in special administrative regions shall be prescribed by law enacted by the National People's Congress in light of the specific conditions." Full text of the constitution can be found in Lieberthal (1995, appendix 1).

8. On ROC skepticism of "one country, two systems," see Chiu (1983).

9. The guidelines are available on the Mainland Affairs Council webpage: http://www.mac.gov.tw/english/english/macpolicy/gnueng.htm (accessed June 16, 2008).

10. As Roy (2003, 185) notes, these actions also weakened the ROC's claim to be the legitimate government of all of China.

11. Goldstein (1999) provides a comprehensive discussion of the events and politics leading up to this meeting and the meeting itself.

12. On Taiwan's democratic development prior to 1996, see Tien (1996).

13. Copper (1996, 12). Note that the figure 85 percent includes both Fujianese and Hakkas.

14. See Roy (2003, 192). The full text of the plank can be found in *Minzhu Jinbu Dang Liang'an Zhengce Zhongyao Wenjian Huibian* (n.d.).

15. On Lee's trip, see, for example, *Free China Review*, May 1994, 30–37.

16. The full text of Jiang's speech is available in Chinese at: http://www.people.com. cn/GB/channel1/14/20000522/72538.html (accessed June 16, 2008).

17. See Sheng (2001); Swaine (2001, 320–21); Ross (2000). I discuss Chinese signaling behavior in this and other episodes in more detail in Chapter 5.

18. Again, I discuss this episode in more detail in chapter 5.

19. Furthermore, unlike the two Germanys and the two Koreas, the size differential between the PRC and Taiwan is vast, further undermining the applicability of those other two models to the Taiwan case from Beijing's perspective. See Chen (1999, 140–41).

20. "Taiwan's President Maintains Hard Line; Chen Rebukes China in Interview," *Washington Post*, March 30, 2004. In LexisNexis.

21. The alliance is referred to as the "pan-green" alliance because the DPP flag is green. A similar alliance between the KMT and the People First Party (PFP) is called the "pan-blue" alliance because the KMT's flag is predominately blue.

22. My own interviews with Mainland Chinese analysts in the summer of 2004 confirmed this general sense of pessimism regarding cross-Strait relations.

23. For the text of the announcement, see "Youguan 'Guojia Tongyi Weiyuanhui' Zhongzhi Yunzuo ji 'Guojia Tongyi Gangling' Zhongzhi Shiyong Zhengce Shuotie" (Notice Concerning the Policy of Terminating the "National Unification Council" and the "National Unification Guidelines"), March 1, 2006. Posted on the Mainland Affairs Council webpage: www.mac.gov.tw.

24. See, for example, "Senior US Official Warns Taiwan Again Not to Hold UN Referendum," *Deutsche Presse-Agentur,* December 6, 2007. In LexisNexis.

25. To be valid, 50 percent of eligible voters must participate in a referendum.

26. The consensus, supposedly reached in 1992 in negotiations in Hong Kong leading up to the Koo-Wang meeting, holds that both sides agree that there is one China but have differing interpretations regarding what "one China" means. Chen Shui-bian's government denied that such a consensus was ever reached. For a discussion, see Lee (2003, 138–39).

27. See, for example, Romberg's (2008) analysis of recent cross-Strait political trends.

28. As Chu notes, these figures understate the actual number of investments since many firms do not use official channels.

29. Taylor (1999); Chu (1997); *Far Eastern Economic Review* (hereafter *FEER*), March 25, 1999, 10–15.

30. The average amount for investment projects approved by the Taiwanese government grew from US$730,000 in 1991 to US$2.2 million in 1995 and US$2.6 million in 1999. See *Liang'an Jingji Tongji Yuebao*, issue 152. By 1996, moreover, it was not uncommon to find individual Taiwanese investments exceeding US$60 million or US$70 million, while some even exceeded US$100 million. See *Jingji Ribao*, August 3, 1996, 4.

31. These statistics come from various issues of *Liang'an Jingji Tongji Yuebao*.

32. Ibid.

33. "Taiwan Government: China Became Largest Trading Partner in 2003," Dow Jones, March 11, 2004. In Taiwan Security Research (hereafter TSR): http://taiwansecurity.org/.

34. For the official figures, see *Liang'an Jingji Tongji Yuebao*. The US$100 billion figure is a common estimate. See, for example, "Taiwan to Screen China Funding," *International Herald Tribune*, March 29, 2006: http://www.iht.com/articles/2006/03/29/bloomberg/sxreview. php (accessed June 17, 2008).

Chapter 4

1. As will become apparent, there has at times been substantial disconnect between Taiwan's policies and actual trends in cross-Strait exchange, as firms often dodge policy restrictions in place. This does beg an important question, however: why has the government not done more to crack down on efforts by firms to evade these restrictions?

2. I interviewed eleven scholars and observers of the Taiwanese political scene, as well as eleven (current and former) government and party officials (from the DPP, PFP, KMT, and New Party) while in Taiwan from fall 2000 to spring 2001. Additional data were collected in several subsequent, shorter trips to the island.

3. Roy (2004) offers a good summary of perceived security-related risks on the Taiwanese side, though he concludes that these risks are probably overstated. For an official government report that considers security concerns, see Executive Yuan (2003).

4. Statistics from various issues of *Liang'an Jingji Tongji Yuebao*. Note that statistics on Taiwanese-contracted FDI (foreign direct investment) as a percentage of total PRC-contracted inward FDI are based on data reported first in the PRC.

5. The former chair of Taiwan's Council for Economic Planning and Development, Ping-kun Chiang, noted in 1996, for example, that too much dependence on the Mainland market made Taiwan "vulnerable to destabilization from Beijing." *FEER*, November 7, 1996, 90. On Taiwanese vulnerability to sanctioning threats, see especially Leng (1998b) and Chen and Chu (2001). Some Chinese analysts are quite frank in pointing to comprehensive trade sanctions as a way to pressure Taiwan (a point discussed in more detail in Chapter 6). Hu Angang, director of the Center for China Studies at Tsinghua University, for example, has suggested that a weeklong trade embargo against Taiwan would cripple the island's economy and force it into concessions. See "Leading China Economist Says Trade War Can Break Taiwan," *China Post*, March 9, 2006: http://www.chinapost.com. tw/asia/2006/03/09/78294/Leading-China.htm (accessed June 17, 2008).

6. For example, Huang Tianlin, an advisor in the Chen Shui-bian administration, suggests that growing economic exchange will muddle Taiwanese consciousness of the enemy, thus fostering eventual reunification. See Huang (2003, 297).

7. *International Herald Tribune*, June 28, 2001, 1.

8. *China News*, November 20, 1996, 7.

9. Tse-Kang Leng (1998b) presents business pressures emanating from cross-Strait integration as analytically distinct from the threat of Mainland sanctions. On the one hand, integration may give the Mainland the opportunity to threaten sanctions against Taiwan if certain political concessions are not forthcoming. On the other hand, businesses engaged in cross-Strait commerce have independent incentives to lobby Taiwanese policymakers to pursue policies consistent with stable cross-Strait economic and political relations. The security concerns highlighted by these interviewees, however, suggest a hybrid of Leng's

two categories. Lam (2001; 2002) argues that Mainland China has encouraged cross-Strait economic integration in part because Beijing officials view Taiwanese businesses as part of a united front against the current Chen administration. For a recent editorial that emphasizes the danger of growing Chinese influence in Taiwanese politics as Taiwan's economic dependence on the Mainland increases, see "Xiaoxin Zhongguo Zhizao Taiwan Neibu Yali Yingxiang Xuanju" (Beware of China Creating Internal Pressures in Taiwan to Influence the Election), *Ziyou Shibao*, December 4, 2007: http://www.libertytimes.com.tw/2007/new/dec/4/today-s1.htm (accessed June 17, 2008).

10. Author's interviews, Taiwan. See also concerns attributed to Ping-kun Chiang in *FEER*, November 7, 1996, 90.

11. "Taiwan Confirms New Rules on China Investments," *Business Times*, May 29, 1997 (in LexisNexis); "Taiwan Bans Investment in Mainland China Infrastructure," *Taiwan Central News Agency*, July 5, 1997. In *Foreign Broadcast Information Service-China* (hereafter *FBIS-China*), July 8, 1997.

12. *International Herald Tribune*, December 28–29, 1996, 1. My list of Taiwanese security concerns is not exhaustive. For example, some officials have expressed concern that direct flights across the Taiwan Strait could make Taiwan vulnerable to "Trojan horse" attacks, in which commercial flights are filled with PLA troops or accompanied by fighter jets. Former vice president Annette Lu has pointed to this possibility (Chao 2004, 702). Former KMT head Lien Chan has argued that the problem could be minimized if flights were restricted to a specific corridor, like that connecting West Berlin to West Germany during the Cold War. See "Academics Shed Light on Lien's Air Lift Plan," *Taipei Times*, September 9, 2003: http://www.taipeitimes.com/News/taiwan/archives/2003/09/09/2003067115 (accessed June 17, 2008). A separate concern is raised by Lin (2003), who writes that China tries to attract Taiwanese investment in part to exacerbate the income gap in Taiwan, and hence contribute to social instability there.

13. See, for example, the transcript of a Washington Post interview with Ma Ying-jeou, December 9, 2008: http://www.washingtonpost.com/wp-dyn/content/article/2008/12/09/AR2008120902788.html?sid=ST2008120902792&s_pos=list (accessed December 10, 2008).

14. Deng (2000, 972–73) also points to this contradiction, and similarly argues that "what worries Taipei most is not a 'hollowing out,' but rather that, as more [of] Taiwan's companies become dependent on the mainland, Beijing will gain political leverage over Taipei." More details of the Go-South strategy will be discussed later. For Lee's 1996 comments, see *Gongshang Shibao*, October 4, 1996, 2.

15. For example, Taiwan allowed investments in only 177 out of 1,266 product categories relating to machinery and electrical equipment and parts. But the government allowed investments in all 203 product categories relating to paper products, and in 861 out of 881 relating to textiles. For a complete list of allowable investment categories as of 1992, see Yan (1992, 89).

16. This overview of Taiwan's democratization is obviously highly simplified. For good reviews, see Roy (2003) and Rigger (1999).

17. Beginning in 2008, legislative elections are conducted under a new single-member district system, with some seats allocated to parties on a proportional basis.

18. In the 1992 legislative elections, thirty-six of the fifty KMT nominees with local faction backgrounds had business origins (Shiau 1996, 218).

19. Shiau (1996, 222) similarly notes that the political influence of small businesses was limited during Taiwan's transition to democracy, though some small businesses sought to increase their influence by giving financial support to new candidates in elections (including members of the Democratic Progressive Party). But candidates to the Legislative Yuan often spent more than US$1 million on their campaigns (Shiau 1996, 221), which put small businesses at an obvious disadvantage in their ability to curry favor. In a 1995 article in *Taipei Weekly*, Yang Chia-hui notes that enterprises used one of two methods when contributing to the KMT: contributing to the central committee and allowing the party to make allocation decisions, or contributing to individual candidates. In general, smaller enterprises gave only to individual candidates; presumably, this was because they believed they could gain influence only by concentrating their limited resources on individual candidates. By giving large donations to the KMT central committee, larger enterprises, in contrast, expected to gain at least some influence within the party center. See "Preparing for the Year-End Election War; Looking for Gold Mines—The Three Parties Show Off Their Talents in Raising Campaign Funds," *Taipei Weekly*, October 8, 1995, 22–25. In *FBIS-China*, "Campaign Fund-Raising by Major Parties Viewed," February 14, 1996, 68.

20. The lifting of martial law and the ban on cross-Strait travel in the mid-1980s probably made it considerably more difficult for the Taiwanese government to enforce restrictions on cross-Strait commerce effectively. As Yun-han Chu argues (1997, 238), many restrictions in place during the late 1980s and early 1990s proved ineffective in stemming the flow of Taiwanese investment to the Mainland. Small-scale businesses increasingly ignored existing bans and invested in China regardless of official policy. Notes Chu (1997, 241), "The adaptable small- and medium-sized enterprises simply rampaged through the official investment ban," forcing the government to change its policies.

21. This strategy was discussed briefly in the previous chapter.

22. For an overview of the plan, and the response by Taiwanese officials, see Leng (1996, 93–97).

23. *Jingji Ribao*, August 3, 1996, 4.

24. *Gongshang Shibao*, July 13, 1996, 9.

25. *Gongshang Shibao*, July 8, 1996, 2.

26. Chu (1997, 241–42) notes several other driving factors behind the trend of larger firms investing in China, including the worries of upstream producers that their sales to downstream producers (that had to a large extent moved to the Mainland already) would be replaced by Mainland producers.

27. *China News*, November 20, 1996, 7.

28. Lee Teng-hui referred to Chang Rung-fa, head of Evergreen, as "my good friend among the people," and it was well known that the two had a close relationship, based in part on their shared native Taiwanese identity and their ability to speak both Taiwanese and Japanese. See *Xin Xinwen*, June 17, 1991, 21. Evergreen would also sometimes offer jobs to former economics officials (*Xin Xinwen*, June 17, 1991, 24–26).

29. See, for example, *Lianhe Bao*, February 28, 1996, 2; *Zhongguo Shibao*, May 20, 1997, 1.

30. The plan called for the establishment of "transshipping zones" in Taiwan. The plan stalled at the time, in part because tensions across the Taiwan Strait escalated in 1995 just as Taiwan was preparing to implement it, and in part because it failed to receive endorsement from the Mainland, which viewed Taiwan's requirement that only foreign-owned ships be used as an effort to internationalize cross-Strait sea lanes (Chu 1997, 243–44). See also "Hsu

Views Kaohsiung Plan, Trade Link Claims," *Taipei Voice of Free China*. In *FBIS-China*, January 6, 1995, 91.

31. *FEER*, April 22, 1993, 75.

32. See also ibid.

33. Yun-han Chu (1997, 242) writes that there was also an unspoken threat by government officials to reduce Formosa's credit line in Taiwanese state-owned banks; this, of course, implies that government officials were not unwilling to apply pressure to major corporations. Still, the bulk of the deal clearly involved carrots and not sticks.

34. "Economic Cooperation with Southeast Asia to Increase," *Taipei Central News Agency*, December 27, 1993. In *FBIS-China*, December 28, 1993, 83.

35. *FEER*, February 24, 1994, 18–19.

36. *Free China Review*, May 1994, 30–37.

37. "Investors to Launch Subic Project," *Taiwan Journal*, July 21, 1995: http://taiwanjournal.nat.gov.tw/ct.asp?xItem=13424&CtNode=122 (accessed June 17, 2008).

38. "Green Light for Subic Bay Project: Taiwanese Industrial Park in Philippines Finally Granted Lifeline Funding," *China News*, April 5, 1997.

39. *Free China Review*, May 1994, 30–37.

40. Ibid.

41. "Twenty-six Local Firms Planning Vietnam Industrial Park," *China News*, October 5, 1996.

42. "Wide-Ranging Tax Pact with Indonesia," *Free China Journal*, March 10, 1994 (in Factiva); "Investment Agreement with Thailand," *Free China Journal*, November 4, 1994 (in Factiva).

43. *Lianhe Bao*, May 29, 1996, 2.

44. *China News*, February 3, 1997, 1; *China News*, April 4, 1997, 5.

45. *China News*, November 20, 1996, 7.

46. "Li Zongtong: Liang'an Jingmao Zhengce Weibian" (President Lee: Cross-Strait Economic Policies Haven't Changed), *Lianhe Bao*, August 21, 1996.

47. "Taiwan Confirms New Rules on China Investments." The ban on investment covered power plants, power distribution facilities, power transmission facilities, incinerators, harbors, airports, railways, highways, water reservation systems, rapid transportation systems, running water supplies, sewage systems, and industrial zones. See "New Regulations for Taiwan Investment in Mainland China," *Taiwan Central News Agency*, July 14, 1997. In World News Connection.

48. *FEER*, March 25, 1999, 10–15.

49. *China News*, February 3, 1997, 7.

50. "Taiwan Confirms New Rules on China Investments."

51. On reports of business lobbying, see, for example, *Lianhe Bao*, May 20, 1997, 9; *Zhongguo Shibao*, May 20, 1997, 1; *Taiwan News*, June 26, 2000, 13; *Taipei Times*, November 26, 2000, 3. Shortly after the Go Slow, Be Patient policy was announced, the Chinese National Federation of Industries conduced a survey of Taiwanese businessmen, and found that most disagreed with the new policy. Over half of the respondents thought the policy would have a negative effect on cross-Strait relations, compared with only 19 percent thinking it would have a positive effect. See "CNFI Releases Survey on Mainland Investment Policy," *Taiwan Central News Agency*, May 30, 1997. In World News Connection.

52. Chase et al. (2004, 7) suggest that disappointing results from the Go-South strategy influenced Lee's decision to announce the Go Slow, Be Patient policy.

53. Both Lin and Hau Pei-tsun (his running mate and a former premier) were expelled from the KMT shortly before the election for supporting New Party candidates in the 1995 legislative elections; they ran as independents (Rigger 1999, 174).

54. Indeed, Lin Yang-kang campaigned on a promise to open direct links with China immediately and to sign a peace treaty with Beijing. *FEER*, March 14, 1996, 18–19.

55. Hsu Hsin-liang, head of the Formosa faction in the party, in particular advocated jettisoning the Go Slow, Be Patient policy in favor of a "Boldly Go West" policy, which would eliminate most restrictions on cross-Strait commerce. In February 1998, the party held a highly publicized and open three-day debate on policy toward China. During the debate, Hsu pushed for a Boldly Go West strategy, while Chiou I-jen of the New Tide faction advocated a more conservative approach to handling cross-Strait economic relations given the political standoff between Beijing and Taipei. Julian Kuo (1998, 145) writes that the party achieved a consensus at the debate to pursue a "Strengthen the Base While Going West" (*Qiangben yu Xijin*) strategy, which meant focusing on strengthening Taiwan's economy while also allowing some liberalization of cross-Strait economic relations. The consensus appeared to split the difference between the two points of view, though press reports at the time suggest that little was actually settled at the debate. Chen Shui-bian, then mayor of Taipei and the most prominent party member, refused to attend, calling it meaningless. See "DPP Leaders Mull," *China News*, February 14, 1998 (in LexisNexis); "DPP United in Lee-Bashing, but Party's Criticism of President Highlights Failure to Resolve Policy Debates," *China News*, February 15, 1998 (in LexisNexis); and "DPP's Seminar on Policy Toward Mainland China Opens," *Taiwan Central News Agency*, February 13, 1998 (in LexisNexis).

56. *Lianhe Bao*, May 20, 1997, 9.

57. During the period 1991–1998, only 21 percent of Taiwan's approved Mainland China investments were in the electronics and electric appliances sector. Statistics from various issues of *Liang'an Jingji Tongji Yuebao*.

58. For example, Zhang Zhenwei reports that when three Taiwanese businessmen in May 1997 went to the economics ministry to protest new restrictions on cross-Strait investment, they also made a point of criticizing the Go-South policy. Why, they asked, did the government insist on driving them toward countries like Vietnam, where they don't even speak the language, when they all have their eye on the flourishing greater-China economic region? *Lianhe Bao*, May 20, 1997, 9.

59. *FEER*, March 25, 1999, 10–15.

60. Ibid.

61. Chao (2004, 696) notes that exact estimates differ somewhat: the government in 2003 estimated 47 percent of Taiwan's IT output to be produced on the Mainland, while the Institute for Information Industry estimated the figure to be 51 percent.

62. *FEER*, March 25, 1999, 12.

63. Ibid.

64. For example, Taiwanese policy prohibited companies from making motherboards on the Mainland with "anything faster than a 486 chip." Companies finished the motherboards simply without the chips on the Mainland, shipped them to a third location, and then added Intel processors there. See ibid.

65. Though the Taiwanese government announced in early 2005 that it was fining Chang for breaking Taiwan's investment laws; Chang's lawyers denied that the government had the authority to do this, since Chang is a U.S. citizen. See *Taipei Times*, April 2, 2005, 11.

66. *Taipei Times*, September 17, 2000, 1.

67. *Zhongguo Shibao*, September 17, 2000, 3.

68. See *Taipei Times*, April 3, 2001, 17; *China Post*, March 14, 2001, 1. Premier Chang Chun-hsiung noted in November 2000 that "under the precondition that it can guarantee national security, the government will do its best to adopt a more relaxed attitude toward direct links and the Go Slow, Be Patient policy." See "Tiaozheng Jieji Yongren, Xin Zhengfu Neibu You Zayin" (Inside the New Government, Sounds That Go Slow, Be Patient Will Be Adjusted), *Zhongguo Shibao*, November 16, 2000.

69. *Taiwan News*, January 5, 2001, 1.

70. Or more precisely, they suggested that Chen likely wanted some opening in cross-Strait economic relations but that he also wanted something in return—like negotiations with Beijing—otherwise he would expose himself to criticism from pro-independence factions in the DPP. Though he recognized that Beijing was unlikely to give him any concessions, Chen nonetheless called for policy change to signal to the business community and moderate voters that he was at least trying. (The three parties were the People First Party, the New Party, and the KMT.)

71. Chen appointed the panel, whose 120 members included a diverse mix of government officials and lawmakers (including members of opposition parties), academics, entrepreneurs, and labor representatives; before the panel met, Chen announced that he would support any consensus decisions that it reached. This was clearly an effort on his part to provide political cover for pursuing liberalization in cross-Strait economic policy. More hard-line elements within his party would find it difficult to oppose policies endorsed by such a distinguished and diverse panel of experts. See "Taiwan Looks to Boost Mainland Trade," *Washington Post*, August 28, 2001 (in LexisNexis); *Taipei Times*, July 4, 2001, 3; "Taiwan Lifts Restrictions on Investments in China," *New York Times*, November 8, 2001: http://query.nytimes.com/gst/fullpage.html?res=9904E1DC1E39F93BA35752C1A9679C 8B63 (accessed June 17, 2008).

72. "Taiwan Looks to Boost Mainland Trade."

73. The Ministry of Economic Affairs announced in the summer of 2002 that the ban on direct investments would be lifted. See "Economics Ministry Says Taiwan to Lift Ban on Direct Investment to PRC," Hong Kong Agence France-Presse, July 31, 2002. In World News Connection.

74. Taiwan's Mainland Affairs Council posts a description (in Chinese) of the new policy: http://www.mac.gov.tw/big5/cnews/emplo1.htm (accessed June 17, 2008). See also Chase et al. (2004); "A Cautious Welcome for Loosening of Restrictions," *Taipei Times*, November 8, 2001: http://www.taipeitimes.com/news/2001/11/08/story/0000110588 (accessed June 17, 2008); and "Taiwan Lifts Restrictions on Investments in China."

75. A larger silicon wafer yields more chips, of course, but is also more efficient: a smaller percentage of the wafer lies in the curved area along its perimeter, meaning a smaller percentage of it is wasted when cut into rectangular microchips. See Chase et al. (2004, 91).

76. The policy change was announced by Premier Yu Shyi-kun on March 29, 2002, and

is available in English on the Government Information Office webpage at: http://www.gio.gov.tw/taiwan-website/4-oa/20020329/2002032901.html (accessed June 17, 2008). For a good discussion, see Chase et al. (2004, 96–101).

77. "Official: Taiwan May Stall on Tech Control," Associated Press Financial Wire, March 16, 2005. In LexisNexis. See also Chase et al. (2004, 114).

78. In a visit to a chip plant in Taiwan, Lee attacked those who "disregard the Chinese Communists' conspiracies, go so far as to put their own economic and political interests above those of the nation, brazenly speak on behalf of the Chinese Communists and talk down to Taiwan . . . Taiwan has become more dependent on the mainland than has any other country . . . and that is extremely risky." "Taiwanese Silicon Chip Debate Arouses Passions," *Financial Times*, March 25, 2002. In Taiwan Security Research: http://taiwansecurity.org (hereafter TSR).

79. Lee was forced to resign as KMT chairman after the KMT candidate, Lien Chan, finished a distant third in the 2000 presidential election. The TSU won thirteen seats in the December 2001 Legislative Yuan elections, and aligned with the DPP in a "pan-green" alliance.

80. "Taiwanese Silicon Chip Debate Arouses Passions."

81. *Taipei Times*, March 10, 2002, 3.

82. *Taipei Times*, March 20, 2002, 4.

83. *Taipei Times*, August 14, 2002, 10.

84. Though officials privately noted that enforcement would continue to be difficult. One official noted that only three or four violations were uncovered the previous year. *Taipei Times*, July 13, 2002, 1.

85. According to Chase et al. (2004, 120), who provide a good overview of the case, He Jian is registered in the British Virgin Islands. The allegations were originally reported in the *Asian Wall Street Journal*, which caught the attention of several TSU legislators.

86. UMC denied that it had broken the law, saying it had not invested in He Jian but rather had only provided "management advice." See *Taipei Times*, April 4, 2005, 10.

87. In 2005 the TSU called on the Chen administration to pressure the legislature into passing the law by making it a top priority. *Taipei Times*, February 25, 2005, 2.

88. "Official: Taiwan May Stall on Tech Control."

89. "Chen No Liberalization of China Investments," *China Post*, January 2, 2006. In LexisNexis.

90. Through April 2005, 433,000 people had traveled to or from Mainland China via the mini three links. Data on the mini three links can be found (on the Mainland Affairs Council webpage) at: http://www.mac.gov.tw/english/english/csexchan/3link9404.htm (accessed June 17, 2008). For anyone who has traveled to the port on Jinmen linking the island to Xiamen, the word "mini" seems highly appropriate.

91. On the 2003 charter flights, see *Taipei Times*, January 4, 2003, 4. On the 2005 and 2006 flights, see "More Direct Flights Across the Strait for Chinese New Year," *Straits Times*, November 19, 2005 (in LexisNexis); also, "Taiwan, China Agree to First Charter Direct Flights," Agence France Presse, January 15, 2005 (in TSR); "Cross Strait Charter Flights Expand," *China Daily Online*, June 14, 2006: http://www.chinadaily.com.cn/china/2006–06/14/content_616989.htm (accessed June 17, 2008).

92. "Negotiations Must Precede Links, Says Premier," *Taiwan News*, January 28, 2003. In TSR.

93. Though Chen did suggest in 2002 that unofficial talks might be possible to resolve the matter, he quickly reversed course (Chao 2004, 699). In its document *Policy for Cross-Strait Exchanges*, Taiwan's Mainland Affairs Council (2005) explains why the Chen administration is opposed, in principle, to private sector talks as a means for resolving issues pertaining to cross-Strait exchanges: "After passing the 'anti-separation law,' the Chinese government has used a variety of means to present its so-called new proposals to promote cross-strait exchanges. The main objective of these proposals is to limit all cross-strait exchanges to the private sector, thus deliberately excluding any involvement of authority by the Taiwanese government. By so doing, it hopes to achieve its goal of treating cross-strait exchanges as Chinese internal affairs, and eventually turning the Taiwan issue into a domestic matter."

94. "Direct Links Could Begin by End of 2004, Chen Says," *Taiwan News*, August 14, 2003. In TSR.

95. Chen stated in 2004: "For the Beijing authorities, 'one China' is a principle, but for Taiwan, it is just an issue, which should be discussed as we seek a resolution." See "Chen: 'One Peace' is New Framework," *Taipei Times*, April 6, 2004: http://www.taipeitimes.com/News/taiwan/archives/2004/04/06/2003116860 (accessed June 17, 2008).

96. See, for example, *Xiang Gang Wen Hui Bao*, March 10, 2000, 6; *Jingji Ribao*, January 14, 2000, 11.

97. *Jingji Ribao*, January 14, 2000, 11.

98. See, for example, *Xiang Gang Wen Hui Bao*, March 10, 2000, 6; Author's interviews, Taiwan.

99. *Zhongguo Shibao*, February 16, 2000, 4; *Jingji Ribao*, January 14, 2000, 11.

100. Tang resigned several months later as it became clear that Chen would try to halt construction of the island's fourth nuclear power plant, which triggered stringent opposition by the KMT and the People First Party.

101. *Zhongguo Shibao*, December 13, 2000, 3.

102. Ibid.

103. Huang Baixue notes in *Xin Xinwen* that Chen Shui-bian and Barry Lam had developed fairly close relations (*bucuo de guanxi*), though Lam had tended to keep his distance from politics in the past. See *Xin Xinwen*, November 30, 2000, 37. Huang also writes that Morris Chang rarely expressed his opinions on cross-Strait relations before Wang's meeting. See *Xin Xinwen*, November 30, 2000, 30–34.

104. *Xin Xinwen*, 30 November 30, 2000, 30–34; "Wang Yung-ching Slams Politicians over Economy," *Taipei Times*, November 24, 2000: http://www.taipeitimes.com/news/2000/11/24/story/0000062822 (accessed June 17, 2008).

105. Wang was frequently critical of the KMT when it was in power, and had developed a fairly close relationship with Chen Shui-bian at the time of his election in 2000. See *Xin Xinwen*, November 30, 2000, 38–40; *Xin Xinwen*, March 30, 2000, 105–7.

106. That is, voters might view them as reliable providers of information regarding the government's economic policy. On the importance of endorsers (or substitutes) as sources of political information, see Lupia and McCubbins (1998) and Milner (1997).

107. The three parties reached a six-point consensus in November 2000. Among the points of agreement reached was that Taiwan should accept the one-China principle as described by the "92 consensus" (one China, with each side holding its own interpretation as to what "one China" means); recognizing a one-China principle would, of course,

remove the key barrier to cross-Strait talks regarding opening direct links. The parties also agreed that the government should not interfere with the market. See *Taipei Times*, November 12, 2000, 1.

108. In October 2000, new premier Chang Chun-hsiung of the DPP announced that the government would halt construction of Taiwan's fourth nuclear power plant. The decision to build the plant was made by the former KMT government, and was already 30 percent complete at the time of the government's decision to stop construction. The DPP has opposed nuclear power for environmental reasons, and Chen Shui-bian in his campaign for the presidency had promised to halt construction. But the decision to halt construction of the plant sparked anger within the opposition parties in the Legislative Yuan and within the business community, which was concerned about a reliable long-term power supply. Chen's effort to stop the project led to a failed attempt by the opposition parties to force him out of office through a presidential recall. See "Controversy over New Nuclear Power Plant Continues," *Taipei Times*, October 5, 2000: http//www.taipeitimes.com/news/2000/10/05/story/0000056087 (accessed June 17, 2008); "Decision on Fourth Nuclear Plant to Be Made by End of Year," *Taipei Times*, October 18, 2000: http://www.taipeitimes.com/news/2000/10/18/story/0000057687 (accessed June 17, 2008); "Cabinet Pulls Plug on Power Plant," *Taipei Times*, October 28, 2000: http://www.taipeitimes.com/news/2000/10/28/story/0000058926 (accessed June 17, 2008); *FEER*, November 16, 2000, 21–22.

109. In fact, the party began as early as 1998 to take steps to change the perception that it was antibusiness. The perception derived in part from an incident in 1998 when Bayer cancelled plans to build a plant in Taiwan after a local official—a DPP member—opposed the project. Party leaders sought to counter the image in early 1999 by arranging weekly meetings between DPP elected officials and business leaders, economists, and other experts to discuss economic policy. See Rigger (2001, 139).

110. One party official emphasized as well that since organized labor is weak in Taiwan, all parties must try to garner business support (author's interviews).

111. *Lianhe Bao*, February 20, 2001, 3.

112. Author's interview with a DPP party official.

113. Author's interviews, Taipei.

114. For example, *Lianhe Bao*, January 3, 2001, 13.

115. Author's interviews, Taipei.

116. The list of participants in the conference is available on the webpage for the Office of the President of the Republic of China (I calculated the percentages based on the affiliations of the different attendees): http://www.president.gov.tw/2_special/economic/e_member.html (accessed June 19, 2008).

117. "Economic Facts Support Direct Links," *Commercial Times*, August 10, 2001 (in TSR); "AmCham Forwards Suggestions Ahead of Economic Meet," *Taipei Times*, August 24, 2001: http://www.taipeitimes.com/news/2001/08/24/story/0000099983 (accessed June 19, 2008).

118. In the mid-1990s, the KMT government developed the idea of turning Taiwan into a regional operations center. The hope was that companies would use Taiwan as a base for their Asian operations—that is, parent companies would assign decision-making authority regarding Asian production, distribution, and research and development to regional offices in Taiwan (Schive 1995, 43). Schive (1995, 44) noted that "because of its

central position in the Asia-Pacific region, its close links with the West, and the strength of its local economy, Taiwan has emerged as an attractive site for companies contemplating the establishment of an Asia-Pacific regional operations center."

119. "Lack of China Ties Worries IPO Head," *Taipei Times*, August 13, 2001: http://www.taipeitimes.com/news/2001/08/13/story/0000098444 (accessed June 19, 2008).

120. "Economic Facts Support Direct Links."

121. "Opposition Says Chen Must Take Action," *Taiwan News*, May 10, 2002. In TSR.

122. The December 2001 elections changed the factional distribution of legislative seats within the DPP. Chen Shui-bian's Justice Faction supplanted New Tide as the party's largest factional bloc in the legislature. See "Zhengyi Lianxian Zhaobingmaima, Yulinjun Chengxing" (Justice Faction Expands Its Forces, the Palace Guards Take Shape), *Lianhe Bao*, December 6, 2001: http://udnnews.com/.

123. Interestingly, the New Tide position on cross-Strait issues, and in particular economic exchanges, has moderated considerably over time. See, for example, "Hsieh Wants China Policy Resolution on DPP Platform," *China Post,* May 23, 2006: http://www.china-post.com.tw/taiwan/detail.asp?ID=82719&GRP=B (accessed June 19, 2008).

124. *Taipei Times,* December 2, 2001, 1.

125. Ibid.

126. Quoted in *Taipei Times*, December 10, 2001: http://www.taipeitimes.com/News/front/archives/2001/12/10/115141 (accessed June 19, 2008).

127. Quoted in *Taipei Times*, March 17, 2002, 3.

128. *Taipei Times,* February 16, 2003, 2.

129. "Taiwan President Declares Re-election Bid," Reuters, November 8, 2003. In TSR.

130. Chen, for example, pressed for a referendum on national security issues at the same time as the 2004 election; campaigned on a promise to hold a referendum on a new constitution; warned that he would withdraw his "5 No's" pledge if China continued to threaten Taiwan; and participated in a rally on February 28, 2004, in which one million Taiwanese formed a human chain along the island to protest China's missiles pointed at Taiwan. On the rally, see "Human Chain Protest Spans Taiwan," Reuters, February 28, 2004. In TSR.

131. *FEER*, February 19, 2004, 22. The head of the Evergreen Corporation, Chang Rung-fa, supported Chen in 2000 but endorsed Lien in 2004. *Taipei Times*, March 20, 2004, 5. Some other prominent Chen supporters in 2000 kept a much lower profile in 2004 (author's interviews with officials and analysts, Taipei, June 2004).

Chapter 5

1. As Robert Ross (2000) argues, the response was intended to signal resolve both toward Taiwan and toward the United States. Beijing wished to convince Taiwan to tone down its activities, and to convince the United States that support for Taiwan was potentially very costly.

2. "ARATS Officials Reassure Taiwan Investors," *Xinhua*, October 29, 1995. In *FBIS-China,* October 31, 1995, 71.

3. "Mainland Official on Ties, Investment," *Tzu-li Wan-pao,* July 21, 1995. In *FBIS-China*, July 31, 1995, 90.

4. "Official Encourages Taiwan Investment on Mainland," *Xinhua*, August 7, 1995. In *FBIS-China*, August 9, 1995, 66–67.

5. *China News*, March 13, 1996, 10.

6. *International Herald Tribune*, August 30, 1996, 4.

7. *Mingbao*, December 31, 1995, A9.

8. *China News*, March 13, 1996, 10.

9. *Lianhe Bao*, December 30, 1995, 1.

10. *China News*, April 4, 1996, 10. Prominent Taiwanese tycoon Y. C. Wang also made a well-publicized trip to the Mainland in November 1995 to examine the feasibility of building a processing plant there; though not immediately announcing his plans, he made a point of emphasizing on his return that the Mainland is "a good place to build" such a plant. *Jingji Ribao*, December 1, 1995, 2.

11. See, for example, "Military Expert Wang Baoqing Envisages War with Taiwan," *Beijing Zhongguo Xinwen She*, September 7, 1999. In World News Connection.

12. "Ta Kung Pao Discusses Danger of Taiwan War," *Ta Kong Pao*, August 10, 1999. In World News Connection.

13. *Taiwan Wenti Duben*, 93.

14. For the white paper, see "Text of PRC White Paper on Taiwan," *Xinhua*, February 21, 2000. In World News Connection.

15. "Official Assures Taiwan Investors of Greater Protection," *Xinhua,* September 8, 1999. In World News Connection.

16. Comments by Wen Zaixing, a spokesman for the China Investment and Trade Fair. "Taiwanese Encouraged to Invest in Mainland," *Xinhua*, September 7, 1999. In World News Connection.

17. "Commentary on Two-State Theory, WTO Entry," *Beijing Central Peoples Radio,* September 18, 1999. In World News Connection.

18. "Cross-Strait Economic Ties Said Unaffected by Tension," *Zhongguo Xinwen She*, September 9, 1999. In World News Connection.

19. "New Law Seeks to Protect Investment from Taiwan," *Beijing Xinhua*, December 15, 1999. In World News Connection.

20. For the text of the new guidelines, see "PRC Law on Protection of Taiwan Investment," *Xinhua Domestic Service*, December 12, 1999. In World News Connection.

21. "New Law Seeks to Protect Investment from Taiwan." Also, "Shi Guangsheng on Taiwan Investment Law," *Xinhua Domestic Service*, December 15, 1999. In World News Connection.

22. At the time, Chen and the DPP especially advocated using a referendum to settle the issue of Taiwan's construction of a fourth nuclear power plant. Chen had, early in his administration, tried to stop the construction of the plant, an effort that failed and that helped to unite the opposition parties against him. See "DPP Reiterates Pledge to Hold Referendum on Nuclear Power Policy," *China Post*, June 24, 2003. In LexisNexis.

23. See, for example, an op-ed by Joseph Wu, at the time the deputy secretary-general to the president: "New Constitution for a New Nation," *Taipei Times*, October 1, 2003: http://www.taipeitimes.com/News/editorials/archives/2003/10/01/2003069997 (accessed June 19, 2008).

24. *Washington Post*, November 27, 2003, A14.

25. "Taiwan Legislators Step Back from Confronting China," *New York Times*, November 28, 2003: http://query.nytimes.com/gst/fullpage.html?res=9801E0DF153AF93BA1575 2C1A9659C8B63&sec=&spon=&pagewanted=1 (accessed June 19, 2008).

26. "Taiwan: China Threat Justifies Referendum," Associated Press, November 30, 2003. In LexisNexis.

27. The official was Luo Yuan, a senior colonel at the Chinese Academy of Military Sciences. See "PLA: Chen Shui-bian Is to Blame if War Breaks Out," *Peoples Daily Online*, December 3, 2003: http://english.people.com.cn/200312/03/print20031203_129595.html (accessed June 19, 2008). See also Mulvenon (2004a).

28. Bush's statement: "We oppose any unilateral decisions by either China or Taiwan to change the status quo … [A]ctions made by the leader of Taiwan indicate that he may be willing to make decisions unilaterally, to change the status quo, which we oppose." The referendum questions asked if Taiwan should purchase more advanced antimissile weapons if China refused to withdraw its missiles aimed at Taiwan, and whether the Taiwanese government should try to negotiate with the Mainland government on the "establishment of a peace and stability framework for cross-Strait interactions." See Suettinger (2004). In early December, Chen had suggested the referendum would demand that China renounce the use of force against Taiwan and withdraw its missiles pointed at the island. See "Taiwan to Hold Historic 'Anti-Missile, Anti-War' Referendum: Chen," Channel NewsAsia, December 7, 2003. In LexisNexis.

29. For example, "Taiwan's President Maintains Hard Line: Chen Rebukes China in Interview," *Washington Post*, March 30, 2004. In LexisNexis.

30. See "Chen Says Defend 'New Constitution,'" *China Post*, June 17, 2004. In LexisNexis.

31. For example, Taiwan Affairs Office spokesperson Li Weiyi argued that "no one should underestimate the determination and capability of the Chinese government and people to safeguard the sovereignty and territorial integrity of the motherland at any cost." See "'New Constitution' Means Timetable for Taiwan Independence: Official," *Xinhua News*, April 14, 2004. In TSR. For a good overview, see Mulvenon (2004b).

32. "Wen: Taiwan Legislation to Be Studied," *China Daily*, May 12, 2004. In LexisNexis.

33. "China Warns Army Can and Will 'Smash' Taiwan Independence," Agence France Presse, August 1, 2004. In TSR.

34. "PLA Troops on Dongshan Island to Soon Enter Stage of Combined Exercises," *Wen Wei Po*, July 23, 2004. In World News Connection. Some military officials in Taiwan downplayed the significance of the drills, viewing them as routine propaganda. See *Taipei Times*, August 10, 2004, 3.

35. "Wen: Taiwan Legislation to Be Studied."

36. "Chen Warns of China 'Mandate' to Invade," Agence Presse France, July 31, 2004. In TSR.

37. "China's Army May Respond if Taiwan Fully Secedes," *New York Times*, December 18, 2004: http://www.nytimes.com/2004/12/18/international/asia/18china.html?scp=1&s q=China+Preparing+to+Enact+Law+Against+Taiwan+Secession&st=nyt (accessed June 19, 2008).

38. For the full text of the law, see "Full Text of Anti-Secession Law," *Xinhua*, March 14, 2005. In World News Connection.

39. "Top Leaders Try to Calm Taiwan Investors," *South China Morning Post*, October 22, 2004. In LexisNexis.

40. *Jingji Ribao*, April 15, 2000, 1.

41. *Taiwan News*, March 12, 2001, 2.

42. "Dalu Bu Huanying 'Luse' Taishang" (The Mainland Doesn't Welcome 'Green' Taiwan Businesspeople), *Renmin Wang*, May 31, 2004: www.people.com.cn/GB/shizheng/1026/2533052.html (accessed June 19, 2008). The article originally appeared in *Huanqiu Shibao*.

43. Deng (1984, 396).

44. "Full Text of Report Delivered by Jiang Zemin at Opening of Party Congress," *Wen Wei Po*, November 9, 2002. In World News Connection.

45. Though Jiang first mentioned the "Three Represents" in a speech to party cadres in the spring of 2000. See Zong (2002, 299). See also Fewsmith (2001, 229–30).

46. Allowing capitalists into the party did provoke sharp criticism from leftists.

47. See, for example, "Hu Jintao Stresses Development at Politburo Study Session," *Xinhua Domestic Service*, April 16, 2005. In World News Connection. Also, "Apparent Text of Hu Jintao Speech on Building Harmonious Socialist Society. Hu Jintao 19 February 2005 Speech at Special Discussion Class for Principal Leading Cadres at Provincial and Ministerial Levels to Study Issues About Building a Harmonious Socialist Society," *Xinhua Domestic Service*, June 30, 2005. In World News Connection.

48. Naughton (1996, 288).

49. "China Overtakes U.S. as Investment Target," *USA Today*, June 28, 2004: http://www.usatoday.com/money/world/2004-06-28-investment_x.htm (accessed June 19, 2008).

50. "Nation Jumps to Be World Third Largest Trader," *China Daily*, January 11, 2005: http://www.chinadaily.com.cn/english/doc/2005-01/11/content_407979.htm (accessed June 19, 2008).

51. For a discussion of the benefits of internationalization more broadly for urban (pp. 60–64) and rural (pp. 124–26) locales in China, see Zweig (2002). Internationalization, for example, "increased the sale price of a key commodity and source of government revenue—land" (60).

52. Tian (2006, 136) writes that in some jurisdictions in Jiangsu Province, local cadres are even evaluated on the basis of how much foreign investment they are able to attract.

53. It should be emphasized that China's integration into global markets was not uniform across regions: central leaders granted some regions access before others (see, e.g., Shirk 1994; Zweig 2002). But as Zweig (2002, 34) writes, because those localities with greater access to global markets reaped disproportionate benefits, a dynamic developed in which officials from other localities "pleaded and lobbied the central administration to grant them" similar status.

54. For a recent case involving a Japanese firm that illustrates this point, see "Firm Battles China Corruption," *Yomiuri Shimbun*, November 19, 2007: http://www.yomiuri.co.jp/.

55. Yang (1997, ch. 7), for example, describes a debate that erupted in China in the mid-1990s concerning special economic zones (SEZs). Interior provinces demanded that SEZs be established in Western China to help that region catch up with the coast, which led to a broader debate concerning the desirability of such zones in China generally. Naturally, coastal officials who benefited from preferential policies vigorously defended the coastal SEZs. In the end, Yang writes, central officials tried to make all sides happy, and in particular "bent backwards to please coastal interests." No SEZs would be allowed in

interior provinces, but more interior cities were to be designated "open cities" with special privileges; certain coastal SEZ privileges would be phased out after 2000, but numerous other concessions reaffirmed their special status (see, esp., pp. 124–29).

56. On this point, see also Tanner (2007, 132): "Some regions of China already benefit greatly from their economic links with Taiwan" and would be "loath to give up those benefits." As such, "many localities or companies might seek a variety of ways to skirt" economic sanctions.

57. *Jingji Ribao*, July 6, 1996, 11.

58. Quoted in Zhao (1999a, 27).

59. For several other, similar versions of the slogan, see Lee (2003, 116).

60. *FEER*, December 31, 1993–January 6, 1994, 14.

61. Arguments along these lines are widespread. See, for example, Zhao (1999a, 26–27); Lee (2003, 116); Bolt (2001, 83); Lam (2001); Tanner (2007).

62. I return to this point, and its implications for signaling arguments linking economic interdependence to peace, in the next chapter.

63. *International Herald Tribune*, June 28, 2000, 1; *Zhongguo Shibao*, March 28, 2005, A4; author's interviews, Taipei.

64. *Gongshang Shibao*, June 28, 2000, 5. Though, as Tanner (2007, 116) writes, Shih also expressed defiance, noting that he could "survive without China . . . [I]f they try to take my small Chinese investment, I'm fine."

65. Author's interviews, Taipei.

66. *Zhongguo Shibao*, March 28, 2005, A4.

67. *Zhongguo Shibao*, March 28, 2005, A4; *Taipei Times*, March 20, 2004, 5.

68. The paper is a major daily newspaper in Taiwan.

69. (*Wushiwuke dou you shushiming chashui renyuan jinzhu.*) *Zhongguo Shibao*, March 30, 2005, A4.

70. "Dalu Bu Huanying 'Luse' Taishang."

71. *Taipei Times*, March 29, 2005, 8; *Zhongguo Shibao*, April 1, 2005, A3.

72. Some in Taiwan suggested that the wording of Hsu's statement suggested it was drafted by authorities in Beijing. The PRC, unsurprisingly, denied this. The Chi Mei corporation also denied that Hsu's statement was related to the company's new applications for Mainland investments. See *Taipei Times*, March 29, 2005, 8; *Zhongguo Shibao*, April 1, 2005, A3; *Zhongguo Shibao*, March 30, 2005, A4.

73. This assessment is based on the author's interviews in Taipei (2001) and Shanghai (2004). Even after the attacks on Chi Mei, several Mainland Chinese analysts doubted that a large-scale crackdown on green businesses was imminent, though they didn't rule it out if cross-Strait relations continued to deteriorate.

74. "PRC to Keep Low-Profile Control on Taiwan Firms," *Ming Pao*, May 13, 2000. In World News Connection.

75. *Taipei Times*, March 12, 2001, 1.

76. "Taiwan Businessmen in Mainland China Not Feeling Heat from Beijing," *Taipei Central News Agency*, June 23, 2004. In *FBIS-China*, June 24, 2004.

77. *Taipei Times*, June 9, 2004, 3.

78. "Chi Mei's Plant in China Operating Normally: Group Spokesman," *Taipei Central News Agency*, June 7, 2004. In *FBIS-China,* June 9, 2004.

79. "Chinese Academic Suggests Possible PRC Economic Embargo on Taiwan, Market Falls," *Ming Pao* (Hong Kong), June 4, 2004. In *FBIS-China*, June 7, 2004.

80. *South China Morning Post*, October 22, 2004, 7.

81. "Wu Yi Urges Improvement in Cross-Strait Trade, Economic Cooperation," *Beijing Zhongguo Xinwen She*, September 13, 2004. In *FBIS-China*, September 29, 2004.

82. "PRC to Keep Low-Profile Control on Taiwan Firms." Huang had noted at the same time that Taiwanese investors should not be allowed to express pro-independence sentiments while in the PRC.

83. Including the vice governors of Shandong and Hainan Provinces and the mayor of Shenzhen.

84. *Ziyou Shibao*, March 13, 2001, 3.

85. "Dalu bu Huanying 'Luse' Taishang."

86. Some statements were issued in the run-up to the 2008 Taiwanese presidential election that suggested possible future threats to Taiwanese businesses. Chen Yunlin is reported to have suggested, for example, that passage of a UN referendum in Taiwan's March 2008 election would potentially change the protected status of Taiwanese investors in China. However, he later indicated that the PRC would continue to keep politics and economics on separate tracks even if the referendum vote were held (the referendum ultimately failed, making the issue moot). See Romberg (2007, 17–18).

87. Indeed, actors who benefit from cross-Strait economic ties often emphasize both the economic benefits of those ties and the potential benefits for national reunification. See, for example, "PRC: Song Defu, Zheng Lizhong Say Fujian, Xiamen Ready for 'Three Links' with Taiwan," *Hong Kong Zhongguo Tongxun She*, November 10, 2002. In World News Connection. By emphasizing the harmony between the economic benefits of openness and the goal of national reunification, local officials presumably aim to garner wider support for open policies. For an interesting anecdote along these lines, see Yang (1997, 123), who writes that in a debate concerning special economic zones that erupted in the mid-1990s, Shenzhen party secretary Li Youwei highlighted the city's deep economic links with Hong Kong—and how that helped to foster the territory's return to Chinese sovereignty—in defending the special economic privileges given to Shenzhen.

88. On this dilemma, see, for example, Zhao (2005).

Chapter 6

An earlier version of this chapter appeared as Kastner (2006b), from the *Journal of East Asian Studies* 6, no. 3. Copyright 2006 by the East Asia Institute. Used with permission of Lynne Rienner Publishers, Inc.

1. On the stabilizing effects of economic interdependence in East Asia more generally, see Wan (2003).

2. In his April 2004, testimony on Taiwan before Congress, former assistant secretary of state James Kelly emphasized that "[i]n the absence of a political dialogue, we encourage the two sides to increase bilateral interactions of every sort. Clearly, there would be economic benefits for both sides by proceeding with direct aviation and shipping links. The increasing people-to-people contacts may also ease tensions." Comments online at: http://www.state.gov/p/eap/rls/rm/2004/31649.htm (accessed June 19, 2008).

3. Gilpin (1987, 57) and Ripsman and Blanchard (1996/97) make similar arguments.

4. For reviews of various arguments linking economic interdependence to peace, see Barbieri (1996), Barbieri and Schneider (1999), Mansfield and Pollins (2001; 2003).

5. On this point, see Mansfield and Pollins (2003). Studies that consider different types of contingent effects include Copeland (1999/2000); Papayoanou (1996); Gelpi and Grieco (2003); and Mansfield and Pevehouse (2000).

6. On the relational specificity of assets, see Lake (1999) and Rector (2009).

7. This sort of opportunity cost argument has a long history: elements of the argument can be found in Kant's works and in the works of nineteenth-century commercial liberals such as Cobden (for an overview, see Russett and Oneal 2001, 127–29). More recently, the argument is endorsed by Viner (1951, 261) and is further developed by Polachek (1980) and Polachek et al. (1999). The argument also appears prominently in the work of Russet and Oneal (2001), Oneal and Russett (1997), and Oneal et al. (1996). Levy (2003) critically analyzes the argument.

8. On sanctions as costly signals, see also Baldwin (1985) and Drezner (1999/2000).

9. As quoted in Gaddis (1982, 38). Deutsch et al. (1957) likewise emphasize the importance of social communication as a condition facilitating the formation of security communities. Deepening economic integration facilitates such contacts, though Deutsch et al. downplayed the role of economic ties per se as a precondition for security communities. Viner (1951, 261), while declining to endorse it himself, attributes this sort of sociological argument to the Manchester School. Some of Cobden's writings do indeed suggest this type of effect (e.g. Cobden 1995, 465–66), though constraint arguments are more prominent. On the Manchester School, see also Grampp (1960).

10. On the effects of commerce on domestic political coalitions, see Rogowski (1989).

11. Solingen (1998; 2003). As noted in Chapter 2, countries sometimes cultivate economic ties with other states in order to harness a transforming effect. See Hirschman (1945); Abdelal and Kirshner (1999/2000); Skalnes (1998); Kahler and Kastner (2006). McDonald (2004) argues that free trade (low protectionist barriers) rather than trade per se has the effect of increasing the relative political clout of actors most likely to oppose war.

12. However, precisely because cross-Strait relations resemble in some ways a "least likely" case, negative findings are unlikely to generalize.

13. According to official Taiwanese statistics (available in *Liang'an Jingji Tongji Yuebao*), in 2004 the Taiwanese government approved investments in China totaling US$6.94 billion, which represented 67 percent of the island's total approved outward investment in that year but only 11.5 percent of total foreign direct investment in China (which totaled over US$60 billion in 2004).

14. The announcement was not anticipated. See "Taiwan's Unnerving President Does It Again," *The Economist*, July 17, 1999.

15. For example, "Chinese Military 'Extremely Indignant' over Li's Remarks," *Beijing Xinhua*, July 14, 1999. In World News Connection.

16. "Taiwan Defence Ministry Report: Threat from Beijing More Serious," British Broadcasting Corporation World Monitoring, October 31, 1999. In LexisNexis.

17. For example, when asked by reporters in August 1999 whether military conflict was likely, Lee smiled and said, "Don't worry!" See "Lee Tells Taiwan: Don't Worry," *China News*, August 12, 1999. In LexisNexis.

18. Indeed, Su writes that the group responsible for crafting the "two states theory," of which he is highly critical, viewed cross-Strait exchanges—including economic exchang-

es—as harmful for Taiwan. As such, if the announcement of the two-states argument were to interfere with events such as Mainland envoy Wang Daohan's approaching trip to Taiwan, this would not be a bad thing. See Su (2003, 85).

19. "China's New Demands 'Unfounded,'" *Taipei Times*, September 10, 1999: http://www.taipeitimes.com/News/front/archives/1999/09/10/1547 (accessed June 19, 2008).

20. "Invasion Fears Are Unrealistic: Tang," *Taipei Times*, August 31, 1999: http://www.taipeitimes.com/News/local/archives/1999/08/31/144 (accessed June 19, 2008).

21. After his presidency ended in 2000, Lee Teng-hui was quite explicit in promoting this underlying logic: the increased costs of war for China enable Taiwan more leeway on the issue of the island's sovereignty. For example, he suggested that Beijing's hosting of the Olympic games offered Taiwan a window of opportunity to take important nation-building steps—implying that Beijing would not dare attack, as the costs (such as an Olympic boycott) would be too high. See "Taiwan's Top Agitator as Bold as Ever," *Washington Post*, October 12, 2003. In LexisNexis.

22. The logic here parallels that developed in Morrow (1999) and Gartzke et al. (2001).

23. Ibid.

24. For example, one recent study found that while 72 percent of respondents support Taiwanese independence if it could be achieved peacefully, 73 percent are opposed if independence would trigger a war with China (Niou 2004).

25. Regarding voter unhappiness with Chen's policies, one survey found that only 15 percent supported Chen Shui-bian's 2006 decision to abolish the National Unification Council, while 57 percent were at least a little worried that the decision would cause increased tension in cross-Strait relations. Poll conducted by the local TV station TVBS, online at: http://www.tvbs.com.tw/FILE_DB/DL_DB/sophia_tsai/200602/sophia_tsai-20060209124200.pdf (accessed June 21, 2006). Meanwhile, Chen's approval ratings began plummeting even before the first family became engulfed in scandal allegations. Ross (2006) attributes recent public opinion and electoral setbacks for Chen and the DPP, and recent successes by the Nationalist Party (KMT), in part to the KMT's willingness to engage the Mainland (in contrast to Chen's continued provocations).

26. "Pro-independence Investors Not Welcome," *China Daily*, June 22, 2004: www.chinadaily.com.cn/english/doc/2004–06/22/content_341316.htm (accessed June 19, 2008).

27. Ibid.

28. "Leading China Economist Says Trade War Can Break Taiwan."

29. In the next section I provide more evidence to this effect.

30. "Green" Taiwanese businesses are obviously less valuable from this perspective and hence are more susceptible to pressure from Mainland authorities.

31. Interestingly, some Taiwanese analysts likewise conclude that comprehensive trade sanctions would be so counterproductive for Mainland China that it is unlikely they would ever be utilized. For example, in response to Hu Angang's comments about China's capacity to cripple Taiwan's economy through a trade war, Lin Chong-Pin, former vice chairman of the Mainland Affairs Council, noted that "technically it is increasingly feasible, but I don't think Beijing will do it because it is counter-productive." Lin also emphasized that the "overall long-term strategic goal is to win the hearts and minds of Taiwanese people." See "Leading China Economist Says Trade War Can Break Taiwan."

32. Indeed, Gartzke and Li (2003b) argue that China and Taiwan were able to avoid a military confrontation during the 2000 Taiwanese elections in part because the two econo-

mies were becoming more globalized. For example, the U.S. Congress at the time was considering granting China permanent normal trading relations (PNTR) status as China prepared to enter the World Trade Organization. The authors argue that Chinese threats directed against Taiwan at the time would harm China's image in the United States, and hence make it less likely Congress would approve PNTR. This danger made the threats more costly and hence more credible to Taiwan.

33. Abdelal and Kirshner (1999/2000), referring to Hirschman (1945). Interestingly enough, Abdelal and Kirschner note that rarely do states that are attempting to use economic means to influence other states actually cut off those ties unless the strategy of influence has failed entirely.

34. The Mainland Affairs Council regularly posts results of polls asking where people stand on the independence/unification issue on its webpage (www.mac.gov.tw). The 61 percent who favored the status quo includes those who say they want to maintain the status quo indefinitely and those who want to maintain the status quo for now and decide sometime in the future which path to pursue. (Those favoring maintaining the status quo for now, but favoring either unification or independence later, are excluded from this percentage.) Note that the percentage does bounce around a considerable amount over time, sometimes dropping below 50. However, it is hard to discern any clear trends.

35. See "Changes in the Taiwanese/Chinese Identity of Taiwanese as Tracked in Surveys by the Election Study Center, National Chengchi University, Taiwan": http://esc.nccu.edu.tw/eng/data/data03–2.htm (accessed June 19, 2008). Chao (2003) cites other polls that point to similar trends.

36. For example, when asked in postelection surveys if they would support independence if peace could be maintained, 37 percent of Taiwanese voters agreed in 1993, while 63 percent agreed in 1996; in 2000, 61 percent agreed. See Benson and Niou (2005).

37. On the conditions under which the Taiwanese public would support independence or reunification, see also Niou (2004).

38. *FEER*, February 19, 2004, 23.

39. "Manufacturers Maintain China Focus," *Taipei Times*, November 13, 2004: http://www.taipeitimes.com/News/biz/archives/2004/11/13/2003210910 (accessed June 19, 2008).

40. The poll was conducted by the local TV station TVBS. See "CNA: Businesses Dissatisfied with Government's M'land Policy: Legislators," *Taipei Central News Agency*, April 25, 2002. In World News Connection.

41. Ibid. The 1992 consensus is discussed briefly in Chapter 3.

42. "Campaign Special (Business Community)—Business Community Looks for Upturn," *Taipei Times*, March 21, 2004: http://www.taipeitimes.com/News/taiwan/archives/2004/03/21/2003107231 (accessed June 19, 2008).

43. See, for example, remarks by Yangda Air Conditioning general manager Liu Zhenlong in "Investors Say Close Commercial Ties with China Future of Taiwan," Hong Kong Agence France-Presse, March 16, 2004. In World News Connection.

44. "Business Leaders 'Hold the Key to President's Fate,'" *South China Morning Post*, February 10, 2004. In LexisNexis.

45. "Young Turks Invest in Cross-Strait Ties; Taiwan's New Generation of Presidential Hopefuls Vows to Open Cross-Strait Trade," *South China Morning Post*, March 12, 2000. In LexisNexis.

46. These promises were detailed in a pamphlet directed to *Taishang* printed by the pan-blue campaign during the 2004 election. The pamphlet had the heading "Wanshan Liang'an Zhengce, Zaixian Taiwan Fenghua" (Perfecting Cross-Strait Relations, Once Again Revealing Taiwan's Talents).

47. *FEER*, July 31, 2003, 12.

48. *FEER*, February 19, 2004, 22.

Chapter 7

1. Some of the findings presented here were earlier published in Scott L. Kastner, "When Do Conflicting Political Relations Affect International Trade?" *Journal of Conflict Resolution* 51, no. 4 (August 2007): 664–88.

2. I use the natural log of bilateral trade flows in constant (real) US$. Data on bilateral trade flows come from Gleditsch (2002). Furthermore, since I use the logged value of trade, I converted $0 values to $2000. The figure is equal to the smallest non-zero value of bilateral trade flows (imports to A from B added to imports to B from A) in the Gleditsch data set. Gleditsch relies primarily on IMF data; he utilizes interpolation, lags, and leads to fill in missing data where possible; the value of trade in dyads for which no data are available is imputed to be 0. As Gleditsch (2002) notes, treating this data as missing could generate misleading results, since missing trade data for IMF members usually indicates negligible or zero trade (Oneal and Russett 1999a, 425). I removed from the data set dyads utilizing five or more consecutive years of interpolation or leads/lags in trade data, countries whose GDP data required five or more consecutive years of interpolation or leads/lags, and countries whose trade data were primarily imputed. Though a large number of countries— including the Eastern Bloc—were not included in this analysis because of data concerns, the sample remains quite diverse: in addition to the OECD countries, it includes a number of countries that have at times had hostile relations with the West and with each other. For example, China, India, Pakistan, and several Middle Eastern countries are all included. The complete sample of countries is listed in Appendix B, Table B1.

3. The measure comes from Gartzke et al. (1999). I transformed the variable to make interpretation of interactive variables easier; Appendix B provides details. For a discussion of this measure, see Gartzke (1998). For works that use the UN measure as an indicator of preference similarity, see, for example, Gartzke (1998; 2000); Pevehouse (2004); Stone (2004); Simmons (2005).

4. Details are provided in Appendix B. Recent works that use this measure as a proxy for trade policy openness include Rose (2004); McDonald (2004); Dutt and Mitra (2005); and Henisz and Mansfield (2006).

5. The basic gravity model posits trade between two countries to be an increasing function of the size of the two economies and a negative function of the distance between them; the model continues to be used widely as the baseline model for testing a range of trade-related hypotheses. See, for example, Gowa and Mansfield (2004); Simmons (2005); Long (2003b); Rose (2004).

6. Data on gross domestic product and per capita income come from Gleditsch (2002). Distance data come from Hengeveld (1996). Entering GDPs in product form is common (Mansfield et al. 2000; Gowa and Mansfield 2004).

7. Here I use Rose's (2004) measure, which for country i with trading partners j is the inverse of the mean value (across the different j) of: the log of j's real GDP divided by the

logged distance between i and j. Data available on Rose's webpage at: http://faculty.haas. berkeley.edu/arose/RecRes.htm.

8. Data on island and landlocked countries come from Rose (2004).

9. Data on arable land come from World Bank (2001); per capita income data come from Gleditsch (2002).

10. The models reported below were estimated in Stata, using ordinary least squares with Huber/White robust standard errors, adjusting for clustering within dyads. Data on democracy comes from the Polity IV dataset (Marshall and Jaggers, 2000).

11. Other simulations conducted using Clarify (King et al., 2000) suggest that, when all other variables are held constant at their mean/median values, a shift from low to high conflict (where the UN variable moves from its 15th percentile to its 85th percentile) starts to have a significant, negative effect on bilateral trade flows when the trade barriers variable reaches its 45th percentile. The effect becomes larger and more significant as trade barrier levels increase beyond that.

12. Pakistan's motivations in this regard are the source of some dispute; see Lamb (1991) and Jha (1996).

13. For a discussion of these crises, see Ganguly and Hagerty (2005).

14. "India and Pakistan Mobilizing Troops Along the Border," *New York Times*, December 25, 2001: http://query.nytimes.com/gst/fullpage.html?res=9C05E4D81531F936A15 751C1A9679C8B63&scp=1&sq=India%20and%20Pakistan%20Mobilizing%20Troops%20 along%20the%20Border&st=cse (accessed June 19, 2008).

15. For a detailed overview of these incidents, see Oberdorfer (2001).

16. *FEER*, July 10, 2003, 6.

17. See, for example, *The Economist*, July 15, 2006, 40.

18. Indeed, India's main business association in the 1950s, the Federation of Indian Chambers of Commerce and Industry, clearly opposed the move toward socialism (Nayar 2001, 74–75).

19. While suspicious of the drastic turn toward socialism and autarky in general, it should be noted that Indian industrialists unsurprisingly did look more kindly on discrimination toward foreign firms in India, and lobbied the Congress to this effect (Desai 1999, 11).

20. Though Jenkins (1999) notes that politicians turned out to be good at finding alternative sources of patronage once the corruption-ridden industrial and import licensing system started to undergo reform.

21. *The Economist*, June 12, 2004, 67.

22. Chhibber (1995) writes that the nature of political competition in India makes it difficult for parties to pursue reforms that aim to rationalize government expenditures. National parties, notes Chhibber (1995, 76), "rely on distributing state resources to mobilize public support." As such, regulatory reforms—like reducing barriers to imports—are more politically feasible in India than are efforts to reduce government expenditures and subsidies.

23. Address by Dr. A. C. Muthiah, President, FICCI, delivered to the Conference on India-Pakistan Trade, July 7, 2003, available online at: www.ficci.com/meida-room/speech-es-presentations/2003/july/july7-ac-pak.htm (accessed December 3, 2006).

24. Guisinger and Scully (1991, 233) devise an index showing that Pakistan liberalized trade policy to a limited extent in the early to mid-1970s, but that liberalization stopped after the mid-1970s.

25. For an extended discussion of *juche*, see Cumings (2005, ch. 8) and Park (2002). While it is often translated as self-sufficiency, Cumings (2005) emphasizes that an accurate translation into English is difficult.

26. Though Solingen (1998) suggests that the reforms of the 1990s could indicate a stronger liberalizing camp than had existed in previous decades.

27. On the strength of the state relative to the business sector, see also Haggard and Moon (1983, 142).

28. These numbers represent estimates and greatly exceed officially reported expenses (see Kang 2002, 195).

29. Cumings (2005, 397) writes that "Kim Dae Jung was never a radical, and did not have a strong base in labor, for two reasons: first, until 1998 it was illegal for labor to involve itself in politics; second, over the years Kim was much more a champion of small and medium business than of labor." But by the same token, "he was clearly more sympathetic to labor demands than previous leaders . . . and labor preferred him to" previous leaders—which, Cumings emphasizes, was not saying much given the labor policies of previous administrations.

30. On the *chaebols'* integration into global markets, see also Kim (2000).

31. On trade in the early 2000s, see *FEER*, May 22, 2003, 38. For the US$1 billion figure, see "Pakistan-India Bilateral Trade Crosses $1US BLN," *Asia Pulse*, March 20, 2006. In LexisNexis. The latter article suggests that actual trade between the two countries is probably closer to US$2 billion when illegal trade is taken into account.

32. Address by Dr. A. C. Muthiah, President, FICCI, delivered to the Conference on India-Pakistan Trade.

33. "Pakistan-India Bilateral Trade Crosses $1US BLN." The estimate comes from a different peak business association in India, the Associated Chambers of Commerce and Industry (Assocham).

34. Pakistan again banned private trade in 1978 (following Zia's coup), in part because the government believed Indian trade was threatening Pakistani industries. Private links were reestablished in 1986. See "India, Pakistan Are So Busy Squabbling They Ignore Their Languishing Trade," *Wall Street Journal*, May 2, 1986; Johal (1989, 205); "India-Pakistan Links Suffer Setback with Trade Mission Ban," *Financial Times*, August 26, 1983. In LexisNexis.

35. See also, "Pakistan's Talks with India Fail to Get Trade Deal; Joint Commission Deadlocked on Key Issue," *The Times (London)*, July 5, 1985. In LexisNexis.

36. "India, Pakistan Are So Busy Squabbling They Ignore Their Languishing Trade."

37. "Additional Items Allowed to Be Imported from India," *The Statesman (India)*, July 17, 1997. In LexisNexis.

38. "Pakistan Not to Extend MFN Status to India," *The Hindu*, May 1, 1998. In Lexis-Nexis.

39. "Pakistan Govt Flayed for Easing Trade with India," *The Statesman (India)*, July 18, 1997. In LexisNexis.

40. "India to Pitch for MFN Status with Pakistan," *The Economic Times Online (India Times)*, November 30, 2006: http://economictimes.indiatimes.com/articleshow/msid-644490,prtpage-1.cms (accessed June 19, 2008).

41. On this point, see also *FEER*, May 22, 2003, 38.

42. "With Pomp and Jeers, India and Pakistan Shut Border," *New York Times*, January 1, 2002 (in LexisNexis); "India and Pakistan Mobilizing Troops Along the Border."

43. "India and Pakistan Mobilizing Troops Along the Border."

44. Ibid.

45. "Tit-for-Tat Bans Raise Tension on Kashmir," *Times of London*, December 28, 2001. In LexisNexis.

46. "With Pomp and Jeers, India and Pakistan Shut Border."

47. "Border with Pakistan Reportedly Sealed." Paris AFP, September 9, 1986 (in *FBIS-India*, September 10); "Indian Embassy Stops Issuing Visas," Hong Kong AFP, November 16, 1986 (in *FBIS-Pakistan*, November 17).

48. *Wall Street Journal*, December 24, 2001, A7.

49. *FEER*, May 22, 2003, 39.

50. "Urdu Daily: Kashmir Issue More Important than India-Iran Gas Pipeline Project," *Rawalpindi Nawa-i-Waqt*, June 15, 2001 (editorial). In World News Connection.

51. *Wall Street Journal*, December 24, 2001, A7.

52. See, for example, "India, Pakistan Holding Talks on Gas Pipeline," *The Globe and Mail* (Canada), June 6, 2005 (in LexisNexis); "Pakistan, India Commit to 2009 Start-up for Pipeline Construction," *Downstream Today*, May 1, 2008: http://www.downstreamtoday. com/News/Articles/200805/Pakistan_India_Commit_to_Start_up__10561.aspx?AspxAu toDetectCookieSupport=1 (accessed June 30, 2008). Other obstacles, besides the often tense rivalry between India and Pakistan, also stand in the way of the project, including possible U.S. objections to a deal with Iran, and the danger of attacks on the pipeline by terrorist groups outside the influence of the Pakistan state.

53. The idea of *Nordpolitik* existed long before Roh's presidency; indeed, Chun's foreign minister had announced in 1983 that Seoul would make establishing relations with Moscow and Beijing a foreign policy priority (Oberdorfer 2001, 187). However, it was only under Roh that substantial steps were taken to achieve these aims.

54. *The Economist*, October 22, 1994, 38. Not surprisingly, some South Korean firms circumvented official bans on direct investment through subsidiaries in third countries. See *Asian Business*, December 1993, 10.

55. *The Economist*, November 12, 1994, 81. *The Economist* suggests that Kim worried that liberalizing too rapidly would allow the *chaebols* to establish a strong foothold in North Korea: he was "loath to give the *chaebols*, which account for more than half of South Korea's private sector, even more power."

56. *Business Korea*, September 1995, 14.

57. *Business Korea*, September 1995, 14. For a detailed account of the negotiations, see Oberdorfer (2001, 365–68).

58. *Business Korea*, September 1995, 14.

59. On the Sunshine Policy as a transformative engagement strategy, see Kahler and Kastner (2006).

60. For details of the Mount Kumgang venture, see Ministry of Unification, ROK (2005, 68–70). The project enabled South Korean tourists to visit Mount Kumgang in North Korea; in the year 2000, over 200,000 South Koreans made the trip (via cruise boat). That number declined drastically as the project hit financial difficulties in 2001, though the addition of an overland route in 2003 led to renewed interest: in 2004 over 260,000 South Korean tourists made the trip.

61. "South Korea to Continue 'Utmost Efforts' for Inter-Korean Complex—Minister," BBC Monitoring International Reports, December 8, 2006. In LexisNexis.

62. "Korea Summit Meeting Paves Way for Joint Projects," *New York Times*, October 5, 2007. In LexisNexis.

63. "2 Koreas Agree on Aid to North and Trains Across Border," *New York Times*, November 18, 2007. In LexisNexis.

64. For events under Lee Myung-bak, see: "Korean Industrial Zone in Spotlight Amid Tension," *Washington Post*, November 25, 2008: http://www.washingtonpost.com/wp-dyn/content/article/2008/11/25/AR2008112501433.html (accessed December 5, 2008); "South Korea Adds Terms for its Aid to the North," *New York Times*, March 27, 2008: http://www.nytimes.com/2008/03/27/world/asia/27korea.html (accessed December 5, 2008).

65. The estimate is from South Korea's Unification Ministry. See "Perils of Investing in N. Korea Become Clear to a Pioneer," *Washington Post,* November 24, 2005. In LexisNexis.

66. Ibid. Hyundai was eventually able to resolve this particular issue with Pyongyang.

Chapter 8

1. I thank an anonymous referee for making this point.

2. This is not to suggest that these firms should be viewed as allies of Beijing at this time. Rather, as far as potential future allies go, these firms are among the most likely candidates.

3. Studies that have considered different facets of the issue of "engaging" China include, for example, Christensen (2006); Friedberg (2005); Papayoanou and Kastner (1999/2000); Shambaugh (1996); Mearsheimer (2001). For a systematic analysis examining whether China should be considered a status quo or revisionist power, see Johnston (2003). For an earlier analysis of the consequences of China's rise, see Goldstein (1997/98).

4. This quote is Romberg's (2008, 8) translation. As Romberg notes, the official English translation is a bit weaker: "Only when Taiwan is no longer being isolated in the international arena can cross-Strait relations move forward with confidence."

5. James Shinn, the U.S. assistant secretary of defense for East Asia, recently warned Congress that the shift in the military balance "materially increase[s] the danger across the Strait." See "Risk of Chinese Attack Has Heightened: U.S. Official," *Taipei Times,* June 27, 2008: http://www.taipeitimes.com/News/front/archives/2008/06/27/2003415884 (accessed June 27, 2008). On the long-term prospects for a PRC-Taiwan unification bargain, see Kastner and Rector (2008).

Appendix A

The appendix expands on the discussion in Chapter 6, Section 3. The model presented here is based on and developed more fully in Kastner (2006a).

1. This application of a take-it-or-leave-it game follows Fearon (1995). For a review of bargaining models of war, see Powell (2002).

2. On this logic, see Morrow (1999) and Gartzke et al. (2001). These authors argue that the increased costs of war associated with economic interdependence are not sufficient to reduce the likelihood of war, because states could simply increase their demands as war's costs rise.

Appendix B

The appendix expands on the discussion in Chapter 7, Section 2.

1. Works that use alliance portfolios as an indicator of preferences are numerous and

date to Bueno de Mesquita (1975). For a discussion, see Bueno de Mesquita and Lalman (1992, 288–94); Signorino and Ritter (1999); and Gartzke (1998). Here again I use Signorino and Ritter's S measure.

2. The end-year for analyses using this variable is 1984, the last year of Tucker's data set.

3. Azar (1980).

4. The end-year for analyses using the COPDAB measure is 1978, the last year of that data set.

5. Bennett (1996); Bennett (1997).

6. Sachs and Warner (1995). For a recent article that uses this measure, see Milner and Kubota (2005).

7. I added "1" before taking the log to ensure only positive values.

References

Abdelal, Rawi, and Jonathan Kirshner. 1999/2000. Strategy, Economic Relations, and the Definition of National Interests. *Security Studies* 9 (1/2): 119–56.

Anderton, Charles H., and John R. Carter. 2001. The Impact of War on Trade: An Interrupted Times-Series Study. *Journal of Peace Research* 38 (4): 445–57.

Azar, Edward E. 1980. The Conflict and Peace Data Bank (COPDAB) Project. *Journal of Conflict Resolution* 24 (1): 143–52.

Baldwin, David. 1985. *Economic Statecraft*. Princeton, NJ: Princeton University Press.

Baldwin, David, ed. 1993. *Neorealism and Neoliberalism: The Contemporary Debate*. New York: Columbia University Press.

Barbieri, Katherine. 1996. Economic Interdependence: A Path to Peace or a Source of Interstate Conflict? *Journal of Peace Research* 33 (1): 29–49.

Barbieri, Katherine. 2002. *The Liberal Illusion: Does Trade Promote Peace?* Ann Arbor: University of Michigan Press.

Barbieri, Katherine, and Jack S. Levy. 1999. Sleeping with the Enemy: The Impact of War on Trade. *Journal of Peace Research* 36 (4): 463–79.

Barbieri, Katherine, and Gerald Schneider. 1999. Globalization and Peace: Assessing New Directions in the Study of Trade and Conflict. *Journal of Peace Research* 36 (4): 387–404.

Baxter, Craig, Yogendra K. Malik, Charles H. Kennedy, and Robert C. Oberst. 2002. *Government and Politics in South Asia*. Boulder, CO: Westview Press.

Beck, Nathaniel, and Jonathan N. Katz. 1996. Nuisance vs. Substance: Specifying and Estimating Time-Series-Cross-Section Models. *Political Analysis* 6 (1): 1–36.

Beck, Nathaniel, and Jonathan N. Katz. 2001. Throwing Out the Baby with the Bath Water: A Comment on Green, Kim, and Yoon. *International Organization* 55 (2): 487–95.

Bennett, D. Scott. 1996. Security, Bargaining, and the End of Interstate Rivalry. *International Studies Quarterly* 40 (2): 157–83.

Bennett, D. Scott. 1997. Measuring Rivalry Termination, 1816–1992. *Journal of Conflict Resolution* 41 (2): 227–54.

Benson, Brett V., and Emerson M. S. Niou. 2000. Comprehending Strategic Ambiguity: U.S. Policy Toward Taiwan Security. Unpublished paper posted online in *Taiwan Security Research*: http://taiwansecurity.org/IS/IS-Niou-0400.htm.

Benson, Brett V., and Emerson M. S. Niou. 2005. Public Opinion, Foreign Policy, and the Security Balance in the Taiwan Strait. *Security Studies* 14 (2): 274–89.

Bertsch, Gary K., and Steven Elliott-Gower. 1991. U.S. Export Controls in Transition: Implications of the New Security Environment. In *Technology Markets and Export Controls in the 1990s*, ed. David M. Kemme, 105–27. New York: New York University Press.

Bolt, Paul J. 2001. Economic Ties Across the Taiwan Strait: Buying Time for Compromise. *Issues and Studies* 37 (2): 80–105.

Bueno de Mesquita, Bruce. 1975. Measuring Systemic Polarity. *Journal of Conflict Resolution* 19: 187–215.

Bueno de Mesquita, Bruce, and David Lalman. 1992. *War and Reason: Domestic and International Imperatives*. New Haven, CT: Yale University Press.

Bush, Richard C. 2005. *Untying the Knot: Making Peace in the Taiwan Strait*. Washington DC: Brookings.

Buzo, Adrian. 1999. *The Guerilla Dynasty: Politics and Leadership in North Korea*. Boulder, CO: Westview Press.

Chao, Chien-min. 2003. Will Economic Integration Between Mainland China and Taiwan Lead to a Congenial Political Culture? *Asian Survey* 43 (2): 280–304.

Chao, Chien-min. 2004. National Security vs. Economic Interests: Reassessing Taiwan's Mainland Policy Under Chen Shui-bian. *Journal of Contemporary China* 13 (41): 687–704.

Chase, Michael S., Kevin L. Pollpeter, and James C. Mulvenon. 2004. *Shanghaied? The Economic and Political Implications of the Flow of Information Technology and Investment Across the Taiwan Strait*. Santa Monica, CA: RAND Corporation.

Chawla, K. L. 2001. India-Pakistan Trade Relations: Viable Options Despite Hurdles. *India Quarterly* 57 (2): 139–56.

Chen, Ming-chi. 2004. Sinicization and Its Discontents: Cross-Strait Economic Integration and Taiwan's 2004 Presidential Election. *Issues & Studies* 40 (3/4): 334–41.

Chen, Qimao. 1999. The Taiwan Strait Crisis: Causes, Scenarios, and Solutions. In *Across the Taiwan Strait: Mainland China, Taiwan, and the 1995–1996 Crisis*, ed. Suisheng Zhao, 127–59. New York: Routledge.

Chen, T., and C.Y.C. Chu. 2001. Cross-Strait Economic Relations: Can They Ameliorate the Political Problem? In *Taiwan's Presidential Politics: Democratization and Cross-Strait Relations in the Twenty-First Century*, ed. Muthiah Alagappa, 215–35. Armonk, NY: M. E. Sharpe.

Chen, Xiangming. 1994. The New Spatial Division of Labor and Commodity Chains in the Greater South China Economic Region. In *Commodity Chains and Global Capitalism*, ed. Gary Gereffi and Miguel Korzeniewicz, 165–85. Westport, CT: Greenwood Press.

Cheng, Tun-jen. 1990. Political Regimes and Development Strategies: South Korea and Taiwan. In *Manufacturing Miracles: Paths of Industrialization in Latin American and East Asia*, ed. Gary Gereffi and Donald L. Wyman, 139–78. Princeton, NJ: Princeton University Press.

Cheng, Tun-jen. 1997. Taiwan in 1996: From Euphoria to Melodrama. *Asian Survey* 37 (1): 43–51.

Chhibber, Pradeep. 1995. Political Parties, Political Competition, Government Expenditures, and Economic Reform in India. *Journal of Development Studies* 32 (1): 74–96.

Chhibber, Pradeep, and Samuel Eldersveld. 2000. Local Elites and Popular Support for Economic Reform in China and India. *Comparative Political Studies* 33 (3): 350–73.

Chiu, Hungdah. 1983. Prospects for the Unification of China: An Analysis of the Views of the Republic of China on Taiwan. *Asian Survey* 23 (10): 1081–94.

Chiu, Lee-in Chen. 1995. The Pattern and Impact of Taiwan's Investment in Mainland China. In *Emerging Patterns of East-Asian Investment in China: From Korea, Taiwan, and Hong Kong*, ed. Sumner J. La Croix, Michael Plummer, and Keun Lee, 143–65. Armonk, NY: M. E. Sharpe.

Chopra, Surendra. 1977. Prospects of Indo-Pakistan Trade. *Indian Journal of Political Science* 38 (4): 476–93.

Christensen, Thomas J. 1996. *Useful Adversaries: Grand Strategy, Domestic Mobilization, and Sino-American Conflict, 1947–1958*. Princeton, NJ: Princeton University Press.

Christensen, Thomas J. 2005. Taiwan's Legislative Yuan Elections and Cross-Strait Security Relations: Reduced Tensions and Remaining Challenges. *China Leadership Monitor* 13: http://www.hoover.org/publications/clm/issues/2903801.html.

Christensen, Thomas J. 2006. Fostering Stability or Creating a Monster? *International Security* 31 (1): 81–126.

Chu, Yun-han. 1994. The Realignment of Business-Government Relations and Regime Transition in Taiwan. In *Business and Government in Industrialising Asia*, ed. Andrew MacIntyre, 113–41. Ithaca, NY: Cornell University Press.

Chu, Yun-han. 1997. The Political Economy of Taiwan's Mainland Policy. *Journal of Contemporary China* 6 (15): 229–57.

Chu, Yun-han. 2000. Making Sense of Beijing's Policy Toward Taiwan: The Prospect of Cross-Strait Relations During the Jiang Zemin Era. In *China Under Jiang Zemin*, ed. Hung-Mao Tien and Yun-han Chu, 193–212. Boulder, CO: Lynne Rienner.

Chu, Yun-han. 2004. Taiwan's National Identity Politics and the Prospect of Cross-Strait Relations. *Asian Survey* 44 (4): 484–512.

Chung, Jae Ho. 2001. Reappraising Central-Local Relations in Deng's China: Decentralization, Dilemmas of Control, and Diluted Effects of Reform. In *Remaking the Chinese State: Strategies, Society, and Security*, ed. Chien-min Chao and Bruce J. Dickson, 46–75. London: Routledge.

Clark, Cal. 2002. Growing Cross-Strait Economic Integration. *Orbis* 46 (4): 753–66.

Cobden, Richard. 1995. *Political Writings* (Vol. 1). London: Routledge.

Copeland, Dale C. 1999/2000. Trade Expectations and the Outbreak of Peace: Détente 1970–74 and the End of the Cold War 1985–91. *Security Studies* 9 (1/2): 15–58.

Copper, John F. 1996. *Taiwan: Nation-State or Province?* Boulder, CO: Westview Press.

Cox, Gary W., and Emerson Niou. 1994. Seat Bonuses Under the Single Nontransferable Vote System: Evidence from Japan and Taiwan. *Comparative Politics* 26 (2): 221–36.

Cumings, Bruce. 2005. *Korea's Place in the Sun: A Modern History*. New York: W. W. Norton.

Davis, Patricia A. 1999. *The Art of Economic Persuasion: Positive Incentives and German Economic Diplomacy*. Ann Arbor: University of Michigan Press.

Deng, Ping. 2000. Taiwan's Restriction of Investment in China in the 1990s: A Relative Gains Approach. *Asian Survey* 40 (6): 958–80.

Deng, Xiaoping. 1984. *Selected Works of Deng Xiaoping (1975–1982)*. Beijing: Foreign Languages Press.

Desai, Ashok V. 1999. *The Economics and Politics of Transition to an Open Market Economy: India*. OECD Technical Papers No. 155. Paris: OECD.

Deutsch, Karl W., and collaborators. 1957. *Political Community and the North Atlantic Area*. Princeton, NJ: Princeton University Press.

Diehl, Paul F., and Gary Goertz. 2000. *War and Peace in International Rivalry*. Ann Arbor: University of Michigan Press.

Dixon, William J., and Bruce E. Moon. 1993. Political Similarity and American Foreign Trade Patterns. *Political Research Quarterly* 46 (1): 5–25.

Drezner, Daniel W. 1999. *The Sanctions Paradox: Economic Statecraft and International Relations*. Cambridge, UK: Cambridge University Press.

Drezner, Daniel W. 1999/2000. The Trouble with Carrots: Transaction Costs, Conflict Expectations, and Economic Inducements. *Security Studies* 9 (1/2): 188–218.

Drezner, Daniel W. 2000. The Complex Causation of Sanction Outcomes. In *Sanctions as Economic Statecraft: Theory and Practice*, ed. Steve Chan and A. Cooper Drury, 212–33. New York: St. Martin's.

Dutt, Amitava Krishna. 1997. Uncertain Success: The Political Economy of Indian Economic Reform. *Journal of International Affairs* 51 (1): 57–83.

Dutt, Pushan, and Devashish Mitra. 2005. Political Ideology and Endogenous Trade Policy: An Empirical Investigation. *Review of Economics and Statistics* 87 (1): 59–72.

Ehrlich, Sean D. 2007. Access to Protection: Domestic Institutions and Trade Policies in Democracies. *International Organization* 61 (3): 571–605.

Executive Yuan, Republic of China. 2003. *Summary of the Main Findings in the Assessment of the Impact of Direct Cross-Strait Transportation (Government Report)*. Taipei: ROC Government.

Fair, Christine. 2005. *India and Pakistan Engagement: Prospects for Breakthrough or Breakdown?* United States Institute of Peace Special Report, No. 129 (January): http://www.usip.org/pubs/specialreports/sr129.html.

Fearon, James D. 1994. Domestic Political Audiences and the Escalation of International Disputes. *American Political Science Review* 88 (3): 577–92.

Fearon, James D. 1995. Rationalist Explanations for War. *International Organization* 49 (3): 379–414.

Fewsmith. Joseph. 2001. *China Since Tiananmen: The Politics of Transition*. Cambridge, UK: Cambridge University Press.

Frieden, Jeffry A. 1991. Invested Interests: The Politics of National Economic Policies in a World of Global Finance. *International Organization* 45: 425–51.

Frieden, Jeffry A. 1999. Actors and Preferences in International Relations. In *Strategic Choice and International Relations*, ed. David A. Lake and Robert Powell, 39–76. Princeton, NJ: Princeton University Press.

Frieden, Jeffry A., and Ronald Rogowski. 1996. The Impact of the International Economy on National Policies: An Analytical Overview. In *Internationalization and Domestic Politics*, ed. Robert O. Keohane and Helen V. Milner, 25–47. Cambridge, UK: Cambridge University Press.

Friedberg, Aaron L. 2005. The Future of US-China Relations: Is Conflict Inevitable? *International Security* 30 (2): 7–45.

Gaddis, John Lewis. 1982. *Strategies of Containment: A Critical Appraisal of Postwar American National Security Policy.* New York: Oxford University Press.

Ganguly, Sumit. 2001. *Conflict Unending: India-Pakistan Tensions Since 1947.* New Delhi: Oxford University Press.

Ganguly, Sumit, and Devin T. Hagerty. 2005. *Fearful Symmetry: India-Pakistan Crises in the Shadow of Nuclear Weapons.* Seattle, WA: University of Washington Press.

Gartzke, Erik. 1998. Kant We All Just Get Along? Opportunity, Willingness, and the Origins of the Democratic Peace. *American Journal of Political Science* 42 (1): 1–27.

Gartzke, Erik. 1999. War Is in the Error Term. *International Organization* 53 (3): 567–87.

Gartzke, Erik. 2000. Preferences and the Democratic Peace. *International Studies Quarterly* 44 (2): 191–212.

Gartzke, Erik. 2003. The Classical Liberals Were Just Lucky: A Few Thoughts About Interdependence and Peace. In *Economic Interdependence and International Conflict: New Perspectives on an Enduring Debate*, ed. Edward D. Mansfield and Brian M. Pollins, 96–110. Ann Arbor: University of Michigan Press.

Gartzke, Erik, Dong-Joon Jo, and Richard Tucker. 1999. *The Similarity of UN Policy Positions, 1946–96.* Version 1.17 (dataset): http://www.vanderbilt.edu/~rtucker/data/affinity/un/similar (accessed 2003).

Gartzke, Erik, and Quan Li. 2003a. War, Peace, and the Invisible Hand: Positive Political Externalities of Economic Globalization. *International Studies Quarterly* 47 (4): 561–86.

Gartzke, Erik, and Quan Li. 2003b. How Globalization Can Reduce International Conflict. In *Globalization and Armed Conflict*, ed. Nils Petter Gleditsch, Gerald Schneider, and Katherine Barbieri, 123–40. New York: Rowman & Littlefield.

Gartzke, Erik, Quan Li, and Charles Boehmer. 2001. Economic Interdependence and International Conflict. *International Organization* 55 (2): 391–438.

Gelpi, Christopher, and Joseph M. Grieco. 2003. Economic Interdependence, the Democratic State, and the Liberal Peace. In *Economic Interdependence and International Conflict: New Perspectives on an Enduring Debate*, ed. Edward D. Mansfield and Brian M. Pollins, 44–59. Ann Arbor: University of Michigan Press.

George, Alexander L., and Andrew Bennett. 2005. *Case Studies and Theory Development in the Social Sciences.* Cambridge, MA: MIT Press.

Gilpin, Robert. 1987. *The Political Economy of International Relations.* Princeton, NJ: Princeton University Press.

Gleditsch, Kristian Skrede. 2002. Expanded Trade and GDP Data. *Journal of Conflict Resolution* 46 (5): 712–24.

Glick, Reuven, and Alan M. Taylor. 2005. Collateral Damage: Trade Disruption and the Economic Impact of War. Cambridge, MA: National Bureau of Economic Research working paper 11565.

Goldstein, Avery. 1997/98. Great Expectations: Interpreting China's Arrival. *International Security* 22 (3): 36–73.

Goldstein, Steven. 1999. The Cross-Strait Talks of 1993—The Rest of the Story: Domestic Politics and Taiwan's Mainland Policy. In *Across the Taiwan Strait: Mainland China, Taiwan, and the 1995–1996 Crisis*, ed. Suisheng Zhao, 197–228. New York: Routledge.

Gowa, Joanne. 1994. *Allies, Adversaries, and International Trade.* Princeton, NJ: Princeton University Press.

Gowa, Joanne, and Edward D. Mansfield. 1993. Power Politics and International Trade. *American Political Science Review* 87 (2): 408–20.

Gowa, Joanne, and Edward D. Mansfield. 2004. Alliances, Imperfect Markets, and Major-Power Trade. *International Organization* 58 (4): 775–805.

Grampp, William D. 1960. *The Manchester School of Economics.* Stanford, CA: Stanford University Press.

Green, Donald P., Soo Yeon Kim, and David H. Yoon. 2001. Dirty Pool. *International Organization* 55 (2): 441–68.

Grieco, Joseph. 1988. Anarchy and the Limits of Cooperation: A Realist Critique of the Newest Liberal Institutionalism. *International Organization* 42: 485–507.

Gu, Weiqun. 1995. *Conflicts of Divided Nations: The Cases of China and Korea.* Westport, CT: Praeger.

Guisinger, Stephen, and Gerald Scully. 1991. Pakistan. In *Liberalizing Foreign Trade: The Experience of Indonesia, Pakistan, and Sri Lanka,* ed. Demetris Papageorgiou, Michael Michaely, and Armeane M. Choksi, 197–282. Oxford, UK: Basil Blackwell.

Haas, Ernst B. 1958. *The Uniting of Europe: Political, Social, and Economic Forces 1950–1957.* Stanford, CA: Stanford University Press.

Haggard, Stephan, and Chung-in Moon. 1983. The South Korean State in the International Economy: Liberal, Dependent, or Mercantile? In *The Antinomies of Interdependence: National Welfare and the International Division of Labor,* ed. John Gerald Ruggie, 131–89. New York: Columbia University Press.

Haggard, Stephan, and Chung-in Moon. 1993. The State, Politics, and Economic Development in Postwar South Korea. In *State and Society in Contemporary Korea,* ed. Hagen Koo, 51–93. Ithaca, NY: Cornell University Press.

Hengeveld, W.A.B. 1996. *World Distance Tables, 1948–1974* [Computer file]. ICPSR version. Amsterdam: W.A.B. Hengeveld, University of Amsterdam [producer], 1983. Ann Arbor, MI: Inter-university Consortium for Political and Social Research [distributor].

Henisz, Witold J., and Edward D. Mansfield. 2006. Votes and Vetoes: The Political Determinants of Commercial Openness. *International Studies Quarterly* 50: 189–211.

Hirschman, Albert O. 1945. *National Power and the Structure of Foreign Trade.* Berkeley: University of California Press.

Hiscox, Michael J. 2001. Class Versus Industry Cleavages: Inter-Industry Factor Mobility and the Politics of Trade. *International Organization* 55 (1): 1–46.

Hiscox, Michael J. 2002. *International Trade and Political Conflict: Commerce, Coalitions, and Mobility.* Princeton, NJ: Princeton University Press.

Hiscox, Michael J., and Scott L. Kastner. 2002. A General Measure of Trade Policy Orientations: Gravity-Model-Based Estimates for 82 Nations, 1960 to 1992. Unpublished manuscript, Harvard University.

Ho, Szu-yin, and Tse-kang Leng. 2004. Accounting for Taiwan's Economic Policy Toward China. *Journal of Contemporary China* 13 (41): 733–46.

Hsing, You-tien. 1998. *Making Capitalism in China: The Taiwan Connection.* New York: Oxford University Press.

Huang, Tianlin. 2003. San Tong, Jingji Jiaoliu yu Jinji Anquan (Three Direct Links, Economic Exchange and Economic Security). In *Liang'an Jiaoliu yu Goujia Anquan* (Cross-Strait Exchange and National Security), 276–303. Taipei: Taiwan Advocates.

Huang, Yasheng. 1996. *Inflation and Investment Controls in China*. New York: Cambridge University Press.

Huang, Yasheng. 2001. Political Institutions and Fiscal Reforms in China. *Problems of Post-Communism* 48 (1): 16–26.

Husain, Ishrat. 1999. *Pakistan: The Economy of an Elitist State*. Karachi: Oxford University Press.

International Monetary Fund. Various Years. *Direction of Trade Statistics*. Washington, DC.

Jenkins, Rob. 1999. *Democratic Politics and Economic Reform in India*. Cambridge, UK: Cambridge University Press.

Jensen, Nathan M. 2006. *Nation-States and the Multinational Corporation*. Princeton, NJ: Princeton University Press.

Jervis, Robert. 1970. *The Logic of Images in International Relations*. Princeton, NJ: Princeton University Press.

Jha, Prem Shankar. 1996. *Kashmir, 1947: Rival Versions of History*. New Delhi: Oxford University Press.

Johal, Sarbjit. 1989. *Conflict and Integration in Indo-Pakistan Relations*. Berkeley: Centers for South and Southeast Asia Studies, University of California, Berkeley.

Johnston, Alastair Iain. 2003. Is China a Status Quo Power? *International Security* 27 (4): 5–56.

Joshi, Vijay, and I.M.D. Little. 1996. *India's Economic Reforms: 1991–2000*. New Delhi: Oxford University Press.

Kahler, Miles, and Scott L. Kastner. 2006. Strategic Uses of Economic Interdependence: Engagement Policies on the Korean Peninsula and Across the Taiwan Strait. *Journal of Peace Research* 43 (5): 523–41.

Kang, David C. 2002. Bad Loans to Good Friends: Money Politics and the Developmental State in South Korea. *International Organization* 56 (1): 177–207.

Kang, Heejoon, and Rafael Reuveny. 2001. Exploring Multi-Country Dynamic Relations Between Trade and Conflict. *Defence and Peace Economics* 12: 175–96.

Kastner, Scott L. 2006a. Rethinking the Political Consequences of Economic Integration in Mainland China-Taiwan Relations. In *Reflections on the Triangular Relations of Beijing-Taipei-Washington Since 1995: Status Quo at the Taiwan Straits?*, ed. Shiping Hua, 255–71. New York: Palgrave Macmillan.

Kastner, Scott L. 2006b. Does Economic Integration Across the Taiwan Strait Make Military Conflict Less Likely? *Journal of East Asian Studies* 6 (3): 319–46.

Kastner, Scott L. 2007. When Do Conflicting Political Relations Affect International Trade? *Journal of Conflict Resolution* 51 (4): 664–88.

Kastner, Scott L., and Chad Rector. 2008. Bargaining Power and Mistrust: Credible Commitments and the Prospects for a PRC/Taiwan Agreement. *Security Studies* 17 (1): 39–71.

Kau, Michael Ying-mao. 1996. The Power Structure in Taiwan's Political Economy. *Asian Survey* 36 (3): 287–305.

Keohane, Robert O., and Joseph S. Nye. 1989. *Power and Interdependence*. New York: Longman.

Keshk, Omar M. G., Brian M. Pollins, and Rafael Reuveny. 2004. Trade Still Follows the Flag: The Primacy of Politics in a Simultaneous Model of Interdependence and Armed Conflict. *Journal of Politics* 66 (4): 1155–79.

Keum, Hieyeon, and Joel R. Campbell. 2001. Devouring Dragon and Escaping Tiger: China's Unification Policy vs. Taiwan's Quasi-Independence as a Problem of International Relations. *East Asia* (Spring/Summer): 58–94.

Kihl, Young Whan. 2006. Staying Power of the Socialist "Hermit Kingdom." In *North Korea: The Politics of Regime Survival*, ed. Young Whan Kihl and Hong Nack Kim, 3–33. Armonk, NY: M. E. Sharpe.

Kim, Eun Mee. 2000. Globalization of the South Korean *Chaebol*. In *Korea's Globalization*, ed. Samuel S. Kim, 102–25. Cambridge, UK: Cambridge University Press.

Kim, Hyung Min, and David L. Rousseau. 2005. The Classical Liberals Were Half Right (or Half Wrong): New Tests of the "Liberal Peace," 1960–88. *Journal of Peace Research* 42 (5): 523–43.

Kim, Ilpyong J. 2006. Kim Jong Il's Military-First Politics. In *North Korea: The Politics of Regime Survival*, ed. Young Whan Kihl and Hong Nack Kim, 59–74. Armonk, NY: M. E. Sharpe.

Kim, Soo Yeon. 1998. *Ties That Bind: The Role of Trade in International Conflict Processes, 1950–1992*. Ph.D. Dissertation, Yale University.

King, Gary, Robert O. Keohane, and Sidney Verba. 1994. *Designing Social Inquiry: Scientific Inference in Qualitative Research*. Princeton, NJ: Princeton University Press.

King, Gary, Michael Tomz, and Jason Wittenberg. 2000. Making the Most of Statistical Analysis: Improving Interpretation and Presentation. *American Journal of Political Science* 44 (2): 347–61.

Kohli, Atul. 1990. *Democracy and Discontent: India's Growing Crisis of Governability*. Cambridge, UK: Cambridge University Press.

Kuo, Julian J. 1998. *Minjindang Zhuanxing zhi Tong* (The DPP's Ordeal of Transformation). Taipei: Commonwealth Publishing.

Kwon, Eundak, and Jae-Cheon Lim. 2006. Crossing the River That Divides the Korean Peninsula: An Evaluation of the Sunshine Policy. *International Relations of the Asia-Pacific* 6: 129–56.

La Croix, Sumner J., and Yibo Xu. 1995. Political Uncertainty and Taiwan's Investment in Xiamen's Special Economic Zone. In *Emerging Patterns of East Asian Investment in China: From Korea, Taiwan, and Hong Kong*, ed. Sumner La Croix, Michael Plummer, and Keun Lee, 123–41. Armonk, NY: M. E. Sharpe.

Lake, David A. 1999. *Entangling Relations: American Foreign Policy in Its Century*. Princeton, NJ: Princeton University Press.

Lam, Willy Wo-Lap. 2001. The Business of Reunification. *CNN.com*: http://archives.cnn.com/2001/WORLD/asiapcf/east/06/06/willy.reunif (accessed June 23, 2008).

Lam, Willy Wo-Lap. 2002. Trade Ties Taiwan to China's Leash. *CNN.com*: http://edition.cnn.com/2002/WORLD/asiapcf/east/01/28/willy.column/ (accessed June 23, 2008).

Lamb, Alastair. 1991. *Kashmir: A Disputed Legacy, 1846–1990*. Hertingfordbury, UK: Roxford.

Laney, James T., and Jason T. Shaplen. 2003. How to Deal with North Korea. *Foreign Affairs* 82 (2): 16–30.

Lardy, Nicholas R. 2002. *Integrating China into the Global Economy*. Washington, DC: Brookings.

Lee, Wei-chin. 2003. The Buck Starts Here: Cross-Strait Economic Transactions and Taiwan's Domestic Politics. *American Asian Review* 21 (3): 107–52.

Leng, Tse-kang. 1996. *The Taiwan-China Connection: Democracy and Development Across the Taiwan Straits.* Boulder, CO: Westview Press.

Leng, Tse-kang. 1998a. Dynamics of Taiwan-Mainland China Economic Relations: The Role of Private Firms. *Asian Survey* 38 (5): 494–509.

Leng, Tse-kang. 1998b. A Political Analysis of Taiwan's Economic Dependence on Mainland China. *Issues and Studies* 34 (8): 132–54.

Leng, Tse-kang. 2002. Securing Economic Relations Across the Taiwan Straits: New Challenges and Opportunities. *Journal of Contemporary China* 11 (31): 261–79.

Levin, Norman D., and Yong-Sup Han. 2002. *Sunshine in Korea: The South Korean Debate over Policies Toward North Korea.* Santa Monica, CA: RAND.

Levy, Jack S. 2003. Economic Interdependence, Opportunity Costs, and Peace. In *Economic Interdependence and International Conflict: New Perspectives on an Enduring Debate*, ed. Edward D. Mansfield and Brian M. Pollins, 127–47. Ann Arbor: University of Michigan Press.

Levy, Jack S., and Katherine Barbieri. 2004. Trading with the Enemy During Wartime. *Security Studies* 13 (3): 1–47.

Li, Cheng. 2001. China's Political Succession: Four Misperceptions in the West. In *China's Political Succession and Its Implications for the United States*, 17–23. Washington, DC: Woodrow Wilson International Center for Scholars, Asia Program Special Report, No. 96.

Li, David D. 1998. Changing Incentives of the Chinese Bureaucracy. *American Economic Review, Papers and Proceedings of the 110th Annual Meeting of the American Economic Association*: 393–97.

Li, Quan, and David Sacko. 2002. The (Ir)Relevance of Militarized Interstate Disputes for International Trade. *International Studies Quarterly* 46 (1): 11–43.

Liang'an Jingji Tongji Yuebao (Cross-Strait Economic Statistics Monthly). Various Issues. Taipei: Mainland Affairs Council of the Executive Yuan.

Liberman, Peter. 1996. Trading with the Enemy: Security and Relative Economic Gains. *International Security* 21 (1): 147–75.

Lieberthal, Kenneth. 1995. *Governing China: From Revolution Through Reform.* New York: W.W. Norton.

Lin, Xiangkai. 2003. Tai, Zhong Jingji Wanglai yu Goujia Jingji Anquan (Taiwan-China Economic Exchange and National Economic Security). In *Liang'an Jiaoliu yu Goujia Anquan* (Cross-Strait Exchange and National Security), 212–75. Taipei: Taiwan Advocates.

Long, Andrew G. 2003a. Does Trade Follow Peace? Postwar Bilateral Trade and Expectations for Recurrent Conflict. Paper presented to the Annual Meeting of the American Political Science Association, August, Philadelphia.

Long, Andrew G. 2003b. Defense Pacts and International Trade. *Journal of Peace Research* 40 (5): 537–52.

Lupia, Arthur, and Mathew D. McCubbins. 1998. *The Democratic Dilemma: Can Citizens Learn What They Need to Know?* New York: Cambridge University Press.

Mainland Affairs Council of the Executive Yuan, Republic of China. 2005. *Policy for Cross-Strait Exchanges*: http://www.mac.gov.tw/english/english/macpolicy/paper9404e.htm (accessed June 17, 2008).

Mansfield, Edward D., Helen V. Milner, and Peter Rosendorf. 2000. Free to Trade: Democracies, Autocracies, and International Trade. *American Political Science Review* 94 (2): 305–21.

Mansfield, Edward D., and Jon C. Pevehouse. 2000. Trade Blocs, Trade Flows, and International Conflict. *International Organization* 54 (4): 775–808.

Mansfield, Edward D., and Brian M. Pollins. 2001. The Study of Interdependence and Conflict: Recent Advances, Open Questions, and Directions for Future Research. *Journal of Conflict Resolution* 45: 834–59.

Mansfield, Edward D., and Brian M. Pollins, eds. 2003. *Economic Interdependence and International Conflict: New Perspectives on an Enduring Debate.* Ann Arbor: University of Michigan Press.

Mansfield, Edward D., and Jack Snyder. 1995. Democratization and the Danger of War. *International Security* 20 (1): 5–38.

Mansourov, Alexandre Y. 2006. Emergence of the Second Republic: The Kim Regime Adapts to the Challenges of Modernity. In *North Korea: The Politics of Regime Survival*, ed. Young Whan Kihl and Hong Nack Kim, 37–58. Armonk, NY: M. E. Sharpe.

Marshall, Monty G., and Keith Jaggers. 2000. *Polity IV Project: Data Users Manual.* Integrated Network for Societal Conflict Research Program, Center for International Development and Conflict Management, University of Maryland.

Martin, Lisa L. 1992. *Coercive Cooperation: Explaining Multilateral Economic Sanctions.* Princeton, NJ: Princeton University Press.

Mastanduno, Michael. 1988. Trade as a Strategic Weapon: American and Alliance Export Control Policy in the Early Postwar Period. *International Organization* 42 (1): 121–50.

Mastanduno, Michael. 1992. *Economic Containment: COCOM and the Politics of East-West Trade.* Ithaca, NY: Cornell University Press.

Mastel, Greg. 2001. China, Taiwan, and the World Trade Organization. *Washington Quarterly* 24 (3): 45–56.

McDaniel, Douglas E. 1993. *United States Technology Export Control: An Assessment.* Westport, CT: Praeger.

McDonald, Patrick J. 2004. Peace Through Trade or Free Trade? *Journal of Conflict Resolution*, 48 (4): 547–72.

McLaren, John. 1997. Size, Sunk Costs, and Judge Bowker's Objection to Free Trade. *American Economic Review* 87 (3): 400–20.

Mearsheimer, John J. 2001. *The Tragedy of Great Power Politics.* New York: W. W. Norton.

Milner, Helen V. 1997. *Interests, Institutions, and Information: Domestic Politics and International Relations.* Princeton, NJ: Princeton University Press.

Milner, Helen V., and Keiko Kubota. 2005. Why the Move to Free Trade? Democracy and Trade Policy in the Developing Countries. *International Organization* 59 (1): 107–43.

Ministry of Unification, ROK. 2005. *2005 White Paper on Korean Unification*: http://www.unikorea.go.kr/english/EUL/EUL0301R.jsp (accessed July 9, 2008).

Minzhu Jinbu Dang Liang'an Zhengce Zhongyao Wenjian Huibian (A Collection of the Main Documents Relating to the Democratic Progressive Party's Cross-Strait Policy) (n.d.). Taipei: China Affairs Bureau of the Democratic Progressive Party.

Montinola, Gabriella, Yingyi Qian, and Barry R. Weingast. 1995. Federalism, Chinese Style: The Political Basis for Economic Success in China. *World Politics* 48 (October): 50–81.

Moon, Chung-in. 1994. Changing Patterns of Business-Government Relations in South Korea. In *Business and Government in Industrialising Asia*, ed. Andrew MacIntyre, 142–66. Ithaca, NY: Cornell University Press.

Moore, Thomas G. 2002. *China in the World Market: Chinese Industry and International Sources of Reform in the Post-Mao Era.* Cambridge, UK: Cambridge University Press.

Morrow, James D. 1989. Capabilities, Uncertainty, and Resolve: A Limited Information Model of Crisis Bargaining. *American Journal of Political Science* 33 (4): 941–72.

Morrow, James D. 1999. How Could Trade Affect Conflict? *Journal of Peace Research* 36 (4): 481–89.

Morrow, James D. 2003. Assessing the Role of Trade as a Source of Costly Signals. In *Economic Interdependence and International Conflict: New Perspectives on an Enduring Debate*, ed. Edward D. Mansfield and Brian M. Pollins, 89–95. Ann Arbor: University of Michigan Press.

Morrow, James D., Randolph M. Siverson, and Tressa E. Taberes. 1998. The Political Determinants of International Trade: The Major Powers, 1907–90. *American Political Science Review* 92 (3): 649–61.

Mulvenon, James. 2004a. The PLA, Chen Shui-Bian, and the Referenda: The War Dogs That Didn't Bark. *China Leadership Monitor* 10: http://www.hoover.org/publications/clm/issues/2904396.html.

Mulvenon, James. 2004b. Anticipation Is Making Me Wait: The "Inevitability of War" and Deadlines in Cross-Strait Relations. *China Leadership Monitor* 12: http://www.hoover.org/publications/clm/issues/2903991.html.

Nanto, Dick K. 2006. North Korea's Economic Crisis, Reforms, and Policy Implications. In *North Korea: The Politics of Regime Survival*, ed. Young Whan Kihl and Hong Nack Kim, 118–42. Armonk, NY: M. E. Sharpe.

Nathan, Andrew J. 1993. The Legislative Yuan Elections in Taiwan: Consequences of the Electoral System. *Asian Survey* 33 (4): 424–38.

Naughton, Barry. 1996. *Growing out of the Plan: Chinese Economic Reform 1978–1993*. New York: Cambridge University Press.

Naughton, Barry. 1997. Economic Policy Reform in the PRC and Taiwan. In *The China Circle: Economics and Electronics in the PRC, Taiwan, and Hong Kong*, ed. Barry Naughton, 81–110. Washington, DC: Brookings Institution Press.

Naughton, Barry. 2000. China's Trade Regime at the End of the 1990s: Achievements, Limitations, and Impact on the United States. In *China's Future: Constructive Partner or Emerging Threat?*, ed. Ted Galen Carpenter and James A. Dorn, 235–60. Washington, DC: Cato Institute.

Nayar, Baldev Raj. 1998a. Political Structure and India's Economic Reforms of the 1990s. *Pacific Affairs* 71 (3): 335–58.

Nayar, Baldev Raj. 1998b. Business and India's Economic Policy Reforms. *Economic and Political Weekly* (September 19): 2453–67.

Nayar, Baldev Raj. 2000. The Limits of Economic Nationalism in India: Economic Reforms under the BJP-Led Government, 1998–1999. *Asian Survey* 40 (5): 792–815.

Nayar, Baldev Raj. 2001. *Globalization and Nationalism: The Changing Balance in India's Economic Policy, 1950–2000*. New Delhi: Sage.

Niou, Emerson M. S. 2004. Understanding Taiwan Independence and Its Policy Implications. *Asian Survey* 44 (4): 555–67.

Noland, Marcus. 2000. *Avoiding the Apocalypse: The Future of the Two Koreas*. Washington, DC: Institute for International Economics.

Noman, Omar. 1990. *Pakistan: A Political and Economic History Since 1947*. London: Kegan Paul International.

Oberdorfer, Don. 2001. *The Two Koreas: A Contemporary History*. New York, NY: Basic Books.

Oneal, John R., Frances H. Oneal, Zeev Maoz, and Bruce Russett. 1996. The Liberal Peace: Interdependence, Democracy, and International Conflict, 1950–85. *Journal of Peace Research* 33 (1): 11–28.

Oneal, John R., and Bruce M. Russett. 1997. The Classical Liberals Were Right: Democracy, Interdependence, and Conflict, 1950–1985. *International Studies Quarterly* 41: 267–94.

Oneal, John R., and Bruce Russett. 1999a. Assessing the Liberal Peace with Alternative Specifications: Trade Still Reduces Conflict. *Journal of Peace Research* 36 (4): 423–42.

Oneal, John R., and Bruce Russett. 1999b. Is the Liberal Peace Just an Artifact of Cold War Interests? Assessing Recent Critiques. *International Interactions* 25 (3): 213–41.

Oneal, John R., and Bruce Russett. 2001. Clear and Clean: The Fixed Effects of the Liberal Peace. *International Organization* 55 (2): 469–85.

Oneal, John R., Bruce Russett, and Michael L. Berbaum. 2003. Causes of Peace: Democracy, Interdependence, and International Organizations, 1885–1992. *International Studies Quarterly* 47 (3): 371–93.

Pandian, S. 2005a. The Political Economy of Trans-Pakistan Gas Pipeline Project: Assessing the Political and Economic Risks for India. *Energy Policy* 33 (5): 659–70.

Pandian, S. G. 2005b. Energy Trade as a Confidence-Building Measure Between India and Pakistan: A Study of the Indo-Iran Trans-Pakistan Pipeline Project. *Contemporary South Asia* 14 (3): 307–20.

Papayoanou, Paul A. 1996. Interdependence, Institutions, and the Balance of Power: Britain, Germany, and World War I. *International Security* 20: 42–76.

Papayoanou, Paul A. 1999. *Power Ties: Economic Interdependence, Balancing, and War*. Ann Arbor: University of Michigan Press.

Papayoanou, Paul A., and Scott L. Kastner. 1999/2000. Sleeping with the (Potential) Enemy: Assessing the U.S. Policy of Engagement with China. *Security Studies* 9 (1/2): 157–87.

Park, Han S. 2002. *North Korea: The Politics of Unconventional Wisdom*. Boulder, CO: Lynne Rienner.

Parkin, Michael. 1990. *Microeconomics*. Reading, MA: Addison-Wesley.

Pevehouse, Jon C. 2004. Interdependence Theory and the Measurement of International Conflict. *Journal of Politics* 66 (1): 247–66.

Pigato, Miria, Caroline Farah, Ken Itakura, Kwang Jun, Will Martin, Kim Murrell, and T.G. Srinivasan. 1997. *South Asia's Integration into the World Economy*. Washington, DC: The World Bank.

Polachek, Solomon William. 1980. Conflict and Trade. *Journal of Conflict Resolution* 24: 55–78.

Polacheck, Soloman W., John Robst, and Yuan-ching Chang. 1999. Liberalism and Interdependence: Extending the Trade-Conflict Model. *Journal of Peace Research* 36 (4): 405–22.

Pollins, Brian M. 1989a. Conflict, Cooperation, and Commerce: The Effect of International Political Interactions on Bilateral Trade Flows. *American Journal of Political Science* 33 (3): 737–61.

Pollins, Brian M. 1989b. Does Trade Still Follow the Flag? *American Political Science Review* 83 (2): 465–80.

Pomfret, Richard. 1995. Taiwan's Involvement in Jiangsu Province: Some Evidence from Joint-Venture Case Studies. In *Emerging Patterns of East Asian Investment in China: From Korea, Taiwan, and Hong Kong*, ed. Sumner J. La Croix, Michael Plummer, and Keun Lee, 167–78. Armonk, NY: M. E. Sharpe.

Powell, Robert. 1989. Nuclear Deterrence and the Strategy of Limited Retaliation. *American Political Science Review* 83 (2): 503–19.

Powell, Robert. 2002. Bargaining Theory and International Conflict. *Annual Review of Political Science* 5 (June): 1–30.

Rawski, Thomas G. 2000. China's Move to Market: How Far? What Next? In *China's Future: Constructive Partner or Emerging Threat?*, ed. Ted Galen Carpenter and James A. Dorn, 317–39. Washington, DC: Cato Institute.

Rector, Chad. 2009. *Federations: The Political Dynamics of Cooperation.* Ithaca, NY: Cornell University Press.

Rigger, Shelley. 1999. *Politics in Taiwan: Voting for Democracy.* London: Routledge.

Rigger, Shelley. 2001. *From Opposition to Power: Taiwan's Democratic Progressive Party.* Boulder, CO: Lynne Rienner.

Ripsman, Norrin M., and Jean-Marc F. Blanchard. 1996/97. Commercial Liberalism Under Fire: Evidence from 1914 and 1936. *Security Studies* 6: 4–50.

Ripsman, Norrin M., and Jean-Marc F. Blanchard. 2003. Qualitative Research on Economic Interdependence and Conflict: Overcoming Methodological Hurdles. In *Economic Interdependence and International Conflict: New Perspectives on an Enduring Debate*, ed. Edward D. Mansfield and Brian M. Pollins, 310–23. Ann Arbor: University of Michigan Press.

Robinson, James A. 1999. What Do You Think About Taiwan's Democracy? *Cosmos Journal*: http://www.cosmos-club.org/web/journals/1999/robinson.html.

Roeder, Philip G. 1993. *Red Sunset: The Failure of Soviet Politics.* Princeton, NJ: Princeton University Press.

Rogowski, Ronald. 1987. Trade and the Variety of Democratic Institutions. *International Organization* 41 (2): 203–23.

Rogowski, Ronald. 1989. *Commerce and Coalitions: How Trade Affects Domestic Political Alignments.* Princeton, NJ: Princeton University Press.

Romberg, Alan D. 2003. *Rein in at the Brink of the Precipice: American Policy Toward Taiwan and U.S.-PRC Relations.* Washington, DC: Henry L. Stimson Center.

Romberg, Alan D. 2007. Applying to the UN in the Name of Taiwan. *China Leadership Monitor* 22: http://www.hoover.org/publications/clm/issues/10263787.html.

Romberg, Alan D. 2008. After the Taiwan Election: Restoring Dialogue While Reserving Options. *China Leadership Monitor* 25: http://www.hoover.org/publications/clm/issues/20099209.html.

Rose, Andrew K. 2004. Do WTO Members Have More Liberal Trade Policy? *Journal of International Economics* 63 (2): 209–35.

Ross, Robert S. 2000. The 1995–96 Taiwan Strait Confrontation: Coercion, Credibility, and the Use of Force. *International Security* 25 (2): 87–123.

Ross, Robert S. 2006. Taiwan's Fading Independence Movement. *Foreign Affairs* 85 (2): 141–48.

Roy, Denny. 2003. *Taiwan: A Political History.* Ithaca, NY: Cornell University Press.

Roy, Denny. 2004. *Cross-Strait Economic Relations: Opportunities Outweigh Risks.* Asia-Pacific Center for Security Studies Occasional Paper Series, April.

Russett, Bruce, and John R. Oneal. 2001. *Triangulating Peace: Democracy, Interdependence, and International Organizations.* New York: W. W. Norton.

Sachs, Jeffrey D., and Andrew Warner. 1995. Economic Reform and the Process of Global Integration. *Brookings Papers on Economic Activity* 1: 1–118.

Saxer, Carl J. 2002. *From Transition to Power Alternation: Democracy in South Korea, 1987–1997.* New York: Routledge.

Schelling, Thomas C. 1966. *Arms and Influence.* New Haven, CT: Yale University Press.

Schive, Chi. 1995. *Taiwan's Economic Role in East Asia.* Washington, DC: Center for Strategic and International Studies.

Schofield, Victoria. 1996. *Kashmir in the Crossfire.* London: I. B. Tauris.

Schultz, Kenneth A. 2001. *Democracy and Coercive Diplomacy.* Cambridge, UK: Cambridge University Press.

Scobell, Andrew. 2006. *Kim Jong Il and North Korea: The Leader and the System.* Monograph: Strategic Studies Institute of the U.S. Army War College (March 1).

Segal, Adam. 2004. Practical Engagement: Drawing a Fine Line for U.S.-China Trade. *Washington Quarterly* 27 (3): 157–73.

Shambaugh, David. 1996. Containment or Engagement of China? Calculating Beijing's Responses. *International Security* 21 (2): 180–209.

Sheng, Lijun. 2001. *China's Dilemma: The Taiwan Issue.* Singapore: Institute of Southeast Asian Studies.

Sheng, Yumin. 2005. Central-Provincial Relations at the CCP Central Committees: Institutions, Measurement and Empirical Trends, 1978–2002. *China Quarterly* 182: 319–37.

Shiau, Chyuan-Jeng. 1996. Elections and the Changing State-Business Relationship. In *Taiwan's Electoral Politics and Democratic Transition: Riding the Third Wave,* ed. Hung-mao Tien, 213–25. Armonk, NY: M. E. Sharpe.

Shirk, Susan L. 1993. *The Political Logic of Economic Reform in China.* Berkeley: University of California Press.

Shirk, Susan L. 1994. *How China Opened Its Door: The Political Success of the PRC's Foreign Trade and Investment Reforms.* Washington, DC: Brookings.

Shirk, Susan L. 1996. Internationalization and China's Economic Reforms. In *Internationalization and Domestic Politics,* ed. Robert O. Keohane and Helen V. Milner, 186–206. Cambridge, UK: Cambridge University Press.

Shirk, Susan L. 2007. *China, Fragile Superpower: How China's Internal Politics Could Derail Its Peaceful Rise.* Oxford, UK: Oxford University Press.

Signorino, Curtis S., and Jeffrey M. Ritter. 1999. Tau-b or Not Tau-b: Measuring the Similarity of Foreign Policy Positions. *International Studies Quarterly* 43 (1): 115–44.

Simmons, Beth A. 1994. *Who Adjusts?* Princeton, NJ: Princeton University Press.

Simmons, Beth A. 2005. Rules over Real Estate: Trade, Territorial Conflict, and International Borders as Institution. *Journal of Conflict Resolution* 49 (6): 823–48.

Skalnes, Lars S. 1998. Grand Strategy and Foreign Economic Policy: British Grand Strategy in the 1930s. *World Politics* 50 (4): 582–616.

Snidal, Duncan. 1991. Relative Gains and the Pattern of International Cooperation. *American Political Science Review* 85 (3): 701–26.

Solingen, Etel. 1998. *Regional Orders at Century's Dawn.* Princeton, NJ: Princeton University Press.

Solingen, Etel. 2001. Mapping Internationalization: Domestic and Regional Impacts. *International Studies Quarterly* 45 (4): 517–55.

Solingen, Etel. 2003. Internationalization, Coalitions, and Regional Conflict and Cooperation. In *Economic Interdependence and International Conflict: New Perspectives on an Enduring Debate*, ed. Edward D. Mansfield and Brian M. Pollins, 60–85. Ann Arbor: University of Michigan Press.

Sridharan, E. 2005. Improving Indo-Pakistan Relations: International Relations Theory, Nuclear Deterrence and Possibilities for Economic Cooperation. *Contemporary South Asia* 14 (3): 321–39.

Stein, Arthur A. 2003. Trade and Conflict: Uncertainty, Strategic Signaling, and Interstate Disputes. In *Economic Interdependence and International Conflict: New Perspectives on an Enduring Debate*, ed. Edward D. Mansfield and Brian M. Pollins, 111–26. Ann Arbor: University of Michigan Press.

Stolper, Wolfgang F., and Paul A. Samuelson. 1941. Protection and Real Wages. *Review of Economic Studies* 9 (1): 58–73.

Stone, Randall W. 2004. The Political Economy of IMF Lending in Africa. *American Political Science Review* 98 (4): 577–91.

Su, Chi. 2003. *Weiji Bianyuan: Cong Liangguolun Dao Yibian Yiguo* (Brinkmanship: From the Two States Theory to One Country on Each Side). Taipei: Tianxia.

Suettinger, Robert L. 2004. Leadership Policy Toward Taiwan and the United States in the Wake of Chen Shui-bian's Reelection. *China Leadership Monitor* 11: http://www.hoover.org/publications/clm/issues/2904106.html.

Sutter, Karen M. 2002. Business Dynamism Across the Taiwan Strait: The Implications for Cross-Strait Relations. *Asian Survey* 42 (3): 522–40.

Swaine, Michael D. 2001. Chinese Decision-Making Regarding Taiwan, 1979–2000. In *The Making of Chinese Foreign and Security Policy in the Era of Reform, 1978–2000*, ed. David M. Lampton, 289–336. Stanford, CA: Stanford University Press.

Taiwan Wenti Duben (Reader on the Taiwan Question). 2001. Beijing: CCP Central Party School.

Tanner, Murray Scot. 2007. *Chinese Economic Coercion Against Taiwan: A Tricky Weapon to Use.* Santa Monica, CA: RAND Corporation.

Taylor, Robert. 1999. China's Emerging Markets: Investment Strategies of Taiwan's Companies. In *China and India: Economic Performance and Business Strategies of Firms in the Mid-1990s*, ed. Sam Dzever and Jacques Jaussaud, 131–50. New York: St. Martin's.

Thompson, William R. 2001. Identifying Rivals and Rivalries in World Politics. *International Studies Quarterly* 45 (4): 557–86.

Tian, John Q. 2006. *Government, Business, and the Politics of Interdependence and Conflict Across the Taiwan Strait.* New York: Palgrave.

Tian, Qunjian. 1999. "Like Fish in Water": Taiwanese Investors in a Rent-Seeking Society. *Issues and Studies* 35 (5): 61–94.

Tien, Hung-mao. 1996. Elections and Taiwan's Democratic Development. In *Taiwan's Electoral Politics and Democratic Transition: Riding the Third Wave*, ed. Hung-mao Tien, 3–26. Armonk, NY: M. E. Sharpe.

Tso, Allen Y. 1996. Developments in the Cross-Strait Economic Relationship. *Issues and Studies* 32 (9): 131–33.

Tucker, Nancy Bernkopf, ed. 2005. *Dangerous Strait: The U.S.-Taiwan-China Crisis.* New York: Columbia University Press.

Tucker, Richard. 1999. *The Similarity of Alliance Portfolios, 1816–1984.* Version 2.50 (dataset): http://www.vanderbilt.edu/~rtucker/data/affinity/alliance/similar/ (accessed 2003).

Vernon, Raymond. 1971. *Sovereignty at Bay: The Multinational Spread of U.S. Enterprises*. New York: Basic.

Viner, Jacob. 1951. *International Economics*. Glencoe, IL: Free Press.

Waltz, Kenneth N. 1979. *Theory of International Politics*. Reading, MA: Addison-Wesley.

Wan, Ming. 2003. Economic Interdependence and Economic Cooperation: Mitigating Conflict and Transforming Security Order in Asia. In *Asian Security Order: Instrumental and Normative Features*, ed. Muthiah Alagappa, 280–310. Stanford, CA: Stanford University Press.

Wang, Qingxin Ken. 2000. Taiwanese NGOs and the Prospect of National Reunification in the Taiwan Strait. *Australian Journal of International Affairs* 54 (1): 111–24.

Wang, Shaoguang. 1994. Central-Local Fiscal Politics in China. In *Changing Central-Local Relations in China: Reform and State Capacity*, ed. Jia Hao and Lin Zhimin, 91–112. Boulder, CO: Westview Press.

Wei, Sung Shou, and Lishui Zhu. 1995. The Growth of Foreign Investment in the Xiamen Special Economic Zone. In *Emerging Patterns of East Asian Investment in China: From Korea, Taiwan, and Hong Kong*, ed. Sumner J. La Croix, Michael Plummer, and Keun Lee, 113–22. Armonk, NY: M. E. Sharpe.

World Bank. 1997. *China 2020: Development Challenges in the New Century*. Washington, DC: International Bank for Reconstruction and Development / World Bank.

World Bank. 2001. *World Development Indicators*. CD-ROM.

World Bank. 2002. *World Development Indicators*. Washington, DC: World Bank.

Wu, Yu-Shan. 1999. Taiwanese Elections and Cross-Strait Relations: Mainland Policy in Flux. *Asian Survey* 39 (4): 565–87.

Xie, Tao. 2006. Congressional Role Call Voting on China Trade Policy. *American Politics Research* 34 (6): 732–58.

Yan, Xuetong. 2004. Origins of the Policy to "Pay Any Price to Contain Taiwan's Independence." *China Strategy Newsletter* (July 20): 39–42.

Yan, Zongda. 1992. *Taiwan Dalu Touzi ji Maoyi zhi Yanjiu* (A Study of Taiwanese Investments in the Mainland and Trade with the Mainland). Taipei: Research Bureau of the Economic Development Council of the Executive Yuan.

Yang, Chyan, and Shiu-Wan Hung. 2003. Taiwan's Dilemma Across the Strait: Lifting the Ban on Semiconductor Investment in China. *Asian Survey* 43 (4): 681–96.

Yang, Dali L. 1996. Governing China's Transition to the Market: Institutional Incentives, Politicians' Choices, and Unintended Outcomes. *World Politics* 48 (3): 424–52.

Yang, Dali L. 1997. *Beyond Beijing: Liberalization and the Regions in China*. New York: Routledge.

Zaidi, S. Akbar. 1999. *Issues in Pakistan's Economy*. Oxford, UK: Oxford University Press.

Zhao, Quansheng. 2005. Beijing's Dilemma with Taiwan: War or Peace? *Pacific Review* 18 (2): 217–42.

Zhao, Suisheng. 1999a. Introduction: Making Sense of the 1995–96 Crisis in the Taiwan Strait. In *Across the Taiwan Strait: Mainland China, Taiwan, and the 1995–1996 Crisis*, ed. Suisheng Zhao, 1–18. New York: Routledge.

Zhao, Suisheng. 1999b. Economic Interdependence and Political Divergence: A Background Analysis of the Taiwan Strait Crisis. In *Across the Taiwan Strait: Mainland China, Taiwan, and the 1995–1996 Crisis*, ed. Suisheng Zhao, 21–40. New York: Routledge.

Zhao, Suisheng, ed. 1999c. *Across the Taiwan Strait: Mainland China, Taiwan, and the 1995–1996 Crisis*. New York: Routledge.

Zheng, Yongnian. 2000. Institutionalizing de Facto Federalism in Post-Deng China. In *China Under Jiang Zemin*, ed. Hung-mao Tien and Yun-han Chu, 215–31. Boulder, CO: Lynne Rienner.

Ziring, Lawrence. 1997. *Pakistan in the Twentieth Century: A Political History*. Karachi: Oxford University Press.

Zong, Hairen. 2002. *Di Si Dai* (The Fourth Generation). New York: Mirror Books.

Zweig, David. 2002. *Internationalizing China: Domestic Interests and Global Linkages*. Ithaca, NY: Cornell University Press.

Index

Studies in Asian Security

A SERIES SPONSORED BY THE EAST–WEST CENTER

Muthiah Alagappa, Chief Editor
Distinguished Senior Fellow, East-West Center

On the domestic political conditions in which bilateral conflict may not decrease trade.